Growing Lawns

Growing Lawns

including Lawn Alternatives and Ground Covers

A.G.W. Simpson

Kangaroo Press

Cover design by Darian Causby using a photograph of a
lawn and mixed border at the factory of Fletcher Jones,
Warrnambool, by kind permission of Fletcher Jones
and Staff Pty Ltd

First published in 1992 by Kangaroo Press Pty Ltd
3 Whitehall Road (P.O. Box 75) Kenthurst 2156
Typeset by G.T. Setters Pty Limited
Printed in Hong Kong by Colorcraft Ltd

ISBN 0 86417 367 9

Contents

PART 1 - GRASS LAWNS

1. Common Questions about Grass Lawns

What in your opinion is the ideal lawn?

The simple answer is that it all depends on the purpose for which the lawn is to be used. A lawn composed of finest bowling green or golf green grasses may be the ideal of one gardener, the lawn, perhaps, being for show only. A lawn composed of hard-wearing grasses to be used by children and dogs may be somebody else's idea of an ideal lawn.

I once worked in a garden where the owner would only allow me to cut the lawns in one direction, using a cylinder-reel, back-roller mower, as he considered that dark green and light green, Wimbledon centre court stripes looked out of place in the naturalness of this famous garden. And the lawn, when observed from the most important viewpoint, looked like a sheet of dark green.

In my opinion, a definition of an ideal lawn is that it be functional and beautiful—a green lung— in fact, an outdoor living-room of top-quality 'grass-carpet', that relaxes the mind and body and revives the spirit. But is also has to be in keeping with the rest of the garden design.

What do you think causes a bad lawn?

1. Haphazard construction of the site.
2. The lawn soil-surface has not been prepared correctly to receive the seed.
3. Sowing cheap seed that contains impure seed, seeds more suitable for a paddock than a fine lawn, seed, even though it may be suitable, that is mostly of poor germinating quality, or using grass seed of a species that is not suitable for the climate.
4. Haphazard and uneven sowing of the seed.
5. Using turf-sods that contain wrong lawn grass species and undesirable weeds.
6. Slapdash laying of the turf-sods, which results in

much time being spent trying to put things to rights *after* the roots have struck into the soil surface.
7. Using the wrong fertilizer, or lack of suitable fertilizer, on an existing lawn.
8. Using a lawn roller too frequently, particularly when the lawn soil is wet, which causes panning of the lawn surface.
9. Using a mower that has blunt blades, or is set so low that it scars the lawn surface, or set too high so that it allows the entry of undesirable weeds and grasses.
10. Inconsistent use of the mower, which results in the lawn grasses not knowing whether they are coming or going.
11. Abuse, or over-use of the lawn by humans and animals.
12. Neglect of the lawn, and using the wrong treatments.
13. Cutting the grass too low in hot weather.
14. Cutting the lawn when it is too cold.

To produce a fine lawn you, the gardener, will have to spend time and money on that lawn, just as you would on the rest of the garden.

Should I use a motorized cylinder-reel mower, or motorized rotary mower on my lawn?

Each are used extensively world-wide. Each has advantages over the other. See section on mowing.

Which is the cheapest and best way to establish a lawn?

Using lawn seed means that you can get exactly the type of grasses you want, although weeds can invade a new lawn, and you have to wait for the lawn to become established. Overall, buying seeds is generally cheaper than buying turf-sods...but each method has its advantages and disadvantages.

What sorts of grasses can I use in my lawn?

Worldwide there are 7500–10 000 species of grass, including wheat, oats, barley and sugar cane, and of these approximately fifty species are used for lawn production worldwide. However, only a few species (and usually selections, varieties, cultivars or hybrids of these), are used for lawns in Australia—some species making better lawns than others.

These species are subdivided into cool-climate (cool season) grasses, and warm-climate (warm-season) grasses.

These in turn are subdivided into: bowling/golf-green type lawns; ornamental lawns; hard-wearing lawns; and rough treatment, or special area lawns.

I will discuss lawn grass species more fully later in the book.

I have been told that water applied to grass lawns in hot sunlight can scorch the grass. Is this true?

Yes and no! If it were true then thousands of hectares of public parks would be scorched each year. Water applied during hot sunlight does not scorch grass. But it must be a deep, sufficient watering as light sprinklings do more harm than good. Also it must soak into the lawn soil and not lie in pools on the surface. See more detailed information concerning irrigation later on.

I am told that I need to top dress my lawn each year with lawn compost to keep it in good health. Is this so?

The word compost can be misleading as, usually, what people mean by 'lawn compost' is applying a lawn top dressing of suitable sand/medium friable soil/finely ground-granulated acid peat. Properly made acid compost can be used, provided it is completely weed free, but more of this in the section on 'top dressings'.

I am told that grass lawns which have suitable strawberry clover or white clover included in their sward make up stay greener. Is this so?

Strawberry clover and white clover are leguminous plants that manufacture their own nitrogen among their roots, and therefore the lawn looks green because nitrogen is a principal element in keeping plants green. There is, however, a down side to using clover, in that bees visit to collect the nectar, which means you will have more bees in your garden and possibly could have problems with stings. Also, clover can be damaged or killed, I repeat killed, by grass lawn selective herbicides.

I have moss on my lawn and my neighbour reckons the lawn needs liming. Is this true?

Moss appears on lawn surfaces that are compacted and poorly drained, and sometimes the soil is impoverished. You can use suitable lawn mosskillers, *(read the label on the product pack)*, but the moss will probably return if the cause is poor drainage. Proper drainage, 'aeration' and the use of the correct fertilizers are usually the most effective ways of curing moss, and obtaining a thick, green, grass sward. Be wary about using lime on lawns as too much lime can lead to worm infestation and lank, coarse grasses predominating. Be aware that certain limes are caustic to grass blades.

What is a selective herbicide (selective weedkiller) for use on lawns? What is a non-selective herbicide (non-selective weedkiller)?

A selective herbicide is one which kills only certain types of plants while a non-selective herbicide kills all plants. Refer to the section on lawn weeds/weeds. When considering selective and non-selective herbicides always *read the label on the product pack before you buy. Check and follow to the letter all safety precautions.*

Should I have my garden soil tested before I sow or turf-sod a lawn? I've heard some say it's a waste of money, as soil is only soil.

I feel that it is a good idea to have your soil tested, for the obvious reason that you'll know what you have in the garden soil. A gardener who knows the soil pH (acidity or alkalinity) of various parts of the garden, the nutrients contained in those various sections, as well as where the sun shines, and for how long, in summer, spring, autumn and winter and from which direction comes the prevailing wind, is in a stronger position to succeed than those gardeners who use trial and error.

A soil test can ascertain such things as pH, salinity, phosphorus, potassium, organic carbon content, and texture. Check which service(s) the soil laboratory offers. The important factor is that the soil testing be accurate and be carried out professionally.

Find out the cost of a soil test before the samples are taken. This doesn't mean that if a soil test costs it shouldn't be carried out, it just means that you are aware of the cost beforehand. And do be particularly exacting when collecting samples, as a laboratory can only test what you send them.

Can I use selective herbicide for use on grass lawns on my new grass seedling lawn to kill off the weeds that have come up?

Generally, no. Firstly, regular mowing will get rid of many of the weeds. Secondly, you've got to wait until the seedlings have established themselves into a reasonable, and stable, sward after several mowings before you can even contemplate using lawn selective herbicides or even fertilizer. Young seedlings, like young babies, are very sensitive. Read the instructions on the manufacturer's product pack.

Can I use selective herbicide for grass lawns on my newly turfed lawns, as the turf contains weeds?

Generally, no. You have to wait for the new turves to become well established before you use selective herbicide for use on lawns on them, as newly laid turves can be adversely affected by these. Read the label on the manufacturer's product pack.

I have moved from interstate, where I had a beautiful lawn. Can I use the same grasses in my lawn as I used there?

Not necessarily. Some grasses will not tolerate cold conditions. It's unlikely that you'll see best Queensland Blue Couch for sale in Victoria or Tasmania, and it is also unlikely that you'll see Fine-leaved Perennial Ryegrass/Chewings Fescue/Browntop Bent turves for sale in the Gold Coast. Cool-climate grasses, generally, will not tolerate hot conditions, except, possibly, under certain special circumstances.

There are many different species of weeds in my lawn. If I spray them with a suitable selective herbicide for use on lawns, before they set seed, will I get rid of the weeds once and for all?

Unfortunately, not all weeds in a given soil germinate in a given year. Therefore these may germinate long after the effects of the selective herbicide have worn off.

I am cursed by the multitude of names given to certain lawn practices and such. What do they mean?

Sward means an expanse of soil covered with lawn-like grasses.

Thatch means the build up of undecomposed grass fibre on the lawn and lawn soil surface, such as can happen if the cuttings of certain grasses are not collected during mowing, or it can be a characteristic of a particular grass, e.g. Kikuyu Grass.

Mat is the same grass fibre that has become intermingled with the top of the lawn soil.

Both thatch and mat, to a thickness of, say, 6 mm (¼ in) may be beneficial to a lawn by absorbing foot traffic, acting as a mulch and cushioning the soil against panning by weather. If too impenetrable, both can be detrimental to the lawn by stifling grasses, habouring insects and disease, causing grass-root layering, preventing moisture from reaching the grass roots, and so on.

Hollow-tining means that a specially designed, hollow metal tube is thrust into the ground, removing a core of grass and soil approximately the size of a small, thin cigar, or middle finger size, to improve aeration and drainage, and sometimes allow for suitable top dressing to be applied and brushed into the core holes.

Hollow tining has good points and bad points. Good points are improving drainage, relieving soil compaction, allowing roots to spread, interrupting layering caused by top dressings, thatch control, better response to fertilizers, and more. Bad points are drying grass around the outside of the core hole in hot weather, a lovely place for weeds to settle and grow, a ready-made home for various 'crawlies', excessive damage to certain fine stolon grasses if done in hot weather; also possible damage to Buffalo (St Augustine) Grass during the grass's dormant season; and if used too often it may cause 'fluffiness' on certain specialized turf surfaces.

Hollow tining is best done when the grasses are growing vigorously, and not during hot weather that could put the grasses under stress. Overall, it is superior to solid tine aeration.

Pricking a lawn means lightly pricking the lawn surface with a fork or special lawn pricking machine to alleviate surface compaction.

Gardeners use the word **aerate** to mean driving a fork or fork-like instrument (solid tines) into the lawn surface to allow oxygen to penetrate to the roots and assist drainage, but this is simplistic. On the practical side I found using a fork to help drain surface water useful on 'hammered' winter playing surfaces.

Pricking and hollow tining are also forms of aeration. Always remember that many of us in Australia have water pipes reasonably close to the surface, which could get damaged by any forking.

Scarifying a lawn means scratching vigorously, but sensibly, at the lawn surface to remove the thatch (build up of dead fibre).

Nap is the 'surface' produced on a lawn after the lawn surface has been brushed gently to raise the grass blades, and then mowed correctly. . . particularly when using the smoothing action of a cylinder-reel mower with front and back rollers. This results in those dark-green and light-green striped lawns we envy, the nap of one stripe lying in the opposite direction to the one next to it.

Ribbing is uneven ridges, usually brought about by the mower jumping over grass, pushing it down, and not cutting it. It could be that the grass is too tall to be cut effectively by the grass cutting cylinder, or the cylinder blades are blunt. Other causes include: a cutting cylinder which is set too tightly on to the bottom blade; blades which are not adjusted correctly; an engine which hasn't sufficient power to cut such grass; an operator not strong enough to push the mower to achieve a clean cut; or a machine which is not suitable for the grasses in the lawn.

Chewing the grass means that the blades are too blunt to cut cleanly, or they are incorrectly set, which results in the grass looking frayed or 'chewed' after mowing.

Uneven cutting means that one side of the mower is higher, or lower, than the other side, or the bottom blade could be damaged, and is out of alignment, or broken.

Note well: Throughout the book metric measurements are given followed by generally only approximate imperial equivalents.

2. The Grass Plant and a Little Lawn History

The Grass Plant

The grass family provides the world's staple diet. It includes cereals such as wheat, barley, oats, rice and maize, and sustains the grass-eating animals which provide milk and meat. Because the grass family is such a large and diverse one, a comprehensive account is beyond the scope of this book. Therefore, I have confined the information below to that which is relevant to lawn grass plants. Grasses are members of the monocotyledon group of plants.

The Grass Family

Grass plants belong to the grass family, Poaceae (synonym Gramineae).

The grass family is divided into genera, such as *Poa*, and these genera are divided into species, such as *pratensis*. For example, Kentucky Bluegrass is *Poa pratensis*.

The species are further divided into varieties (variations produced by nature) and cultivars (cultivated varieties bred by plant breeders).

There are between 7500 and 10 000 different grass species, however, only approximately 20 species are used for lawns in Australia.

Annual, Biennial and Perennial Grasses

Some lawn grasses are annuals. A famous, albeit notorious, annual lawn grass is Crabgrass *(Digitaria sanguinalis)*.

I cannot think of any true biennial grass that is used for top lawn production. A biennial will grow vegetatively for the first year, then flower and die the next year.

Most lawn grasses are perennial, living for more than two years.

Grass Root Systems

Lawn grasses have fibrous (adventitious) roots that grow from the base of the stems down into the soil in fibrous tufts.

Much of the grass's fibrous root-mass dies naturally each year to be replaced by fresh fibrous root, and this continues year in and year out.

The Stem

The stem (culm) arises from the roots and is sheathed by leaves. The stem, as you may have observed, looks similar to a drinking straw, or a semi-flattened drinking straw, or a completely squashed drinking straw.

The stem is enclosed by the base of the leaf, known as the sheath.

Stolons

Stolons are usually overground, creeping stems that clamber over the top of the soil sending out fibrous (adventitious) roots into the soil from a junction in the stolon known as a node. Aerial plantlets also grow from a node. These rooted plantlets, when separated from the parent, are capable of growing independently. An example is Kikuyu Grass *(Pennisetum clandestinum)*.

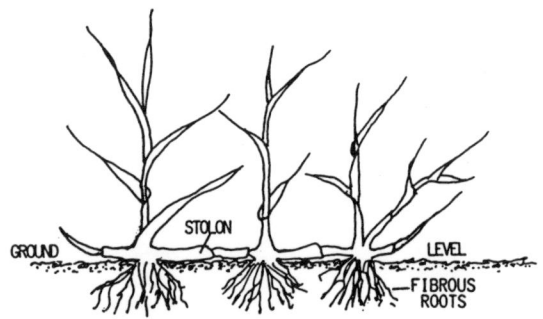

Grass roots: stolons and fibrous roots

Rhizomes

Rhizomes are usually underground creeping stems that travel through the soil at varying depths below ground level, and send fibrous (adventitious) roots further down into the soil from rhizome junctions (knuckles). They also send plantlet shoots straight up from the junctions of the rhizome. An example is Kentucky Blue Grass *(Poa pratensis)*.

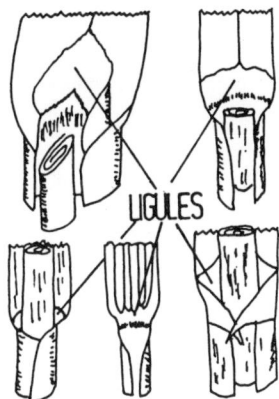

Ligules of grass plants are important identification factors

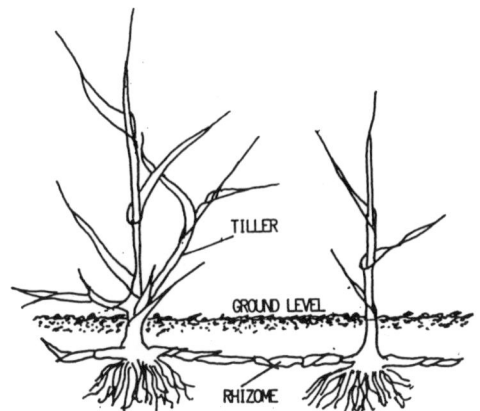

Grass roots: rhizomes

The Leaf

The leaf area is made up of the blade, sheath, veins, auricle and ligule.

Leaves are borne alternately along or up the grass stem, and if you look closely you will see that the leaf seems to be wrapped around the stem.

Leaves are an important feature in identifying grasses. The leaf blade can be smooth or rough, or smooth and rough. It can be rolled, or rolled-flattened, or flattened and wide, either blunt-pointed like a spoon, or sharp-pointed like a needle, and variations of these.

The veins in the leaf blade run parallel up the leaf, like railway lines, as opposed to dicotyledon plants, which have spreading veins like crazy paving.

The leaf sheath embraces the grass stem and can be complete, split, ridged and so forth.

Some leaf sheaths have claw-like auricle projections, like the collar ends of a shirt.

The ligule is a membrane tissue that appears when the sheath is pulled away from the stem. Ligules are remarkably varied, and can be an important identification point. In some grasses the ligule is very obvious, but in others it seems to be non-existent, or the merest fringe of hairs.

Growth

New buds and grass blades appear from the base (crown) of the plant, which is why it is possible to cut lawn grasses to a reasonable height without killing, or unacceptably stunting the plant. Some grasses, such as those used on cricket wickets, can be cut lower than others and still survive, albeit under protest.

If certain grass plants are allowed to grow without mowing, then their root extent is proportionately as great as their aerial growth. Because gardeners want a reasonably close-mown lawn they have to accept that they will not get the same extensive grass root growth as for uncut grass.

Those grasses, however, that tend to grow naturally close to the soil surface are less affected by cutting than those that are more erect in their growth habit. Even so, if these grasses are scalped to ground level to produce a special playing surface, then their roots will react accordingly. Be aware, then, that lawns will generally be healthier if cut at suitable heights.

Nodes

Spaced along or up the stem at regular intervals are nodes (like the knuckles on your fingers). The node is usually blocked, but still allows moisture and nutrients to pass through. These nodes are like staging posts in the grass plant's growth. The section of stem between the nodes is known as the internode.

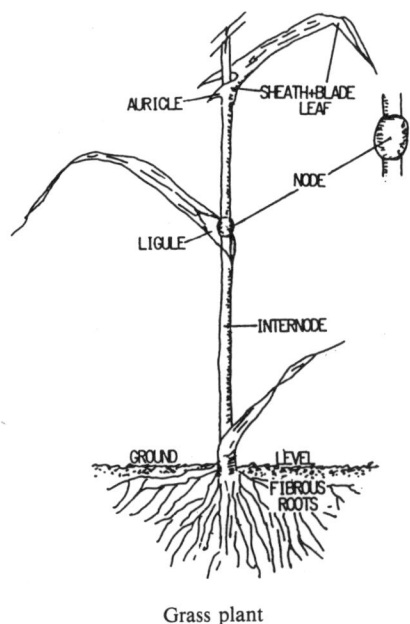

Grass plant

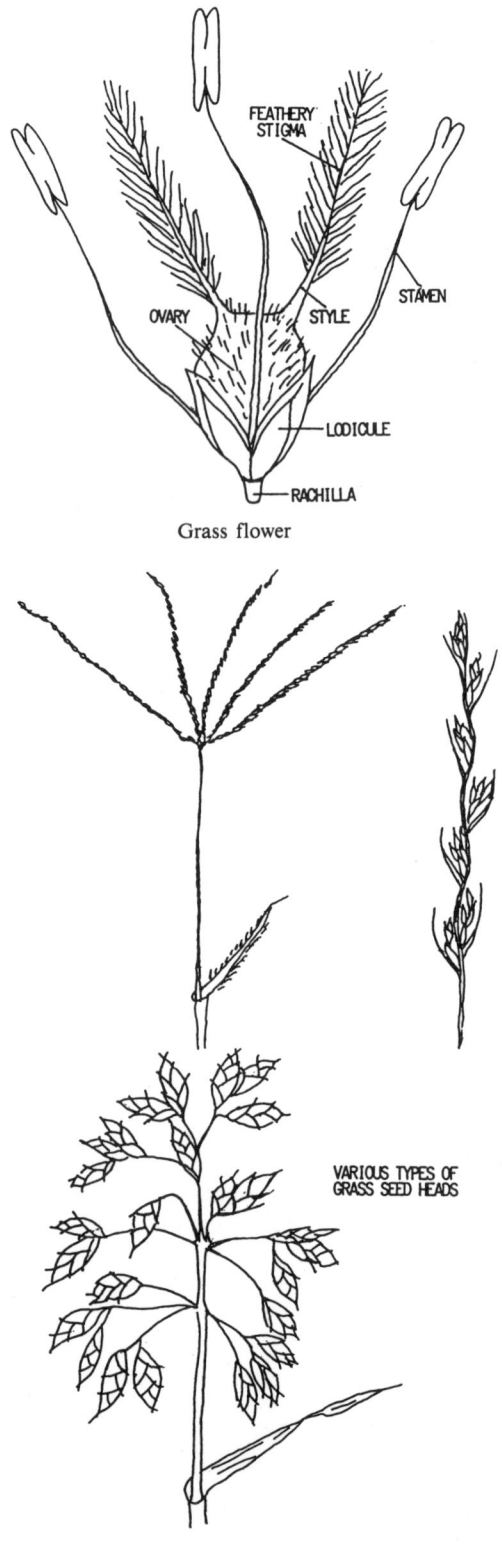

Grass flower

Bunching, Tillering

If the grass plant is kept low it will either bunch, mat or tiller, depending on the nature of the plant. Bunch grasses do not necessarily make a good lawn, indeed some can form foot-tripping tussocks.

When lawn grass mixtures are compounded they often include suitable bunching, running and tillering grasses.

The Flower

The stem ends in an inflorescence, which can be in the form of a spike, raceme or panicle. These flowers eventually form seed.

The grass plant, generally, is adapted to being pollinated by wind-borne pollen, which makes it a very successful plant away from woodland and forest areas.

The flower consists of a pistil, comprising the two stigmas, style, ovary and three anthers-stamens. The feathery stigmas catch windborne pollen, which is transferred to the ovary. Pollination takes place and the whole then becomes the grass seed.

The mature seeds may be harvested and used for future sowing.

Seed (Caryopsis, Dry Fruit)

The quickest, easiest, usually cheapest, and sometimes the best way to grow a lawn, is by using

VARIOUS TYPES OF GRASS SEED HEADS

Various types of grass seed heads

suitable, top-quality lawn-grass seeds, with suitable 'purity' and 'germination' potential.

It is interesting to note that fine lawn Bent Grasses (Creeping Bent, Browntop Bent) can have roughly sixteen to eighteen million seeds to the kilogram, whereas Perennial Ryegrass can have only approximately 460 000 seeds to the kilogram.

Buying Grass Seed

Mixtures of species-varieties-cultivars, or blends of the same species, or even a single species or cultivar are used by seed firms to provide a particular lawn surface for a particular use. Grass seed can be purchased in different forms.

1. Single species. Such a lawn is composed of a single species, variety, or cultivar which can form a tightly-knit hard-wearing turf-sward. Examples include Browntop Bent *(Agrostis tenuis)*, Creeping Bent *(Agrostis stolonifera* syn. *A. palustris*; syn. *A. s. palustris)*, or Couch (Bermuda) Grass *(Cynodon dactylon)*.

2. Single species, using various varieties or cultivars. Cultivars and/or varieties of one species are blended in proportion to make a lawn. For example, using various Kentucky Bluegrass *(Poa pratensis)* cultivars.

3. Mixed species, varieties or cultivars. Various species, varieties or cultivars are mixed in proportion to make a suitable lawn. For example, suitable cultivars of Chewings Fescue *(Festuca rubra commutata)* and Browntop Bent *(Agrostis tenuis)* are mixed in proportion, say 80% Chewings Fescue to 20% Browntop Bent, by weight, to make a fine, cool-climate (season) lawn.

Suitable cultivars of Chewings Fescue, Browntop Bent and Kentucky Bluegrass *(Poa pratensis)* are mixed in correct proportions to make a top-class ornamental lawn.

And lawn-suitable cultivars of Fine-leaved Perennial Ryegrass *(Lolium perenne)*, Chewings Fescue, Browntop Bent and Kentucky Bluegrass are mixed in the correct proportions to make a compact, harder wearing lawn.

Generally, a mixture of intertwining grasses gives more scope, because it is possible that some grasses in the mix will suit your particular site and soil conditions. Many factors come into the reckoning such as purity and germination, soil, suitability for available light, disease resistance or disease susceptibility, natural vigour, potential loss of fine, small seeds and so on.

Grass seed mixing and blending is best left to those experts who are aware of suitable grasses for a particular locality and soil type.

Good seed mixtures or blends must contain a high percentage of viable seeds, which under the correct growing conditions will germinate freely and grow strongly. The seeds must be free from dangerous, noxious or nuisance weeds that could establish in any future lawn. They should be acceptably free from dirt, dust, chaff and other inert matter. The seeds must be true to those grass species, varieties and cultivars listed on the label.

It is important to sow those top quality grasses that will stabilize and become suitable, permanent lawn grasses, and not be swayed by offers of vast quantities of unsuitable grass seeds at give-away prices.

And I make the point that 'top quality' does not refer only to super bowling/golf green lawn grasses, but also to those less glamourous grasses such as Fine-leaved Perennial Ryegrass cultivars, Tall Fescue cultivars, Improved Couch (Bermuda) Grass cultivars, Kentucky Bluegrass cultivars and so on, that are used for lawns.

Runners, Rooted Runners, Blocks, Plugs and Turves

Some of the finest lawns are grown from runners, rooted runners, small blocks of turf, small round plugs of turf or whole turves, because the seeds of that particular grass are not viable (such as some popular bowling green Hybrid Couches), are unable to produce the same quality of grass as the parent, or are too slow to germinate and form a suitable lawn surface.

A Little Lawn History

Was Sir Francis Drake playing bowls on a chamomile, or a grass lawn, when the Spanish Armada arrived? Nobody knows, but it is generally thought that he was playing on a chamomile lawn, which, possibly, illustrates that fine grass lawns were not then in vogue.

However, it was also around Drake's time, with the emergence of more and more prosperous landed gentry, that garden turf lawns composed of fine grasses began to appear...not necessarily as lawns...but as walks and garden paths.

But it wasn't until the eighteenth century, with

the advent of the great gardeners such as Capability Brown, that the lawn as a feature took on such prominence.

For generations, lawns were a feature of the country houses of the rich; the poor using what little garden space they had to produce food to survive. And in the beginning these country house lawns were made from selected, finest pasture-meadow, or hill-pasture turves, that were capable of withstanding the constant mowing of a hand-scythe.

Occasionally, some of the larger lawns, which were not too close to the house, were kept mown by sheep, the sheep being contained by a ha-ha (a sunken fence).

Lawn maintenance was revolutionized in the early nineteenth century with the advent of the cylinder-reel push-mower, a machine fundamentally similar to the cylinder-reel machines we see used today on golf and bowling greens. It was patented by Edwin Budding, a textile engineer, who realized that the cylinder-reel machine used for cutting wool-nap from carpets could be adapted to cutting grass.

Lawn mowers were produced cheaply, and this was important, particularly following the two world wars when the working and middle classes, as well as town planners, demanded more amenity garden space, which usually included a lawn.

A suitable petrol-engined mower did not appear until the very early twentieth century. Electric cylinder-reel and rotary mowers, and petrol rotary mowers, suitable for the home lawn, then made their appearance.

Lawn Grass Selection

Selection of grasses suitable for greens or lawns, began in the eastern United States in the late nineteenth century, when it was established that certain of the finer Fescues and Bent Grasses made the finest lawns. American agricultural colleges, universities, the Sports Turf Research Institute, Bingley, Yorkshire, among others, carried out intensive lawn/sports grass research. The Dutch were, and are, in the forefront in developing lawn grasses, as were, and are, many famous seed firms.

South African turf experts began their experiments in the early twentieth century, and New Zealand was well into turf research before the Second World War. Much turf research has been carried out, and still is being carried out, in Australia for our own particular collection of climatic conditions.

And all this time fertilizer and chemical firms were producing lawn products to nourish or protect lawn grasses.

Finally, let us not forget those groundsmen/greenkeepers, past and present, who have done so much in putting the results into practice.

3. Lawn Grasses

Cool-climate grasses, also referred to as 'cool-season' grasses, are those that grow normally in 'cool' countries such as the United Kingdom. Grasses such as Perennial Ryegrass, Browntop Bent, Creeping Bent, Red Fescues and Kentucky Bluegrass.

These grasses also survive successfully in colder areas of Australia, for example, certain areas of the New South Wales Tablelands, Victoria and Tasmania.

These cool-climate grasses will, however, grow successfully during the colder-wetter months in certain warmer parts of Australia (for example, Adelaide, hence the 'cool-season' tag). They may also survive during the summer period, but only if certain growing conditions are met, e.g. copious water. Selected cultivars of Tall Fescue are more adaptable, but they still need adequate water.

It is unlikely that you would see cool-climate grasses growing in the warmer parts of Queensland or in Darwin.

Warm-climate grasses, also known as 'warm-season' grasses, are those that will survive in the warmer parts of Australia, but will not do much in colder areas, such as certain parts of Victoria or New South Wales. Grasses such as Couch (Bermuda) Grass, Hybrid Couch, Kikuyu Grass and Buffalo Grass.

To complicate things a little more there are warm-climate grasses that will grow successfully in Darwin and subtropical Queensland, but will not be so successful, if at all, in the warm climate of Adelaide, grasses such as Carpet Grass, Queensland Blue Couch and Bahia Grass.

Important Points

The common names of grasses begin with capitals throughout the book merely to highlight them.

Genera (e.g. *Poa*), species (e.g. *pratensis*) and a plant variation that has been produced naturally, are usually written in italics, e.g. *Poa pratensis* var. *simpsoni* (*Poa pratensis* is Kentucky Bluegrass), whereas a cultivated variety (i.e. produced by plant breeders), which shortens to 'cultivar', is written in Roman script, starts with a capital letter, and is enclosed with inverted commas, i.e. *Poa pratensis* 'Bill Simpson'.

Words of Caution

What some people may refer to in one part of the country or world as a particular plant, may be different elsewhere. For example, in some countries Creeping Bent is referred to as *Agrostis stolonifera*, in others as *Agrostis palustris* and in others as *Agrostis stolonifera* var. *palustris*.

The world of botany is in a state of flux, and many family, generic and species names are being changed.

Cultivars

Grass plant cultivars are not given for the simple reason that by the time you read this book a suggested cultivar may have been superseded by a better one, although some cultivars do seem to last. However, I will list a few 'landmarks'; names which have stuck in my mind over the past 40 years. Some are no longer available, some are still going strong, while others are more recent:

'Aberystwyth S.23', 'Pelo' and 'Elka' Perennial Ryegrass; 'Highland' Bent; 'Egmont' Browntop Bent; 'Penncross' Creeping Bent; 'Highlight' Chewings Fescue; 'Aberystwyth S.59' and 'Dawson' Slender Creeping Red Fescue; 'Novorubra' and 'Boreal' Strong Creeping Red Fescue; 'Merion' and 'Monopoly' Kentucky Bluegrass (Smooth-stalked Meadow Grass); 'Biljart' and 'Scaldis' Hard Fescue;

'Arid' and 'Shortstop' Tall Fescue; 'Pensacola' and 'Argentine' Bahia Grass; 'Greenlees Park' Couch Grass; 'Tifdwarf' and 'Santa Ana' Hybrid Couch.

There are many, many more cultivars as well as strains and selections.

Stripes

It is possible that you may want a lawn that will produce those dark green and light green 'centre court' stripes so much admired on the television. These are produced by using a cylinder-reel mower with front and back rollers. Bear in mind that some grasses are so tough that cutting them with a cylinder-reel machine would be impractical, or even impossible. Also some fine grasses don't seem to produce such distinct dark green and light green striping as others.

Cool-climate Grasses

Annual Meadow Grass *(Poa annua)*
Synonym Annual Bluegrass

Annual Meadow Grass appears in certain areas as a lawn weed grass. It is a low-growing grass that seeds below the mower blades. Generally, it is considered an annual, but I'm not sure whether it can be an annual, as I have a plant from seed which is eighteen months old, but struggling. *Poa annua* is easily recognized throughout the sward by the whitish appearance of its seed.

Kentucky Bluegrass *(Poa pratensis)*
Synonym Smooth-stalked Meadow Grass

A rhizomatous, 'Roman-sword', spoon-leaved grass which is coarser than fine fescues, but which will not tolerate the same close mowing. It is a lovely, dark-green (variable), hard-wearing grass which prefers a well-drained, moist, slightly acid (not too acidic) to neutral soil, and requires adequate fertilizer during the spring flush, and adequate water during dry spells. It is usually used in grass mixtures for particular situations, but selected cultivars are used on their own, or as a blend.

Many superb cultivars/varieties have been produced by Dutch and American breeders.

Mature Kentucky Bluegrass cv.

Rough-stalked Meadow Grass *(Poa trivialis)*
Synonym Rough Bluegrass

As the name suggests, a slightly rougher-looking grass, but similar to Kentucky Bluegrass. It tends to spread by stolon runners and is rather patchy in appearance, but is used in seed mixtures for shady, moist, fertile soil areas. It can become almost weed-like in turf, as it doesn't 'sit' well with other species cultivars. Indeed, it is a weed in the finest turf swards.

Browntop Bent *(Agrostis tenuis)*
Synonym Common Bent, Colonial Bentgrass, New Zealand Bent, Oregon Browntop, Highland Browntop

A famous, fine-leaved, adaptable, tufted or creeping grass that can produce moisture-seeking short rhizomes on dry (but not hot-dry) soils, and above-ground creeping stolons on moist soils, but prefers a well-drained, slightly acid to acid soil and reasonable fertility.

Mature Browntop Bent cv.

Browntop Bent

Chewings Fescue

Creeping Bent Grass

Hard Fescue

Kentucky Bluegrass

Fine-leaved Perennial Ryegrass

Tall Fescue

Buffalo (St Augustine) Grass

Carpet Grass

Couch (Bermuda) Grass

Hybrid Couch Grass

Kikuyu Grass

Queensland Blue Couch Grass

But choose only desirable cultivars for fine lawns as some selections can be coarse. Suitable Browntop Bent cultivars will tolerate close mowing, and in combination with fine Chewings Fescue cultivars and possibly Slender Creeping Red Fescue cultivars, are used extensively for the finest cool climate lawns.

Browntop Bent can be used on its own, however, as it does produce a tight-knit, compact sward. But remember the peril of using one species of grass: when disaster strikes in the form of disease, the destruction can be total.

I have read recently in a professional turfculture magazine that the old cultivar 'Highland' (Oregon) Browntop may be considered a separate species, *Agrostis castellana*. Dryland Bent has also been placed under this species. Remember, if you want the finest Browntop Bent lawn then discuss it with an expert on lawns and modern lawn seeds.

Creeping Bent Grass *(Agrostis stolonifera)*
Synonym *A. palustris, A stolonifera* var. *palustris*

Some creeping Bent strains are loose of habit and unsuitable for fine turf, but better cultivars have been produced and will result in a fine lawn; indeed even good enough for certain famous golf greens.

Creeping Bent Grass grows reasonably vigorously in moist soils, provided this soil moisture is

Mature Creeping Bent cv.

supplemented in dry spells by sufficient irrigation, to keep the grasses growing well.

Some cultivars are better propagated vegetatively, others by seed.

Velvet Bent *(Agrostis canina)*
Synonym *A. canina* ssp. *canina*

An extremely fine-leaved, some consider the most beautiful, lawn grass, predominantly of heathland, but not readily available for lawns. However, because of its beauty, its development as a commercial lawn grass is being pursued by lawn seed breeders.

Mature Chewings Fescue cv.

Chewings Fescue *(Festuca rubra* ssp. *commutata)*

A most useful, relatively low-growing, bunchy dense-turf, fine-leaved Red Fescue. It is used in mixtures with other suitable fine grass cultivars for fine turf mixtures. Prefers a well-drained, acidic soil.

Creeping Red Fescue *(Festuca rubra* ssp. *rubra,* ssp. *litoralis* and ssp. *tricophylla)*

There are two distinct forms of Creeping Red Fescue: Strong Creeping Red Fescue (ssp. *rubra*) with 54 chromosomes; and Slender Creeping Red Fescue (ssp. *litoralis*, also known as ssp. *tricophylla*) with 42 chromosomes.

Mature Creeping Red Fescue cv.

Strong Creeping Red Fescue has stronger root rhizomes, coarser, darker-green grass blades, and a more vigorous growth than the Slender Creeping Red Fescue.

Slender Creeping Red Fescue (ssp. *litoralis*) is a fine-leaved, low-growing fescue with short, slender root rhizomes. This form of Creeping Red Fescue is the type used, for example, in seed mixes for many United Kingdom and New Zealand fine lawns. Although not much used in Australia it is, nevertheless, used in certain grass seed mixtures for lawns and moderately shaded areas.

Creeping Red Fescue prefers a well-drained, partially shaded site, and acidic soil. It deteriorates in a highly fertile soil.

Fine-leaved Sheep's Fescue *(Festuca tenuifolia)*
Synonym *F. ovina* var. *tenuifolia*

Suitable for acidic soils, this fine-leaved plant is of dwarf habit and forms slight tufts. It is hard wearing but is not used on its own. Not much used for lawns in Australia, as it is not a true lawn grass.

Mature Fine-leaved Sheep's Fescue

Hard Fescue *(Festuca longifolia)*
Synonym *F. ovina* var. *longifolia*

A tufted, hard-wearing, fine-looking grass which is not suitable for fine lawns, but is used in combination with other suitable grasses for cool-climate 'hard-dry' areas. Hard Fescue is not much used in

Mature Hard Fescue cv.

Australia, but seed is possibly available from specialist suppliers.

Tall Fescue *(Festuca arundinacea)*

In the wild, a hard-wearing, deep-rooting grass that is coarser than the other fescues mentioned. However, selected, versatile, finer-leaved cultivars have been produced (but still not as fine as the fescues mentioned above) that stand up to reasonably hard use, and reasonably dry conditions, such as those of Adelaide, provided that the grass is not mown too closely, and receives sufficient water during dry spells.

Do try to see modern cultivar Tall Fescue lawns before buying the seed or turf to ascertain leaf quality. Reasonably quick germination.

Mature Tall Fescue cv.

Crested Dogstail *(Cynosurus cristatus)*

A hard-wearing, deep-rooting, low and slow growing grass, similar in appearance to the fine ryegrasses. It has, however, been largely superseded by the best of the modern Fine-leaved Perennial Ryegrass cultivars. Crested Dogstail is not much used in Australia, if at all.

Perennial Ryegrasses *(Lolium perenne)*

Perennial Ryegrass can be split up into three groups: hay Perennial Ryegrass; hay-pasture Perennial

Mature Fine-leaved Perennial Ryegrass cv.

Ryegrass; and pasture Perennial Ryegrass. Those strains-varieties that came within the pasture group were, originally, selected for lawn grasses.

Fine-leaved (Amenity) Turf-Type Perennial Ryegrass cultivars suitable for lawns are superior to some of the pasture Perennial Ryegrasses. I shall refer to these as Fine-leaved Perennial Ryegrasses.

Fine-leaved Perennial Ryegrass is used for lawns that are expected to take more wear and tear than the fine Fescue-Bent, or Kentucky Blue Grass lawns. It prefers a moist, cool climate, without severe summer temperatures.

Perennial Ryegrass is adaptable, but succeeds best in a slightly acid, moist, fertile soil. It needs adequate fertilizer, particularly in spring, and irrigation during dry spells to succeed.

Note well: There are many Perennial Ryegrass cultivars, but choose only fine-leaved cultivars suitable for lawns. Rapid germination.

Smaller Catstail *(Phleum bertolonii)* Synonym *P. nodosum*

Certain dwarf cultivars are used in combination with finer grasses for hard-wear areas. It needs reasonable fertilizer during growth periods and adequate irrigation during dry spells. Not much used in Australia, if at all.

Timothy, Synonym Catstail, *(Phleum pratense)* is a larger-leaved, tufted grass with distinctive catstail seed heads, which is not much used in lawn grass mixtures because of its tufted habit.

Warm-climate Grasses

Be careful when selecting grasses from this group, although some grasses may grow well in, say

Darwin, those same grasses may not succeed in Adelaide, though both are classed as warm-climate areas. Therefore, check with a lawn expert to see if a particular grass will survive in your part of the world before buying it.

Bahia Grass *(Paspalum notatum)*

Bahia Grass is not much used in Australia, and its use is restricted to the northern areas, Darwin for example.

It is a hard-wearing, coarse-leaved grass, with both stolon and rhizome roots being reported.

It has been used as an 'expedient' grass for sandy, slightly acid soil. 'Pensacola' is a well-known variety, and 'Argentine' cultivar seeds are available in Australia but, at the time of writing, are expensive.

Buffalo Grass *(Stenotaphrum secundatum)* Synonym St Augustine-grass

A trailing, stoloniferous grass which produces a loose-textured, greyish blue green, even thatchy, turf after a time. This coarse, hardwearing type of lawn is still grown in many areas of Australia, even though it is not the prettiest of grasses, and not all that pleasant to walk on.

Mature Buffalo (St Augustine) Grass

Lawns are usually planted from runners (stolons), rooted runners and turves. This grass grows well in a well-drained, but moist, sandy, slightly acid, reasonably fertile soil, and needs irrigation during dry spells.

Do not confuse what Australians call Buffalo Grass, and what Americans call St Augustine-grass, with Buffalograss USA *(Buchloe dactyloides)*, although I cannot recall seeing *B. dactyloides* or its selections in Australia.

Carpet Grass (*Axonopus* species)

Carpet Grasses are naturalized grasses from the West Indies and the tropical areas of the southern parts of the United States. Their leaves are large, light green, shiny and folded. Their use is confined in Australia to frost-free areas, for example the Darwin area and parts of Queensland.

Two species are used for lawns—Narrow Leaf or Common Carpet Grass *(Axonopus affinis)* and Tropical or Broad Leaf Carpet Grass *(Axonopus compressus)*.

Narrow Leaf Carpet Grass is a prostrate grass that usually spreads by stolons, and its use is sometimes restricted to those acidic-sandy areas where a better looking grass would not survive.

Tropical Carpet Grass *(Axonopus compressus)* is coarser-leaved than the Narrow Leaf Carpet Grass.

Thoroughly discuss the pros and cons of using Carpet Grasses, including the mowing, with a local lawn expert before using.

Centipede Grass *(Eremochloa ophiuroides)*

To the best of my knowledge Centipede Grass isn't much used in Australia, although suitability tests were being carried out by various organizations many years ago. The grass blades are a sort of cross between the finer grass blades of Couch Grass and the coarser Buffalo Grass (St Augustine-grass). It spreads by stolons, and is used for poor, often sandy, soils.

Couch Grass *(Cynodon dactylon)*
Synonym Bermuda Grass

Couch (Bermuda) Grass is the most celebrated of the warm-climate grasses, and it spreads rapidly by overground runners. Cultivars, selections, varieties and hybrids have been produced so that now there is a range of forms from coarse-leaved to fine-leaved. Rhizomes are also produced.

Australian groundsmen/greenkeepers, forced by circumstances, have in the past selected and 'nursery-grown' their own fine-leaved forms of Couch (Bermuda) Grass. Indeed, some prefer these selections to Hybrid Couch Grasses for a specific soil-use situation. Commercial growers have also produced selections, and this work is ongoing.

Selected Couch (Bermuda) Grass is available as seed either with hulls, or with hulls removed for speedier germination. It is also available as selected runners, rooted runners, small turf blocks, small turf

Mature Hybrid Couch Grass

Mature Couch Grass

plugs or whole turves, and these are generally used when the seed does not produce the same quality leaf as does the vegetative overground runner.

Other *Cynodon* species have been crossed with Couch (Bermuda) Grass *(Cynodon dactylon)* to produce Hybrid Couch Grasses, the best known being those hybrids between Couch (Bermuda) Grass and Germiston Couch, also known as South African Couch Grass—*(Cynodon dactylon × Cynodon transvaalensis)*. 'Santa Ana' and 'Tifdwarf' are Hybrid Couch cultivars.

While producing fine greens using Hybrid Couch is a great art, these hybrid grasses can produce excellent swards. In the correct climate the resulting lawn should be fine-leaved and excellent to look at, although in winter, in some areas, the sward does tend to brown off.

Couch (Bermuda) Grass will not tolerate shade. Thatch will have to be controlled in fine Couch (Bermuda) Grass lawns.

There is a down side to Couch (Bermuda) Grass, in that it becomes one of the world's worst weeds when it is allowed to escape.

Durban Grass *(Dactyloctenium australe)*

Durban Grass is shade tolerant. Its blades are large and soft looking, but it will not take close mowing. Used mainly as a shade grass.

Kikuyu Grass *(Pennisetum clandestinum)*

Many gardeners have Kikuyu Grass lawns; not by choice necessarily, as in the right climate Kikuyu Grass is a great invader. It produces a very coarse lawn, but if kept mown, watered and fertilized can produce a remarkably green lawn during hot spells, although thatch build-up is a major problem. Mid-winter in areas such as Adelaide, it may be eye-achingly green. Although I wouldn't recommend planting one, I have seen some fine Kikuyu Grass lawns.

Kikuyu Grass is available as runners, turves or seed. The seed is expensive and is sown at very low rates. Rhizomes are also produced.

Mature Kikuyu Grass

Queensland Blue Couch Grass *(Digitaria didactyla)*

Queensland Blue Couch has been used, as the name suggests, in Queensland, but also in parts of northern New South Wales and similar climates. It is a hot weather grass suitable mainly for warm, moist areas, and produces a reasonably fine sward. It is not used to any great degree in other parts of Australia, where it can be prone to cold snaps. Seed can be expensive, but turf is readily available where it grows prolifically.

Salt Water Paspalum *(Paspalum vaginatum)* Synonym Seashore Paspalum

This grass is useful for certain problem soils in warmer areas, but out of its environment Salt Water Paspalum is not particularly adaptable. Check its suitability in your area with a local expert on lawns.

Zoysia Grass

Zoysia Grass leaf tissue is usually extremely fibrous, and if cut with a light mower, or mower with blunt blades, can result in a finished lawn that looks ragged and torn. Check out local Zoysia Grass lawns, find out frequency of cut, and type of mowers used.

Japanese (Korean) Lawngrass *(Zoysia japonica)* produces a moderately coarse, hardy turf, that grows well on a well-drained, slightly acid soil with reasonable fertility. It is more tolerant of cold than the following, but needs irrigation during hot, dry spells.

Manila Grass *(Zoysia matrella)* produces a reasonably fine turf in moister, hotter climates.

Mascarene Grass *(Zoysia tenuifolia)*, as the Latin name suggests, produces a fine-leaved turf. It is slow growing.

At first glance Zoysia Grasses are similar to Couch Grass. They produce a tightly packed, hard-wearing turf from rhizomes and stolons. They are very slow growing, and therefore initially subject to weed competition. They prefer a slightly acid soil, and irrigation water that is not limy. The leaf blades turn straw-coloured during cold weather.

Choosing the Correct Grasses

Bear in mind that the climate of your locality, the pH of your lawn soil, the guaranteed availability of irrigation water in summer, the quality of the water, or expected drought conditions, will affect the choice of a grass seed mixture. This is where it is logical to seek local professional advice on lawn grasses, as the local lawn professional should know the best grasses to use for a given area, and, importantly, for a particular lawn surface. You should make abundantly clear what type of lawn surface you want.

You should also make growing a beautiful lawn as easy as possible, as this is not an easy goal, and choosing the correct grasses is an important step in this direction.

Use only top quality strains/varieties or cultivars/hybrids of grass, as unclean mixtures, coarse strains, etc. will result in an unsatisfactory lawn.

Allergies

Are you, or is anybody in your family, allergic to certain types of grasses? This, no doubt, has to be considered before starting a lawn.

What Type of Lawn Do You Want?

Before you begin a lawn decide exactly what you want to use it for. Is it to be a fine lawn like a bowling green or golf green? A medium-textured ornamental lawn that will take a certain amount of wear and tear? Or a coarse-textured harder wearing lawn?

Bear in mind that maintaining a lawn to bowling green/golf green standards is an exacting and arduous business; a 'journey' not to be embarked upon lightly.

Below are a few suggestions, but the choice depends, considerably on your local climate. Generally, but not always, species and cultivars are mixed to form a more compact or suitable grass sward.

Suitable grasses for various lawn types

Cool Climate	Warm Climate
Bowling Green-Golf Green Type Lawn	
Creeping Bent cvs only	Fine Hybrid Couch Grasses cvs only
Browntop Bent cvs only	
Browntop Bent cvs Chewings Fescue cvs	
Browntop Bent cvs Chewings Fescue cvs Slender Creeping Red Fescue cvs	

Cool Climate	Warm Climate
Ornamental Lawn	
Kentucky Bluegrass cvs only	Specially selected fine-leaved Couch (Bermuda) Grass cvs only
Kentucky Bluegrass cvs Chewings Fescue cvs Browntop Bent cvs	Specially selected Queensland Blue Couch Grass only
Crested Dogstail Browntop Bent cvs Chewings Fescue cvs	Zoysia Grass only
Second Class Ornamental Lawn	
Fine-leaved Perennial Ryegrass cvs Chewings Fescue Kentucky Bluegrass	
Fine-leaved Perennial Ryegrass cvs only	
Intermediate Ornamental Lawn	
Tall Fescue – finest cvs only	
Coarser Texture Lawn	
Suitable Pasture Perennial Ryegrass cvs only	Buffalo Grass (St Aug.) only
	Common Couch (Bermuda) Grass only
	Kikuyu Grass only
	Narrow Leaf Carpet Grass only
	Broad Leaf Carpet Grass only
	Bahia Grass cvs only

Note well: cvs = only suitable cultivars to be used

Special seed mixtures are usually available for partially shaded areas.

4. Preparing the Site

Is the lawn to be used for pure visual pleasure? Is it to be used by yourself, children and dogs as a playground? Or is it to be used for croquet, bowls and the like?

The use a lawn is to receive goes some way toward deciding the types of grasses you will use, and could determine to a considerable extent how your garden will be laid out. Therefore, consider the lawn's uses and have a clear plan before you begin work.

Are You Fit Enough?

I think it pertinent to point out that producing a lawn could be dangerous or damaging work for those who are not fit enough. Therefore, you should be aware of your physical capabilities before attempting lawn construction, and here I include young and old, male and female. Also, wear suitable protective clothing when working in the garden.

Underground (and Above-ground) Services

Before you attempt to work in any area below soil level, you must make sure that you know where all the services lie; services such as electricity, gas, water, sewer, phone, existing land drainage, and any others installed by you, or previous inhabitants, as damaging such services may lead to serious

The site before preparation for a lawn

complications, injury and worse. Also check for overhead services.

Perhaps you haven't had any of these services installed yet. Obviously it is not a good idea to construct a lawn if somebody is going to dig trenches all over it, so have the services installed first. Make sure that any trenches are well stabilized, have a sufficient depth of suitable soil, and will not sink after the lawn is laid.

Caution

I am not a lawyer or insurer, and can only suggest the following. If you are having persons coming to your property to carry out work, then make sure that they are properly insured (public liability, worker's compensation), licensed, registered, qualified and so on.

All the above may entail a lot of running around and phoning, but it is better to spend time checking such matters *before* any work is done, rather than sorting out problems after the event.

Find out what these persons are going to charge before they start work in your garden, by obtaining a properly written quotation.

Find out where you stand legally if an accident happens on your property to friends and neighbours who have volunteered to give you a hand.

If you are a tenant, you should probably get approval from your landlord in writing, before considering alterations to the propery.

Grading

It is reasonable to state that most home garden lawns are flattish, or sloping with a flat plane, but this may not always be possible, or desirable, due to the landscaping of the area.

Therefore, certain lawns are graded gradually so that they can be negotiated easily by the mower, and by the person mowing, without the mower scalping any bumps or humps in the lawn.

Although such a lawn can be undulating, it must be free-draining without hollows, as hollows can retain water and hamper mowing. Awkward corners should be avoided as these tend to make mowing difficult and possibly dangerous.

Analyse and stack any suitable topsoil to one side, usually in a heap or heaps, and grade the subsoil to the desired contour levels, finally replacing the topsoil. The work should be done in dry conditions to avoid ruining and compacting the subsoil.

As stated, gradients should be gentle enough to allow for easy mowing. The home gardener should aim to provide say 150 mm (6 in) of suitable topsoil over the site to cater for adequate grass root growth and development.

You may only have to make minor grading adjustments, by moving and regrading existing topsoil, or adding fresh but suitable, compatible topsoil to obtain the desired finish.

Trees

Trees situated in lawn and garden areas where extensive grading is being carried out should be protected against damage, and it is quite easy to protect them from minor punishment.

Roots and soil cut away by machinery, for example, can endanger the health of the tree. Even a few centimetres of soil graded over the top of existing roots, or up against the bark, may harm or eventually kill the tree.

Ask yourself, or seek professional opinion on such matters as: 'Is the tree in danger?' 'Is it economically viable to save the tree?' 'Is it possible to transplant the tree?' 'Is the tree protected by a tree preservation order, encumbrances or similar?'

Working from Fixed Points

Each garden has fixed points to work to, or from. It could be a footpath that surrounds the house, the concrete of a driveway, an outbuilding, or a tree, and so forth.

Water Drainage Points

It is vital, when you grade a lawn, that water runs away to the correct drainage points. You would not grade a lawn so that water runs into the living-room, into the garage, into underground cellars, etc. I make the point that you have to be aware exactly where the water will drain once you have constructed a lawn.

Finished Levels

The height of the finished soil base, when seeding, should be just above the level of obstructions such as concrete footpaths, so that the finished lawn height eventually will be just above the height of the footpath. If the concrete were slightly higher than the lawn it could ruin the mower blades, and could be potentially hazardous in other ways.

Any settling of the lawn should be replenished with fresh soil. It is important to ensure that the soil will not sink after seeding.

Conversely, the finished lawn height should not be too high above the concrete (or-what-have-you) as the mower could slip off the grass and scalp the lawn edges. Therefore, if you are going to use turves allow for their thickness when levelling the soil. Again, the final turf height should be just above the concrete level.

Common sense is necessary when deciding final soil height; also bearing in mind that lawn compost top dressings may be added in the future.

Soil

A good soil for a lawn is a slightly acid, sandy loam containing a suitable quantity of humus. It should also be of a suitable crumbly nature. Surplus water should drain freely, but at the same time the soil should retain and hold sufficient moisture and nutrients, retain pore-air spaces, and be a minimum overall depth of 150 mm (6 in), although 225 mm (9 in) would be preferred.

Soil pH

A soil can be acid, neutral or alkaline. A scale, known as the pH scale, has been devised to measure acidity and alkalinity. The number 7 is considered neutral. From 7 down to 0 is becoming progressively more acidic. From 7 up to 14 is becoming progressively more alkaline.

Increasing Acidity   Neutral   Increasing Alkalinity

↓

0 1 2 3 4 5 6 7 8 9 10 11 12 13 14

Most lawn grasses, provided everything else in the soil is as it should be, succeed in a slightly acid soil pH 6 to pH 6.5, with pH 6 being preferred. However, there are certain grass species which prefer, or can cope with, a slightly more acidic soil.

Kits for testing soil acidity-alkalinity are available at nurseries. Make sure you get a good soil testing kit; get advice from your local Department of Agriculture/Primary Industries/Primary Production or Botanic Garden expert on soils.

Carefully read the instruction given on the label or pamphlet that comes with the soil testing kit.

Difficulty in Using the pH Kit

Some people have difficulty in reading a soil testing kit's chemical reactions on soil, and come up with wrong readings; sometimes hair-raising ones! If you have any doubt as to your ability to read a colour soil testing kit correctly then get the soil checked by a suitable, professional laboratory.

Most Garden Soils

Most garden soils are in the range pH 5.5 to pH 7.5. If you have a soil that has a wide variance, or has an unusually high or low soil pH, then check the soil again, and recheck the soil. And if in any doubt get the soil checked professionally, as widely varying soil pH and high or low soil pH are not the norm.

Testing for Soil Nutrients

Testing soil for the quantity of various plant nutrients is a complicated business, and best left to soil laboratory analysis. You can have your soil tested at a recognized, reputable laboratory. Check your local Department of Agriculture, Primary Industries or Primary Production for details concerning soil analysis services.

Soil Depth

Lawn grasses, mostly, inhabit a layer approximately 150 mm (6 in) deep into the soil, but this depends on the grass species. Given the opportunity many grasses will reach much further into the soil.

The amount of green grass leaf and suitable soil will decide the quantity and depth of grass roots, as the leaf feeds the roots with carbohydrates and proteins, and an open soil will allow the roots to move freely.

But generally 150 mm (6 in) is a reasonable depth for the concentration of lawn grass feeding roots.

Spoil and Compaction

You may find that builders have buried all sorts of things around the new house. It can be a long, tedious job to remove and dispose of this spoil but it should probably be done.

Digging over the lawn area, removing weeds and incorporating peat and suitable sand (wear suitable gloves)

Lawn area completely dug over

Any spots where sand and cement have been stored or mixed will have to be cleared in the case of cement, or scattered in the case of sand to prevent layers that could impede drainage.

It could be that the site levelling carried out by the builder has resulted in a compacted soil layer, which could lead to impeded drainage.

This compacted soil has to be broken up to allow moisture penetration, and this is done using a hand fork or a suitable rotary cultivator. Very large areas call for special machinery.

Sand

Sand for the purpose of lawn construction should be coarse, inert, clean-washed, lime-free, saline-free, sharp sand, and in some areas suitable river sand is available. In other areas coarse, inert, clean-washed, lime-free, saline-free, sharp sand may be obtained from suitable quarries, special sand pits or mines.

It may be possible to visit the area where you intend buying your sand and to examine the various grades, as sand can be divided into various particle diameters, and can be conveniently classed as fine sand, medium sand or coarse sand.

Sharp Sand and Children

Sharp sand, particularly if coarse, when used as a lawn top dressing may cause problems as children's delicate skin (also adults' and animal paws) and sharp-edged sand just do not mix. But remember, too fine a sand may cause drainage problems.

Sea Sand

Sea sand may be readily available, but usually it is unsuitable as it can contain, among other things, much lime (calcium carbonate deposits), which will raise the soil pH.

Seek local professional advice on suitable sands for lawn construction.

Mixing Sand with Clay Soil

A small amount of clean, coarse, sharp sand mixed with a large quantity of clay is not very effective; indeed it could be counter-productive.

To improve drainage in a clay soil, coarse, inert, clean, lime-free, salt-free sand has to be added in such vast quantities as to completely enclose the clay particle groupings, which means that the sand is in continuous contact with sand.

Advice should be sought from a professional soil scientist before remotely considering embarking on the extensive labour and cost of ameliorating clay soil with sand. Just stop and reflect on the enormity of the project. (Also check out the cost of a sand/soil grass root zone laboratory physical analysis beforehand).

When you consider the vast quantities of clean, coarse sharp sand needed to improve a clay soil, it may be more feasible to consider adding approximately 150 mm (6 in) of suitable, free-draining, sandy loam on top of the subsoil.

If so, then you could first consider ameliorating the clay subsoil surface before adding the topsoil, to help improve drainage and grass root penetration.

Crumb Structure

Lawn soils have to have what is known as a good 'crumb' structure, where the soil is aggregated into crumbs, or soil granules, with smaller and larger air spaces between the crumbs.

The larger airspaces fill with water, but soon allow much of this water to drain away, while the smaller air spaces fill with water and hold it for the plant. Once the water has drained from the larger spaces they are again filled with air, which supplies the plant roots with the oxygen they need for healthy growth.

Heavy Soil Plus Organic Matter

Heavy soils could have a suitable amount of acidic, organic, weed-free material, such as acid peat, incorporated into the top few centimetres of soil, but again we are looking at considerable quantities of peat. For example, a 50 mm (2 in) layer of peat incorporated in the top 100 mm (4 in) of soil represents a large investment.

Peat

Peat is usually sedge or sphagnum. Both are usually acidic but, as a precaution, always check the pH level.

Suitable acid sedge peat is used extensively on lawns, as generally it has a reasonable pH, has high humic quantities, and can be finely ground or granulated by the supplier to form organic particles easy to apply and quick to break down. Finely ground moss peat is also used.

You can incorporate moist peat in the lawn bed preparation, at say 2 to 3 kg/m² (4½ to 6½ lbs/yd²) for the seeded lawn, mixed in with the top 50 to 75 mm (2 to 3 in) of soil, and 1 kg/m² (2¼ lbs/yd²) mixed in the same depth for the lawn that is to be turfed. Do read the instructions given on the pack of peat. If you use peat then make sure it is moist before application. Peat that has been allowed to dry out completely can be extremely difficult to wet.

Sandy Soils

Sandy soils can be too free draining and need a top quality organic loam or organic material such as acid peat mixed into the top spit to help retain moisture.

Sandy soils can also be non-draining because sand fines have filled the pore spaces and thus impaired drainage. The addition of weed-free, acidic organic matter could help alleviate this problem.

Reasonable quantities of acid peat, weed-free, and well-rotted acid farmyard manure or well-rotted, weed-free acid compost can be added to sandy soils to aid water retention.

Too much organic bulk, however, added to any one area at any one time can lead to these lumps eventually breaking down into humic material, with the result that the lawn level can be affected. Therefore, organic matter such as peat, farmyard manure and compost should be broken down into reasonable-sized particles, before mixing with the soil, so as not to cause subsidence problems.

Adding a 50 mm (2 in) layer of organic matter which is mixed into the top 100 to 125 mm (4 to 5 in) of seedbed, should be beneficial. You may need to obtain the use of a rotary tiller cultivator to do this work, but pick your time carefully. On easy-to-work loam and sandy loam soils the garden fork or spade can be used.

And the expression 'weed-free' means exactly that. Using materials that contain weed seeds or weed particles may cause formidable lawn problems later on. Manure from animals which have been fed agricultural hay grasses may contain seeds which could prove to be a headache in a Fescue-Browntop Bent or other fine grass lawns. Also, if Couch (Bermuda) Grass clippings have been dumped on to the compost heap, then the stolon-nodes they contain, if not destroyed by the composting process, could sprout in your fine Hybrid Couch or fine Fescue-Kentucky Bluegrass lawn.

Topsoil and Subsoil

If on your existing lawn area you have a few centimetres of suitable topsoil then do not, I repeat *do not*, mix this topsoil with clay subsoil when preparing the lawn.

Move the topsoil to one side and treat the subsoil separately for all operations, such as grading, adding weed-free, acidic organic materials, or gypsum, or any amelioration you want to achieve with this subsoil. Then replace the topsoil.

Bringing subsoil up to the future lawn surface is fraught with problems, such as a lumpy seed bed, uneven lawn surface, drainage problems, user problems, and more.

Heavy Soil Tilling

Heavy soil will have to be tilled properly and carefully to produce a suitable bed for the grass. Choose your time, otherwise instead of breaking down the heavy soil into a reasonable tilth you end up with a surface of brickbats.

Conversely, don't pulverize the surface into a brick-dust that will cake at the first watering.

Heavy soils are far from ideal for lawn production.

Imported Soil

It's possible to build up your lawn area with imported soil, but it is imperative that the soil you buy is suitable and compatible.

Some silty soils become like concrete after a while, and have to be removed. Some soils are very saline. Some are too limy.

Deal with a reputable soil supply firm and seek professional advice, for example, from suitably qualified people at the State/Territory home garden advisory service, Department of Agriculture, Primary Industries, Primary Production, or Botanic Garden advisory service, on the suitability of local soils for the type of lawn you have in mind.

Prevent Layering

If you do intend placing a layer, say 150 mm (6 in), of suitable loam over a clayey subsoil, then fork-mix say 50 mm (2 in) of this new soil into the top 50 mm (2 in) of the clayey subsoil. This may help prevent layering, and give the grass roots more scope for development. Then add the rest of the soil on top. Remember, although, to avoid mixing the subsoil with the top layer of topsoil.

Weeds and Stones

Remove as many tap-rooted, bulbous and other perennial weeds as possible when preparing a lawn soil to help prevent future weed problems. Remove stones and the like, that could become dangerous flying objects during mowing.

If the lawn area is full of weeds then it is advisable, if possible, to eliminate them before you

begin preparing for the lawn, and methods for doing so are outlined below.

Fallowing

Allowing the area to lie fallow is an old-fashioned and still practised remedy, involving hoeing out weeds as they appear.

Digging over the lawn soil prior to winter in cold-climate areas to allow the winter weather to work the soil, to help settle it, and account for any weed seeds that germinate, is another method of preparing a lawn surface.

Non-selective Herbicide

Using the non-selective herbicide 'glyphosate' that will kill the weeds but will not poison the soil is another method of preparing a lawn soil.

It is vital to read the label on the herbicide product, absolutely vital, as a mistake here using the wrong herbicide could lead to disaster, with the soil being poisoned for a long, long time.

Fumigation

Having the soil fumigated by a firm officially registered and licensed by the State/Territory government for this type of work is another method.

Be warned, fumigating soils using certain chemicals can be a very, very hazardous task, and it will kill everything in the lawn area, including tree and shrub roots if they have penetrated into the area. Certain soil-fumigating chemicals are also extremely toxic to humans and animals.

Levelling and Finishing

Check on pH

The pH of the lawn soil should be determined as most grasses grow well in a slightly acid soil.

Don't add ground limestone unless the soil is too accidic for the grasses you have in mind. Worms are more active in an alkaline soil than an acid one, and coarse grasses will go beserk in a fertilized, alkaline soil.

Funguses, however, will readily attack grasses that are growing in a soil that is too acidic for them. But it is pointed out that funguses will also attack lawns growing in ideal conditions.

Tilling

Soil that has been recently tilled will usually settle and the level has to be adjusted before seeding. Break the soil down to a fine tilth suitable for taking grass seeds.

Consolidating the Soil

The lawn has to be levelled and firmed thoroughly, and the professional lawnmaker may, on a dry day when the soil is thoroughly dry, and wearing a stout pair of boots, walk carefully over the loose soil mostly on his or her heels, the balls of the feet being used to retain balance. Heelmark should slightly overlap heelmark.

Heeling loose soil, which is an ancient method of consolidating soil, can be, I can assure you from painful experience, a leg-taxing business, and should not be attempted unless you are sure that your legs can take the strain.

Heeling soil to make it firm

Area completely heeled in

An alternative is to walk over the ground to and fro, as you would walk slowly down the street, but taking small steps.

You may feel it advisable to use a roller to consolidate a lawn surface, but pulling a roller over loose soil can also be very taxing indeed, and you should be aware of this.

Practicality, when constructing lawns over very large areas, demands that rollers designed for this purpose be used.

The lawn surface must be firm otherwise the seeds will disappear into the soil crevices and, eventually, the lawn surface level will be out.

If your lawn is in a low area where water will lie, then drainage should be considered, as any water-holding areas will lead to a deterioration in the lawn. See Chapter 6 for a detailed discussion of drainage.

Lawn Levels

To obtain a level lawn you can use a spirit level and a straight edge. Buy a piece of suitable hardwood, planed to an exact straight edge, and say 75 mm × 25 mm × 3 m (3 in × 1 in × 10 ft), or whatever sensible length you consider, from a reliable local timber merchant. Then you can check the finished job by eye; that is, holding the wood up to your eye and sighting down the edges looking for deviations, twists, bends and so on. It has to be exact or your levels will be out. You also have to make sure that your spirit level is correct.

Pegging Out

When levelling, a large area is difficult to work with, so divide your area into smaller squares. Knock in pegs say at every 2 m (6 ft), thus making 2 by 2 m (6 × 6 ft) squares, and level them up using the straight edge and spirit level. You can make smaller squares if you prefer.

A lawn soil surface should have a fall away from the house, or any areas that could get flooded during rain.

One type of 'level' peg

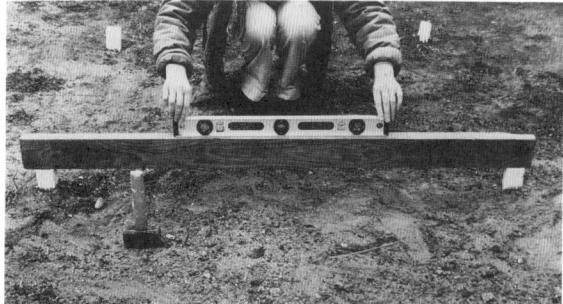

Levelling pegs using straight edge and spirit level

Using string to keep pegs in line

Lawn area boxed in; also showing level pegs

Perhaps, a lawn should be slightly raised in the middle to create a slight fall that will shed water away from the centre to the sides, provided there is adequate drainage to remove the run-off. Or you can have a 'flat' lawn, but with a slight fall to one side to take away the surface water.

The lawn pegs could be 100 to 150 mm (4 to 6 in), preferably 150 mm (6 in), above the subsoil level to allow for subsequent soil being added.

Screeding

You can bring the level of the soil up to the level of the pegs. You then use a method I call screeding.

Screeding soil is similar to how a concrete worker levels concrete, with a sawing action, using a straight edge across two 'railway line' shuttering guides. These so-called railway lines can be straight lengths of wood fixed so that they will not move out under pressure, and the height of these guides is the same as the pegs.

Levelling soil using the 'railway line' screeding method. This method is very taxing on the arms, elbow joints, etc.

Firstly you rake the soil into the area between the pegs in shallow layers and firm these layers, gradually working up to the peg height. Trying to firm deep layers of soil is not as successful, and could result in subsequent uneven settling.

Place and firm small layers of soil until you have reached the top of the pegs, and then screed the topsoil in a sawing movement across the two 'railway lines' using a straight-edged screeding board.

This screeding work can be very taxing to the arms, elbow joints and back, causing strained muscles and possibly worse. Two people working together, one on either end of the screeding board, should lessen the strain, but even so moving soil is heavy work.

If you intend using this method then level out the

Levelling a lawn using the rake to bring soil to peg height

soil as much as possible using a rake or shovel, a little at a time. Work with small quantities of dry soil only, when using the screeding method, and if feasible have somebody help you. Take your time and work carefully.

Consolidate

Consolidate the screeded soil by walking over it on your heels, or with flat feet, or by using a roller if suitable. Rake out the screeded soil lightly to get rid of any indentations. Add more soil if need be and screed it again. You should be able to walk over the soil and just leave the merest suggestion of a footprint. This work must be done only when the soil is dry.

An Easier Method

You can lessen the strain of levelling the lawn soil by still having the pegs close to each other as suggested above, but by taking your time and raking small quantities of soil level to the tops of the pegs, and forgetting about the screeding method.

Then carry out the procedure of consolidating the soil, re-rake and add soil if necessary.

Gradual Sweeps and Undulations

You don't have to have a level lawn, but can have one with gradual sweeps and undulations. (They must be gentle to avoid scalping the lawn with the mower.) You still have to work from a fixed starting point, otherwise how will you know where you are going?

Pegs are usually knocked in at the correct heights above the lawn to guide you over the lawn. You may think that working without pegs, using your eye to

ascertain levels, is a good idea, but working to pegs is easier and I imagine more accurate.

Stakes and lines can be laid out to guide you and indicate just how to graduate and mould the surface of the lawn. You can modify the stakes and strings, adjusting the system to arrive at your final lawn surface finish.

You should still aim to have the 150 mm (6 in) of suitable top soil, if possible and feasible, no matter how you grade.

For larger areas you may need to extend the distance between the pegs and hire suitable earth grading equipment. And you may need to hire a professional land surveyor to gauge the site levels accurately.

Finishing Up

Re-firm the soil, rake out any footprints and heel marks. Remove all pegs that have been inserted in the surface, and fill and firm the holes that are left with free-draining soil. The soil is now ready to receive the pre-seeding fertilizer and seed.

Area completely levelled ready for seeding

Depth of surface soil and subsoil after lawn preparation

Irrigation

This is the time to consider whether to install an irrigation system for the lawn. Why leave it this late in the lawn's installation? You now have all your working levels, so you know at what height you want the sprinkler heads installed.

If, however, you are laying a turf lawn then you have to allow for the height of the turves. It is important to check the turf thickness with the supplier before you install irrigation.

Discuss the practicalities with an irrigation expert well before you begin the lawn, and before you buy and install. Irrigation is discussed in detail in Chapter 12.

Pre-seeding Fertilizer

It is a good idea to add a suitable, balanced, pre-seeding lawn fertilizer to the soil surface before seeding, and rake it carefully into the top 12 mm (½ in). Read the directions on the manufacturer's label. The fertilizer should contain balanced proportions of nitrogen, phosphorus and potassium, and be recommended as a lawn pre-seeding fertilizer. Phosphorus is vitally important for the successful establishment of a lawn.

Applying fertilizer to prepared surface

Browntop Bent cultivar lawn

Creeping Bent cultivar lawn

Couch (Bermuda) Grass fine cultivar lawn

Hybrid Couch Grass lawn

Mostly Fine-leaved Perennial Ryegrass lawn

Tall Fescue lawn

Kikuyu Grass lawn

Strawberry Clover, Kentucky Bluegrass and Red Fescue lawn alternative

Kikuyu Grass turf showing thatch build up

Coated and uncoated grass seed: (1) Fine-leaved Perennial Ryegrass cv. (2) Fine-leaved Perennial Ryegrass cv. coated (3) Chewings Fescue (4) Creeping Bent Grass cv. coated (5) Kentucky Bluegrass (6) Browntop Bent (7) Hard Fescue coated (8) Creeping Bent Grass cv. coated (9) Tall Fescue cv. coated (10) Tall Fescue cv. (11) Couch (Bermuda) Grass (12) Kikuyu Grass

Grass seeds sown in punnets. *Top row left to right:* Fine-leaved Perennial Ryegrass cv; Fine-leaved Perennial Ryegrass cv.; Tall Fescue; Kentucky Bluegrass; Hard Fescue. *Bottom row left to right:* Kikuyu Grass; Browntop Bent; Couch (Bermuda) Grass; Creeping Bent Grass; Chewings Fescue

Same grasses eight weeks later. *Top row left to right:* Fine-leaved Perennial Ryegrass cv; Fine-leaved Perennial Ryegrass cv; Tall Fescue; Chewings Fescue; Kikuyu Grass. *Bottom row left to right:* Browntop Bent; Kentucky Bluegrass; Couch (Bermuda) Grass; Creeping Bent Grass; Hard Fescue

Creeping Bent Grass *(Agrostis palustris)* cv. seedling lawn

Same Creeping Bent Grass *(Agrostis palustris)* cv. seedling lawn several weeks later

5. Banks and Slopes

The bank must be properly prepared and correctly levelled to accept the turf or seed, as a problem bank which is wavy and bumpy not only looks bad, but can be difficult, if not impossible, to mow. The bank should have the same topsoil cover as the rest of the lawn.

Before you even think about starting work on a bank ask yourself: 'If it is going to be a grass bank then how am I going to maintain it?' 'Am I fit enough to maintain it?'

A bank with a gradient of up to, say, 20 degrees can be negotiated reasonably by the person mowing. Between 20 and 25 degrees the going gets progressively harder because of lack of foothold. Between 25 and 30 degrees, however, is very hard going and is the maximum gradient even for the fit home gardener.

Problems with Mowing Banks

You need to be aware that some lawn mowers lack the ability to provide sufficient engine oil lubrication on banks. Check your manufacturer's instructions,

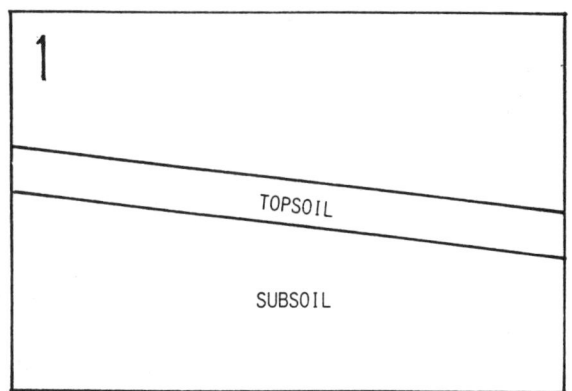

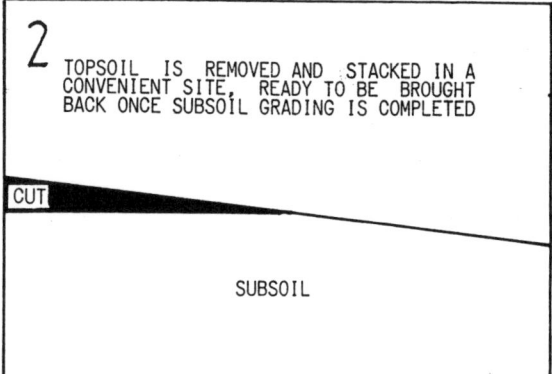

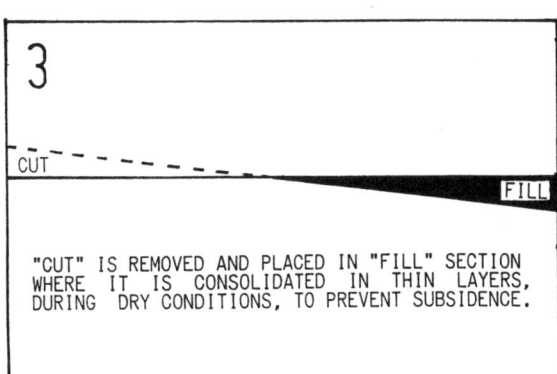

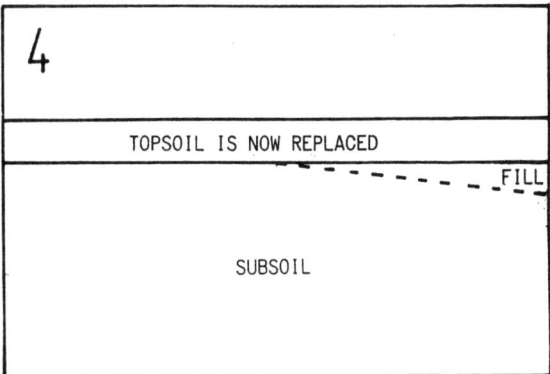

Levelling a slope

and discuss the problem with a properly qualified mower mechanic.

Further, there is a certain amount of danger to be considered before attempting to mow banks.

Mowers can slip and roll, as can mower operators. This can be particularly hazardous when pushing-walking up a bank behind a working wheeled rotary or cylinder mower, as the operator may slip, or the mower may lose traction, and roll back down the bank over the operator's feet (or worse). Although it is difficult to comment without seeing the site, pushing-walking behind mowers up banks is not advised, and mowers can run away out of control going down a bank, which could be hazardous to anybody or anything at the bottom of the bank. Usually, banks are mown across the face of a sloping incline, using a suitable mower, but even so mowers and operators can slip and roll. Read the manufacturer's instructions concerning the use of the mower on banks. It is possible that certain banks can only be cut safely by hand.

Ask yourself:

'Am I doing the right thing; is there a better alternative than a grass bank, such as planting it with suitable shrubs or ground covers, or have a suitably qualified professional construct terracing?'

'Am I creating an erosion problem where one doesn't currently exist?' Soil erosion on banks can cause massive problems to home owners through damage to, or undermining of, foundations and so on, so be aware of this.

'Do I need the advice of a professional soil engineer?' Masonry-brick walls that hold up a bank may act as a dam to water running off or draining through the bank soil. This build-up of water behind such a wall could push it over.

And while we're discussing walls and grassy banks, be aware of the danger of falling from such a wall while constructing a bank, or mowing or weeding it.

Other Problems

Lawns on banks can drain rapidly without allowing water to soak into the lawn surface, which results in the grass being drought stressed.

Establishing the seed or turf can become a problem because of soil washout. Fertilizers, selective herbicides and pesticides can drain off, or run off down the bank.

So before grassing a bank, ask yourself, 'How can I maintain it?' It may be wiser to choose a lawn substitute or ground cover. See Part 2 for ideas on this.

Seeding a Bank

Seeding a bank can be frustrating as the seed/seedlings can be washed away before they become established. A method sometimes used, with varying results, to help prevent soil sliding from top to bottom, is to fix wooden laths across the face of the bank, at suitable distances apart, and remove them once the seed is established.

Turfing a Bank

If you do intend turfing a bank then lay the turves across the face of the sloping incline, with the joints staggered in the same way that brick joints are staggered in the walls of most houses.

You can start from the base of the bank and work upwards. Carting heavy turf up (or down) an incline is difficult in the extreme, as heavy turf can be awkward to handle, particularly if wet. Reducing the size of the turves to more manageable proportions could help alleviate this problem.

The turves should be carefully beaten into place with a suitable wooden punner, similar in shape to a square frying pan, to anchor them to the soil.

Since the weight of the turves can be considerable, particularly if they come with 25 mm (1 in) of soil, and once turves get wet they become much heavier, the gravitational drag down the banks can be great. These turves may need to be pegged securely into the bank soil to help stop them sliding *en masse* down the bank. You can use small wooden stakes or pegs 150 to 175 mm (6 to 7 in) long (or whatever length is suitable for anchorage), driven in vertically for maximum turf anchorage with their tops flush with the turf soil surface; flush enough to avoid tripping over them. The pegs must be strong and long enough, and placed correctly, to keep the turves secure.

Remember that the pegs are there, and remove them carefully once the turf roots have struck adequately into the soil below. Some people drive the pegs deeper into the soil and forget about them. Others try to remove them if only to avoid encouraging 'fairy ring' funguses.

Turves on banks have to be carefully, but thoroughly, watered at all times as they soon dry out.

The correct mowing of turves and seedling grasses is critical, as any ham-fisted mowing could cause real problems.

Spray-on Lawns

Spray-on lawns are coming into prominence of late, but this is not a new idea. One method was, and probably still is, used extensively for banks, where a mixture of suitable seeds, together with an organic matter mulch, fertilizer and water are sprayed over a given area. The mulch acted as a moisture reservoir and protection for the seeds, and a grass-lawn could be produced in the most inaccessible of areas. But ask yourself, 'How are you going to maintain the grass?'

It is possible that there are firms in your area specializing in spray-on lawn establishment for the home garden.

Weed Control

Do not use selective herbicides on a new lawn until the grasses are properly established, as new grass and newly laid turves may be affected by such treatment. *Read the label.*

The label could tell you how long to leave a newly seeded or newly turfed lawn before using selective herbicide on it.

Traffic

Do not use the lawn until it is strong enough to take such wear and tear as foot traffic. Also restrict use of the lawn during inclement weather, as heavy traffic over a wet lawn soon ruins the crumb structure.

Bare Patches

Bare patches can be reseeded using the same grasses as the lawn. On 'runner' lawns use suitable runners.

6. Drainage

A continuously wet soil surface accompanied by algae and moss growth can be an indication that your garden is suffering from natural waterlogging.

It also has to be stated that draining soils is a difficult, exacting, heavy and demanding job, and shouldn't be undertaken by the amateur unless he or she is fully cognizant of the problems that can be encountered.

It is not avoiding the issue to suggest that land drainage should be left to properly qualified, suitably insured/registered professionals, as it is a fact that it requires considerable expertise, with many factors having to be taken into consideration.

Points to Consider

Any necessary drainage should be considered when planning and constructing the lawn, and not after the lawn has been turfed or seeded.

Other points to heed when contemplating drainage are:

1. Are you physically and technically capable of doing the work, or do you need the services of a professional drain layer?

2. Where is the water outlet going to be, and is the outlet point suitable for the drainage you have in mind?

3. Can you place a suitable interceptor drain to capture and redirect the water before it reaches the lawn? Interceptor drains come in various forms, including precast ones covered with a grating to allow the entry of water, and strong enough to take foot or, possibly, vehicular traffic.

4. All drainage trenches should be in straight lines without sharp bends as sharp bends can impede water flow, and may cause silt build up and impede any rodding.

5. Do you need suitable inspection pits so that you can rod and inspect drains that may have become blocked?

6. Any excavated drain soil or subsoil should not be laid on existing turf as it will smother the turf.

7. Subsoil should not be mixed with topsoil.

8. Keep a plan of the drainage system so that in future years you, or any future occupant, knows where and what the system is.

9. Porous pipes that run close to trees could become blocked by tree roots. If necessary use different, but suitable pipes that will help prevent this. Discuss this with the supplier or installer.

10. Cutting tree roots may damage the trees, and possibly you. Be aware of this and seek suitable professional advice if need be.

11. Is the drainage pipe-layer suitably qualified, registered/insured etc. for this type of work?

12. Remember to find out where any services (such as gas, phone, water, electricity and sewer) run on your property, as drainage usually means digging trenches in the garden soil.

13. On the subject of trenches, remember that gardens are frequented by children and animals, and suitable protection should be provided to prevent children, animals or indeed adults from falling into open trenches. Water falling or running into impervious clay trenches can build up quickly, thus creating a water hazard.

Small Lawn Areas

It is uncommon, but not unheard of, that a complicated drainage system is needed for small lawn areas. However, many drainage problems may be solved by the installation of a simple drainage system, such as a soakaway or vertical drainage, installed at the lowest part of the lawn site where

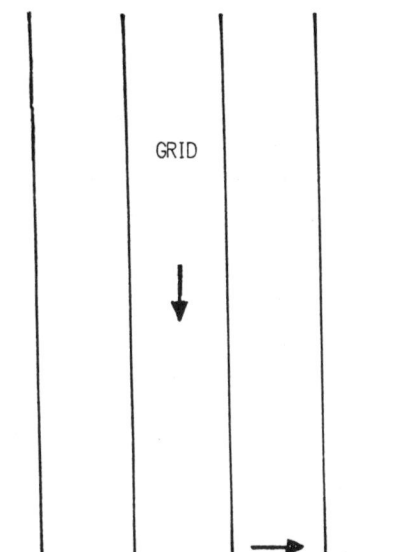

GRID

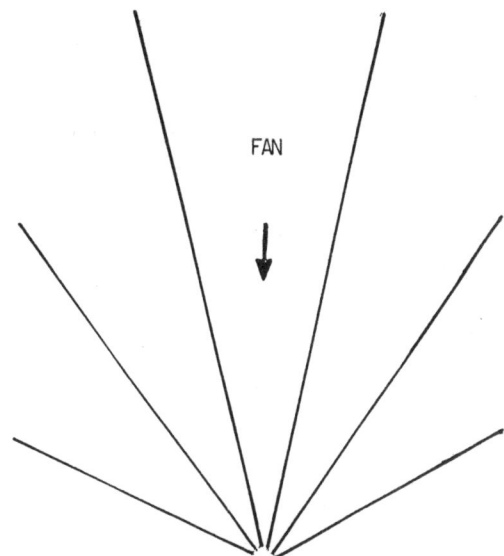

FAN

Methods of lawn drainage. *Left to right:* grid and fan for small lawn areas; grid laterals drain to main drain, which in turn drains to suitable outlet to take away surplus water. Fan drains to suitable outlet to take away surplus water

flooding occurs. The floor of the soakaway or vertical drainage has to be above water table height, and water must drain away naturally, and quickly enough, into a porous subsoil.

Soakaways

A soakaway can be a small hole, e.g. 600 mm to 1 m (2 to 3 ft) square, 1 to 1.25 m (3 to 4 ft) deep, that is filled with clean, hard drainage materials which allow rapid water dispersal: clean materials such as inert stone, broken bricks and the like, which are added to within 300 mm (12 in) of the top. A 100 mm (4 in) layer of suitable small aggregate (large enough not to run through and block up the stone/broken brick aggregate, but also small enough to prevent sand washing through) is laid on the top of the hard drainage material which in turn is blinded by a 50 mm (2 in) layer of coarse sand.

These top layers should help prevent soil from infiltrating the soakaway. Finally, the hole is topped with say a 150 mm (6 in) layer of free-draining sandy loam top soil. Soakaways vary in depth, width and length depending on the problem.

Vertical Drainage

Where small holes, say two spade widths square (or use a suitable post-hole auger), are dug at the lowest part of the lawn site, where flooding occurs, down to a more permeable layer. The hole is filled with small stone, then blinded by grit and then coarse sand, and topped with 100 to 150 mm (4 to 6 in) of free-draining topsoil.

However, a soakaway or vertical drain may not be sufficiently free-draining or have adequate permeability for the amount of water that falls, in which case rain could fill up the soakaway, then back up and still flood the lawn area.

The water from the soakaway should not, I repeat *not* be allowed to drain under building foundations, footpaths and the like, for this may lead to foundation subsidence and other problems. If you have any doubts you should seek professional advice on such problems.

Raising the Lawn Soil Level

You can, if you have a small level lawn (the logistics of treating a large lawn are formidable) that has, for example, a 100 to 150 mm (4 to 6 in) topping of suitable free draining top soil overlying a wet clay soil, adopt one of the following methods.

1. Remove the top soil to one side and stack it, then grade the subsoil, if necessary. Lay pipe drains (which flow to a suitable outlet) in trenches in the clay subsoil with suitable washed stone—say 13 mm (approximately ½ in)—to the level of the surrounding subsoil. Place a layer of suitably sized (large enough not to run through and block up the pipe trench drainage stones, but also small enough

to prevent soil washing through and blocking up this top layer), clean, inert, coarse gravel-stone material, over the entire lawn area. This drainage layer is in immediate contact with the washed stone in the drainage trenches, and is in turn topped with the layer of 100 to 150 mm (4 to 6 in) suitable top soil.

Theoretically, water drains from the lawn surface into the drainage layer, through the drainage layer, from there into the stone-filled drainage trenches and then into the pipes which take it to the outlet. Aerating the soil layer, for example with a garden fork, will help get the surface moisture through to the drainage layer and into the drainage trench.

2. Remove the layer of topsoil, grade the sub-soil if necessary, then spread a practical layer of porous, inert, small drainage aggregate—coarse gravel or stone (large enough to allow water to drain through, but also small enough to prevent soil washing through and blocking up this layer)—over the lawn site, and then replace the topsoil, so that eventually the lawn surface is above the soil surrounds.

3. Remove the layer of topsoil and stack it. Grade the subsoil if necessary. Spread a 100 mm (4 in) layer of clean, inert, drainage rubble over the surface. Top this with a 50 mm (2 in) layer of clean inert small stones/grit. Then top this with a 50 mm (2 in) layer of coarse sand, which in turn is topped with the topsoil.

A problem that may accompany these methods if that you may be left with steep/high lawn edges. Perhaps you can enclose the lawn with boards or concrete edging to contain the soil, but still allow enough weep holes for water to drain away. Grass roots, eventually, will tend to hold the soil, but with steep sides you create another problem in that the mower, and you, may slip off the lawn during mowing.

However, after using any of these methods if the water cannot get away from the garden area, then the problem of waterlogging still exists, even though it may be shifted to a different part of the garden. It may be possible to lay a suitable land drainage system around the outside of the lawn, which can be directed to a suitable outlet.

Planning Drainage

Any lawn drainage should be considered when the lawn is being planned, and installed when the lawn site has been levelled, so that you have the correct levels to work to.

Often a solitary diagonal drain that runs in the direction of fall towards a suitable outlet is sufficient; or even one that collects water at the bottom of the slope, and then transports it to the soakaway or outlet; or one that falls down the slope of the land to a suitable soakaway that drains effectively.

Pipe Drains

Unglazed, porous, burnt-clay (clayware) agricultural drainage pipes and concrete drainage pipes have been mostly replaced by suitable plastic pipes, either smooth and slotted or corrugated and slotted. A chat with a local expert on land drainage should explain what is available.

Plastic drainage pipe

Corrugated, slotted, plastic drainage pipe has slots in the valley of the corrugations to allow the entry of water, which is transported via the pipe to a drainage outlet. The corrugations help maintain external load resistance, and the pipe is flexible to absorb some ground movement. It comes in various coil lengths and pipe diameters. These coils are usually light to manage.

Drainage Patterns

The water could fall on to the lawn, then drain off the surface of the lawn naturally, into a drainage pipe, and from there to the outlet. Or it could be a 'herringbone' system, where the side drain branches enter the main drain (backbone) at an angle, these side branches pointing in the direction of the flow, and the main drains to the outlet. Or a 'fan-shaped' system, where the pipes converge to the drainage outlet, provided the gradient is suitable.

In the 'grid' system usually the gradient falls away to one side of a lawn and the pipes run down the gradient to a main drain on the boundary. All main drains have to be of sufficient diameter to take away the water from the laterals.

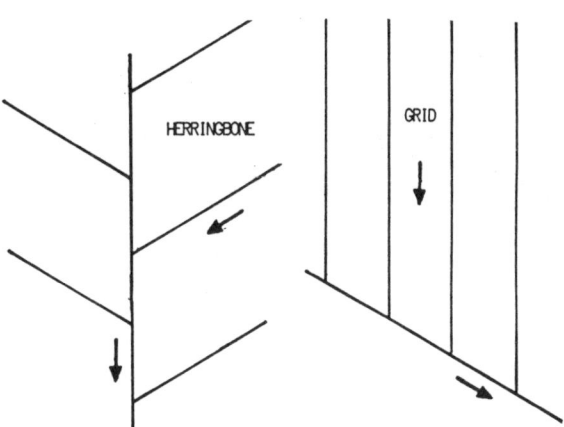

Methods of lawn drainage. *Left to right:* herringbone; grid. Laterals drain to main drain

Angles of Pipes

The angle at which pipes enter the main drains is of paramount importance, and the actual angle is decided on site.

Distance Apart for Pipes

The distance drainage pipes are spaced apart depends on the type of soil. For example: Is it clay? Is it clay loam? Is it sandy loam? Is it fine sandy loam? And so on. It all comes down to the particular conditions of your site.

Therefore, the type of soil, and any other characteristics peculiar to your garden will decide, usually, the depth and spacing of land drains. This is possibly where professional land drainage opinion could be sought.

Pipe Depths

Drainage trenches (piped) in the lawn have to be at a sufficient depth to provide suitable, adequate drainage, have sufficient depth of soil medium for the grass to grow properly and sufficient fall to take the drainage water away.

The main drain has to collect the water, and also have sufficient fall to effectively take the collected water from the laterals away to the outlet.

Pipe manufacturers/suppliers may provide information concerning the 'correct' installation of their lawn drainage pipes.

Storm Water Drains and Council Permission

It is possible that the water could be directed into a convenient storm water drain.

Storm water can also be collected before it reaches the lawn, and directed through a storm water pipe, under the Council footpath, and into the street. However, it is vitally important that you check with local authorities before you shed water from your property. Remember that various services can run under footpaths.

You may not direct water into the street without checking with your local council and obtaining their written permission to do so.

You may not direct water into a storm water drain without checking with your local council or water board authority and obtaining their written permission to do so.

You may not direct water on to other people's property.

You may not direct storm water into the sewer.

Therefore, check with your local council authority and your local water board before you consider shedding water from your propery.

Laying Pipes

After the trenches have been correctly excavated take particular care connecting the laterals to the main drain, particularly if using porous clay drainage pipes, as many systems break down because of a silt build-up in these areas.

If a drainage trench runs through the lawn, then there must be an adequate amount of suitable soil for the grass roots to thrive, say a minimum of 150 mm (6 in) of free-draining, sandy loam, otherwise you could end up with brown trench outlines across the lawn during hot weather. Even with adequate soil these trench outlines may occur during hot weather, although with irrigation, theoretically, they shouldn't.

Narrow trenches help when sand is used at the top of the trench, as the grass roots can reach the more accommodating, moister, surrounding soil sooner.

The material selected for backfilling the trenches is of paramount importance as it should allow moisture to drain quickly, and maintain this drainage facility for a considerable time.

A discussion with the pipe manufacturer or supplier regarding backfill could be useful, as backfill should not be so fine that it: prevents moisture percolating through the drainage material; blocks up the holes in the drainage pipe; or goes through the holes and blocks up the pipe.

7. Establishing a Lawn Using Grass Seed

When to Sow the Grass Seed?

The obvious time to sow cool-climate grasses in cold areas is prior to the autumn-winter rains so that they germinate and are established before the winter cold, or in early spring, once the soil has warmed up sufficiently, so they become established before the summer.

Warm-climate grasses are sown in spring and on into summer provided adequate irrigation is available.

Most cold climate grasses in warm climate areas can be sown autumn and spring, although Tall Fescue in some areas may have an extended sowing period. But climates are so variable: in Darwin, for example, grass seed sown during December-March could be subjected to heavy monsoonal rains and subsequent wash-out. Seek local professional advice on suitable times to sow particular grass seeds.

Estimating Seed Requirements

You can work out how much seed you need by measuring the lawn area and by checking how much is recommended on the pack for a given area.

If your lawn is an awkward shape and your maths is rusty, get somebody to work out the area for you, or split the area up into convenient squares, say 1 m by 1 m, and then separately work out the awkward sections that are left, remembering to add everything up at the end.

Marking Out the Seed Bed

Grass seeds should only be sown on a calm day, and then only if the seed bed soil surface is dry enough to walk on.

To ensure even distribution, mark off the lawn in squares, say 1 m by 1 m, using strings.

You can use strings as 'railway lines' and lay canes as 'sleepers' at 1 m intervals, or, using string as a guide, you can lightly scratch 1 m squares on to the lawn surface. When I say lightly I mean lightly, otherwise seeds will gravitate into the scratched lines and you could end up with a lawn with marked squares of concentrated grass, like a crossword puzzle.

Portioning Up the Seed

Weigh out the portion of seed for each square metre and then divide the portion of seed for each square metre into halves, each half to be spread in an opposite direction, to ensure even distribution.

If necessary, add a small amount of fine, dry lime-free sand as a carrier to facilitate spreading the grass seed.

Sowing fine seeds like Browntop Bent and Creeping Bent (estimated to contain between sixteen and eighteen million seeds to the kilogram) calls for great care. A suitable carrier has to be used and well mixed with the seed to obtain such fine adjustments, and a light-coloured, very fine sand carrier may help indicate where the seeds have fallen.

Seed Spreaders

You can use a fertilizer-seed spreader to sow larger grass seed, but make sure that it is capable of spreading grass seeds correctly with even distribution. Check, and double check, to ensure that the machine is distributing the seed correctly. As a control, you can mark out 1 m² on brown paper, or whatever. Check the amount of grass seed the supplier recommends per square metre. Weigh out this amount exactly. Carefully and exactly spread this amount of grass seed evenly over the brown paper. This gives you an indication of what the recommended amount per square metre looks like for comparison.

Some seeds are too fine for certain seed spreaders.

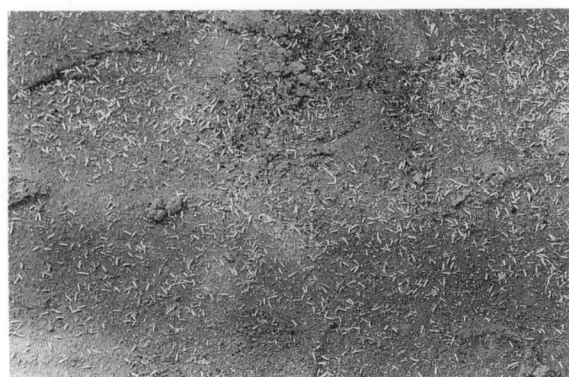

Seed spread evenly over area

Lightly rolling in grass seed

Tumbling grass seed into prepared surface with back of lawn rake

Finishing Off

Once the seeds have been distributed over the lawn surface, very gently using, for example, the back of a leaf rake, tumble-rake or very lightly rake the seeds into the very top of the soil surface, taking great care not to bury them too deeply, as a deep soil covering is not recommended for grass seed.

Some grass seeds, such as Browntop Bent and Creeping Bent *(Agrostis tenuis; Agrostis stolonifera,* syn. *A. palustris,* syn. *A. s. palustris)* are so fine that they will become exhausted if buried too deeply, and will not produce seedlings. In my opinion fine seeds like *Agrostis tenuis* and *Agrostis stolonifera* should not be buried at all. Certain tests have indicated that this loss of fine seed can be dramatic.

Then, provided the soil surface is perfectly dry, roll the seeds with a very light roller to anchor them. On heavy soils, usually, rolling is best omitted.

If you don't want to roll the lawn, then gently water in the seed with a fine rose on the hose. The seed must be watered immediately to trigger the germination process.

Early Problems

One problem with seed sowing is that any subsequent heavy rainfall, if severe enough, can wash seed out of the soil. I don't know what one can do about this, except to check the weather forecast and possibly delay sowing.

Birds may descend on the lawn once you have seeded it, and they can upset the level of the lawn by dusting and scratching, and may eat the seed. Don't do anything that will harm the birds. Try to consider birds as nature's twelve-months-a-year 'flying flowers'.

Hopefully, the bird will lose interest in your grass seed once the starch in it turns to sugar, and remember that birds may help keep many injurious lawn insects at bay. I do, however, appreciate that they can be a bigger problem in some areas than others.

Cats may be under the delusion that you provided the beautiful lawn soil just for their benefit, or your dog may suddenly remember that he has buried a bone in the centre of the lawn, so be aware of these possibilities.

Watering Seeds

You have properly prepared the lawn soil. You have included a correctly balanced pre-seeding fertilizer. You have sown the seeds. And now you must ensure that all this work was not in vain.

Keep the lawn soil moist, but not flooded, at all times until the seedlings have germinated and are well established. Then water the lawn when need be.

I, personally, wouldn't use lawn sprinklers on a newly seeded, *small* lawn area to establish the grass seedlings, but not everybody would agree with this. Some would consider it more practical to use fine-spray sprinklers. If feasible water the seeds by hand using a gentle, fine spray on a hose, giving the lawn a thorough, gentle soaking, at least until the seedlings are established well enough to take heavier sprinkler jets or other lawn sprinklers.

Lawn grass seedlings are kept permanently moist as their young roots are extremely susceptible to drying out. It is possible that they may get adequate rainfall. Once the seedlings appear as an overall, not patchy, green haze continue to water them gently, thoroughly and copiously.

Be alert for hot weather and drying winds which can decimate seedlings, and if the seedlings appear to be drying out then water accordingly, but do not heavily flood them, washing them out of the ground. Keep the new lawn adequately watered until it becomes established as a mature lawn.

The time taken for the seeds to braird (shoot) depends on the grass seed used. Some species/cultivars are quicker to germinate than others.

First Mowing

It is time to tip-cut the seedling grasses once they have grown to approximately 25 mm (1 in) above the established cutting height. The established cutting height is the grass height the established lawn would be kept at normally, and here we are concerned with normal home lawns.

Inspect the lawn before mowing, as stones and other debris must be removed. Stones and other hard objects can become very dangerous missiles when slung-shot by the mower; they can also damage the blades of a cylinder mower.

Lightly roll the lawn surface on a dry day when the lawn soil is dry. Grasses such as the finest Bent Grasses can be smothered if the soil is not perfect for rolling. What you are doing by rolling is eliminating small bumps, and providing a surface for the mower wheels to run on.

After rolling, wait until the grasses are standing up before mowing. Make sure that the mower wheels do not sink into the lawn soil or the seedlings will be scalped.

Tipping the grass blades keeps the young seedlings tillering or shooting or budding out from the base. The amount of grass blade to remove depends on the grass species concerned. Remove say 10 mm (½ in) of the taller grasses mentioned above. Barely tip the shorter growing grasses.

Do not remove more than one-third of a grass blade at a single cutting, as tests have indicated that grass root regeneration has stopped for some time when more than one-third of the grass blade has been removed; much more so when the grass has been scalped. Common sense is vital to prevent ruining the new lawn.

Many weeds that appear will disappear under mowing as they cannot take the competition.

The grass and the lawn soil surface have to be dry when you cut the grass. If the soil is wet then leave cutting the lawn until a more suitable time.

It is also ridiculously easy for blunt mowers to pull young grass seedlings out of the soil. Therefore, ensure that the blades are sharp as grass that has been bruised by a blunt mower can also be prone to disease attack.

Keep the mower blades at the correct height for the first cut which, I repeat, is higher than the final cutting height. You are only tipping the grass blades to keep them in check. All grasses need plenty of green leaf to help manufacture roots.

If feasible, use a wheeled cylinder mower with grass catcher for the first cut, as opposed to a mower with front and rear rollers, which can flatten down the grass prior to cutting it. A properly sharpened wheeled cylinder mower cuts the grass in a scissor-like action, which gives a cleaner cut than the striking blade action of the rotary mower.

Once your lawn has had its first haircut, continue to mow the lawn when it needs it, still keeping the blades at the correct initial cutting height. After a suitable time the cutting height can be gradually lowered to the final cutting height for the type of lawn grasses you have. (Also see Chapters 10 and 11.)

Damping-off Disease

The biggest disease problem in the lawn's early stages is *Pythium* (damping-off disease) which can decimate or completely destroy seedlings. The disease can be treated with a suitable lawn fungicide. Secondary damping-off diseases can attack again a few weeks later, so be on the look out for this. (Also see Chapter 14.)

8. Runners, Rooted Portions, Blocks and Plugs

Runners are overground clambering stems (stolons) of certain grasses that can root at the nodes (knuckle joints); rooted portions are individual stems of grass containing a few roots, blocks of rooted turf can be 50 mm (2 in) square, or less; plugs are small scone-sized sections of rooted turf.

Hybrid Couch, Couch (Bermuda) Grass runners or rooted portions or plugs are usually planted in the spring, if it is warm enough, so that spring rains or irrigation, plus the warm weather to follow will assist in their establishment. However, this depends on local climate as some areas don't have cold winters; therefore discuss this with local experts.

Planting a runner lawn

If the runner had four nodes then, using an old screwdriver, or similar, as a dibber to make the hole, I would insert one or two nodes firmly in the hole, say 25 to 50 mm (1 to 2 in) or possibly more, deep to anchor the runner and to force it to root, while the other future growing tip nodes rested on the surface. It is important to make sure that the rooting node is firmly anchored in the soil. I would point out that I have also had failures, i.e. non-rooting runners.

You can also make a shallow slit in the soil, lay the centre of the runner in the slit, making sure it contains a node or nodes, with the future growing tip exposed, and then ease the soil to make firm contact with the node/nodes that was/were underground. The rows can be 250 mm (10 in) apart.

Alternatively, you can draw out straight, shallow trenches, say 50 to 75 mm (2 to 3 in) deep, and 250 mm (10 in) apart. Runners approximately 100 to 150 mm (4 to 6 in) long are laid, reasonably thickly, in the trench, then covered with soil, firmed, and watered; again leaving future growing tips exposed.

Rooted portions, runners, blocks and plugs need sufficient fertilizer in the soil for their roots to establish quickly.

Runners, rooted portions, blocks and plugs are extremely vulnerable to drying out before planting and must be kept moist at all times. Often gardeners will set about planting a lawn, with the box full of runners and rooted portions drying out in the blazing sun. You can place them in a bucket of water while you are planting down the rows, to keep them turgid prior to planting.

I repeat, runners must be planted firmly in the soil so that the rooting nodes are in contact with the soil. They must be kept regularly/properly watered, as at this stage they are vulnerable to drying out, but not permanently sodden.

Other grasses such as Bahia Grass *(Paspalum notatum)*, Manila Grass *(Zoysia matrella)*, Salt Water Couch *(Paspalum vaginatum)*, Buffalo Grass (syn. St Augustine-grass) *(Stenotaphrum secundatum)* and Kikuyu Grass *(Pennisetum clandestinum)* are also used in certain areas.

Check with local experts on the best time to plant these rooted portions, runners, blocks or plugs, and whether they are suitable for your locality and situation, and the correct method of planting them.

Spacing

Rooted portions, runners, blocks or plugs should be planted at the correct distance apart; a distance which provides for a lawn forming in a suitably quick time. The higher the density of planting the quicker the runners fill the gaps.

Blocks and plugs of Hybrid Couch can be planted say 300 mm (12 in) apart; their roots underground, their green leaves exposed to sunlight. An average of 200 mm (8 in) apart is reasonable for runners or rooted portions. You could go a little closer, say 150 mm (6 in) apart with Hybrid Couch, Couch (Bermuda) Grass, Salt Water Paspalum and Zoysia Grass.

Stretch out a string in a straight line across the lawn and plant rooted portions or runners or blocks or plugs at the required distance apart along the string. Stagger the plantings so that a plant in one row comes between the two plants in front of it, like the five spots on dice.

The above does at least three things: it prevents waste; it allows for the correct distance between each plant; and it looks better while the lawn is forming.

Rooted portions of turf are usually a surer bet than runners as their roots are already established before you plant them. Blocks and plugs are a better bet still as their roots are established in soil.

Chopped Runners

An alternative to planting rooted portions, runners, blocks or plugs, where the availability and cost of runners is not a problem is to use chopped runner particles of, for example, suitable Couch (Bermuda) Grass, complete with nodes capable of forming roots.

These particles can be scattered broadcast fashion, like seed over the lawn area, and covered with suitable lawn soil or compost, or very lightly mixed into the very top surface, then lightly rolled to press the runners into contact with the soil.

The ground is kept adequately watered (but very carefully so as not to wash out the grass particles) as the runners are extremely vulnerable to rapid drying out.

Watering

Rooted portions, runners, blocks and plugs should never be allowed to dry out in these early stages of lawn formation, as this could be disastrous or at best result in a patchy lawn, but if adequate rain is falling then artificial irrigation is not necessary. Don't be fooled by a few spits of rain, as a useful rain has to be a good, gentle, thorough, soaking rain.

9. Turfing—an Instant Grass Lawn

A most important factor when buying turves is that they be of top quality, true to description, and free from weeds, undesirable grasses and the like. Therefore, dealing with a reputable supplier is paramount.

Even so, check turves before you lay them, just in case the odd weed or weed grass may have sneaked into the sward. Remove any pernicious weeds and weed grasses in the turves before you lay them, as removing weed grasses once the turf is established can develop into a major problem.

Laying turves is practised extensively in cool-climate gardens, where gardeners use grasses such as Chewings Fescue, Browntop Bent, Fine-leaved Perennial Ryegrasses, or Chewings Fescue-Browntop mixtures, or Kentucky Bluegrass or Tall Fescue.

In warm climates gardeners use, according to area, selected Couch (Bermuda) Grass, Queensland Blue Couch, Kikuyu Grass and others, and to a lesser extent, because of cost, Hybrid Couch.

Grasses Suitable for Your Area

It is important to establish the mixture of grasses contained in the turf sward, and whether they are suitable for your particular localized climate and the particular type of lawn you have in mind. For example, turves containing pedigree Fine-leaved Perennial Ryegrasses, plus a mixture of other top quality grasses, will not form a top-class bowling green lawn.

The turves may be a blend of Kentucky Bluegrass cultivars. Or a mix of Fine-leaved Perennial Ryegrass cultivars, suitable Fescues, Browntop Bent and Kentucky Bluegrass, and so on. Check with the supplier.

With or Without Soil

Some turves come cut to approximately 25 mm (1 in) in depth. Others are sold with soil washed from their roots, which means that the roots are hungry to strike into soil.

Turves that are cut with too much soil attached take longer to root and are heavier to lay.

For many years experiments have been carried out using thinner turves with sufficient root fibre, and it has been reported that good results have been obtained by using suitable turves 19 mm (¾ in) thick.

The practicality of turf laying depends on the length and breadth of the single turf. I have laid thousands of 1 m × 300 mm × 25 mm (3 ft × 1 ft × 1 in) turves, and when I had been laying such turves for the best part of the day, I knew I had been laying turf. More so when the turves were wet.

Some turves are cut longer, say 1.2 m (4 ft). Some are cut even longer. Check with your supplier on the length, width, depth and weight *before* you buy the turves and, indeed, before you construct the lawn.

Soil Preparation

The lawn surface has to be prepared properly to take the turves, as discussed in Chapter 4, and this surface has to be ready before you order the turf. It is of little use having turf delivered if you can't lay it.

You need a suitable depth of either a sandy loam top soil or say a mixture of 75% suitable coarse sand to 25% suitable, friable garden loam, for the turf roots to strike into, and in my opinion 100 mm (4 in) would be the minimum, but 150 mm (6 in) would be better.

It is usually advisable to apply a suitable (NPK) pre-turfing fertilizer (read the label on the fertilizer pack) to the lawn soil base, say a few days before you intend laying the turves, and rake it lightly into the prepared surface.

If you have properly prepared the soil, but the surface has caked a little, you can gently scratch the soil surface with the garden rake prior to turfing.

Laying Turf

Remember turves are very vulnerable to drying out and could be destroyed if not adequately watered. Also, laying turves is hard work and should be approached carefully, particularly if the turves are wet.

Laying amputated turf roots on hot soil comes as somewhat of a shock to them. The soil shouldn't be wet or muddy as this could lead to soil compaction.

Lay the first row of turves from the most obvious side or corner, and work across the area to be turfed, using a string if necessary to keep the line of turves straight.

If this turf abuts a concrete or brick path or drive, or similar, then the turves must be just a little above the concrete to prevent the concrete interfering with subsequent mowing, causing damage to the mower etc.

If, however, the turf is too high above the concrete then the mower will slip off the lawn, particularly wheeled mowers, and scalp the edges of the turf.

Don't forget where your underground irrigation is, if you have already installed it; this is easily done. Make a plan and keep the plan in a safe place.

If your lawn is informal and you do not have straight sides to work from, then you could run a line down the centre of the lawn, lay the first row of turves, and work from this centre line of turf out on both sides. However, do not have narrow strips or small pieces of turf on the outside perimeter of the lawn. Not only can this look unattractive, but it may be dangerous if these small pieces are walked over and they tip. Narrow strips and small pieces of turf should be contained further into the lawn.

Using Planks

On reasonably level surfaces you work from the first row of turf by placing a clean wooden plank or planks on the turves, and doing all your walking on that rather than on the turves or the prepared soil.

The reason you work forward from a plank away from the turf already laid is that you do not mess up the soil base, particularly if it is too damp, and also do not unnecessarily damage the turves.

This plank should be removed from the turf when you have finished for the day, or you have left the area for any length of time, to prevent the grass sweating and yellowing, or you'll end up with a lawn full of yellow plank outlines. And don't leave a hose

on the lawn, as this will also produce a yellow 'snake' outline.

Keep the planks clean, otherwise any slippery mud may be a problem to you, and for the turf that has been laid.

The turves should be laid with the end joint of one turf coming in the centre of the turf behind it, similar to the staggered pattern of bricks in most houses. The next line of turves must be laid up close

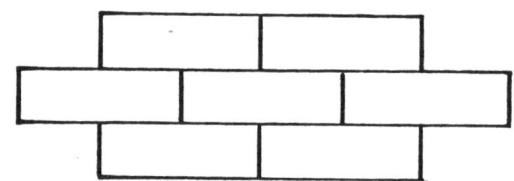

THE RIGHT WAY TO LAY TURF WITH JOINTS STAGGERED

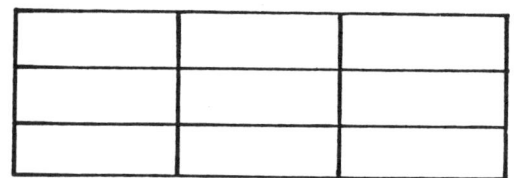

THE WRONG WAY TO LAY TURF

The wrong and right way of laying turves/sods

to the first row of turves, and so on until you have laid all the turves.

Any surplus turf can be cut off by using a 'half-moon' edging iron, which is a specially made tool for cutting turf. Some gardeners use an old bread knife or similar to cut turf edges, but should you do so then be extra careful and avoid cutting yourself as soil and open wounds don't mix.

Some gardeners lightly beat the turves to help settle them, and should you do this then you would use a proper turf beater, which is an easily-managed, clean block of wood fixed to the end of a stout broom handle. And when I say lightly, I mean lightly—do not knock the stuffing out of the turf.

Some gardeners have used the back of a spade to 'level' turf, but when you hit the turves using this method the spade handle may break and be redirected at your head, and there is always the possibility of clouting a fellow turf layer accidentally.

After completing the turfing, a light dressing of suitable sand is run along the turf joints and worked carefully into the joints and surrounding grasses without stifling grasses. This will help the turves knit together, as this sand should wash into the joints. (Remember what has been said previously about sharp sand and injury to future lawn users.)

Rolling the turves with a light roller will help settle them into the lawn soil. The soil must not be wet or compaction will result.

Don't be too ambitious with the roller as over-compacting the turves will also knock the stuffing out of them. Rolling may be heavy work for some, and they may need assistance. Be sure to use only a light roller.

Watering Turf

The turves must be thoroughly watered after you have finished laying them. Give them a good saturating drink. When I say a good saturating drink I mean just that. If adequate rain falls then consider this a bonus, but don't be fooled by a sprinkling.

Water the turves thoroughly, if sufficient rain hasn't fallen, the following day.

Turves must be kept adequately watered as they are very susceptible to drying out in these early stages, but given adequate watering the roots soon strike into the properly prepared soil bed below.

You can check this rooting by gently seeing if a selected number of turves lift off from the soil, and if white turf roots are beginning to appear. But even so, turves that have struck but do not receive adequate water from then on and are allowed to dry out form the most hideous open joints. It is only when the roots of one turf have thoroughly integrated with the roots of the adjoining turf that the incidence of 'open jointing' is lessened.

Hopefully, you have installed automatic irrigation properly, or set up traditional lawn sprinklers, and these can water your lawn. Keep a wary eye open as lawn turf edges can dry out rapidly, and curl up like grand viziers' toe-caps.

Once the roots have struck into the soil surface and the turves are well and truly anchored, you can regulate your watering.

Problems

It could happen that during the turf laying those turves already laid are drying out rapidly, and you still have turves to lay. You would have to water the turves to keep them alive, of course, but do this work carefully and sensibly as you don't want to mess up the area that is still to be laid.

Stacked turves exposed to the elements may be drying out too rapidly in the stack. Don't allow this to happen. It goes without saying that any turfing should be carried out in conditions that are favourable for turf laying.

If the turves are delivered and for some reason cannot be laid for some time then these turves have to be laid out, exposed to light, in a convenient spot, for they will turn yellow if kept rolled. Also remember that rolled out turves such as these are extremely, I repeat extremely, vulnerable to drying out.

Talk these problems over with the supplier *before* you buy the turves, and most important make sure that the lawn surface is ready to receive the turves before you order them.

Rolling

New turves can look pretty bumpy in these initial stages. After a while, and when the roots have struck into the soil, the turves begin to 'make' and the area can be rolled to prepare the lawn for mowing. If the turves are loose, then mower wheels can sink into them and scalp the grass. Check the turf to see if the roots have struck into the lawn soil bed.

Cut the grass reasonably high until the sward thickens into a turf, then gradually reduce the cutting height to the desired level.

After Care for Turf

Newly laid turves need occasional rolling to settle the roots and provide a suitable sward to receive the mower, but excessive heavy rolling will do no good and should be avoided. A cylinder mower with a back roller rolls the lawn each time it is cut. Mow the new turves regularly, but do not cut too low, as scalped turf can rapidly become colonized by weeds and moss.

The turf lawn will need fertilizing in due season, and very soon it is treated in the same fashion as an established lawn.

If the turf has not settled to the desired finish, you can top dress the lawn using a suitable sandy loam. Do not smother the grasses, but carefully rub and brush the top dressing into the lawn surface, so that the grasses stand up above the top dressing.

As soon as the grass blades have established

thoroughly above this top dressing, if need be you can apply another light dressing, and so on, taking care not to smother either the grass blades or the grass crowns. If the lawn has been laid properly then too many top dressings should not be needed.

If one spot has sunk too low for light top dressing to be effective, then slit the turf and roll it back, still leaving an end attached to the lawn, as by doing so the slit turf will recover that much more quickly. Add the necessary quantity of soil needed to establish the level and roll back the slit turf, making sure that it is level, and gets ample water for its roots to become re-established.

10. Mowing

Mowers

There are two basic types of mowers for lawns—the rotary mower and the cylinder-reel mower.

Most petrol-driven lawn mower engines are either four-stroke engines or two-stroke engines, and if you don't know the difference between the two then carefully check the manufacturer's manual and discuss lawn mowers with a properly qualified mechanic, who specializes in lawn mowers, before you buy or use one.

Some engines must have the correct petrol-oil mix, otherwise they can seize up. Some mowers must not be used on certain banks or slopes as serious problems because of the lack of engine lubrication may occur.

Rotary Mowers

The cutting blades of the rotary mower, which are contained under a protective cover, spin round horizontally—parallel to the lawn surface—and slash the grass stalks at incredibly high speeds.

A rotary mower, usually, has less working parts than a cylinder-reel mower and its initial purchase and upkeep can be less costly. It's engine tends to get through much work per cutting season.

Generally, a rotary mower cannot cut as effectively low as some of the finer cylinder-reel mowers. The rotary mower's height is usually easy to adjust. Rotary mowers are mostly supplied with rear-

Rotary mower

Cylinder-reel mowing showing striping

Area to be turfed showing plank, punner and rake

Lightly raking tilth prior to laying turf

Rolling out a turf (wear suitable gloves)

Lightly punning turf to settle it

Turf is laid over odd-shaped area, and using half-moon edger, cutting around outside of turf

Running sandy loam into turf joints. Surplus loam is removed

Rolling new turf

New turf being irrigated by pop-up sprinklers

Same lawn (mostly Fine-leaved Perennial Ryegrass) some months later

mounted grass catchers, but some have side-mounted catchers, whereas others do not have a catcher.

Pedestrian operated rotary mowers are divided into 'self-propelled' where the wheels and cutting blades are driven by the engine, and 'hand-propelled' by the operator, where the petrol-engine drives the cutting blades only.

1. The four-wheeled, petrol-engine driven, hand-pushed mower, for example with a 440 to 450 mm (17 to 18 in) cutting width, is a popular type of mower.

2. The pedestrian-controlled, 'self-propelled' petrol-engine driven rotary mower, for example with a 500 mm (20 in) width is also used on lawns.

3. There are electrically operated rotary mowers, perhaps with less wide cutting widths. Be alert, if using a mower powered by electricity, to cut away from the electrical cord to prevent running over and cutting through the cord.

4. The petrol-driven engine, air-cushion rotary mowers have no wheels but float on a cushion of air and at the same time cut grass in a fashion similar to other rotary mowers. There are electrical versions of the air-cushion mower.

5. The smaller, ride-on 610 to 660 mm (24 to 26 in) width rotary mowers are used on large lawns. The 760 to 915 mm (30 to 36 in) width ride-on mower can be used on much larger lawns. Some ride-on mowers come equipped with a grass catcher.

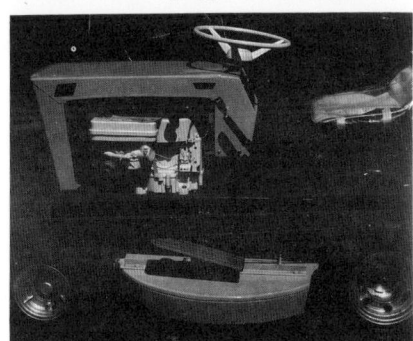

Ride-on mower

Cylinder-reel Mowers

Some refer to the following as 'cylinder' mowers others as 'reel' mowers.

Cylinder-reel mowers have cutting blades made with a spiral twist which, as they revolve, trap the grasses and cut (shear) them against a fixed bottom blade in a scissor-like action.

Cylinder mower

The pedestrian-operated, power-driven cylinder-reel machine, properly sharpened, properly adjusted, equipped with suitable front and back rollers will give those dark green and light green patterned stripes we see on professional playing surfaces such as golf greens.

Cylinder-reel mowers can be: (a) self-propelled; (b) petrol-engine driven cutting blades but hand-pushed; or (c) hand-pushed, i.e. with no engine.

A bowling green cylinder-reel mower has many blades.

Remember, many fine-bladed machines are made specifically for only the finest of grass lawns, and would jib at coarse grass lawns.

There are mowers that are used to give a quality finish to ornamental private lawns, but have less blades than a bowling green mower, for example six or seven blades on the cylinder. They have a cutting width of, say, between 430 and 510 mm (17 and 20 in).

Mowers with wider cutting widths, say 600, 650 or 700 mm (24, 26 or 28 in), can be used for mowing larger formal lawns.

The 750 or 915 mm (30 or 36 in) cutting width petrol-driven cylinder mowers with front and back rollers are used for cutting very large lawns.

The manufacturer usually indicates for which lawn area a particular machine is to be used.

Lawns must be cut very regularly by cylinder-reel machines to avoid the appearance of any unsightly stalks and ribbing.

Some of the self-propelled mowers mentioned above can also be supplied with a 'trailing seat' attachment, which allows the operator to sit down, being towed behind the mower. The manufacturers should indicate this in their instructions, and brochure, and specify the correct form of trailing seat.

Most of the above machines are provided with front grass catchers.

If you intend buying a cylinder-reel mower then refer to the manufacturer's specifications on width of cut, number of blades, for use on particular lawn areas (i.e. size and quality of grass), cuts per linear metre, and so on, before you buy.

Indeed, no matter what machine you intend to buy, always refer to the manufacturer's specifications to find out about the mower you have in mind.

Various battery-operated cylinder-reel mowers are also available, some operated by electric motors.

The 'hand-pushed' cylinder-reel machine with front and back rollers can also produce the dark-green and light-green striped effect.

It's extremely hard work—practically impossible—to use these mowers on a small lawn comprising tough grasses.

Hand-pushed cylinder-reel mowers come in various cutting widths, usually from 250 to 450 mm (10 to 18 in), and have from 6 to 12 blades. These mowers are not seen as often in Australia as they are in Britain.

Side-wheel Cylinder-Reel Mower

The smaller, pedestrian-operated, petrol-driven cylinder mower with wheels on either side of the cutting cylinder is also used for cutting home lawns.

Two-wheeled cylinder mowers, usually, do not give those dark-green and light-green stripes.

The 'hand-pushed' side-wheeled cylinder mower is still used for cutting small lawns, but only where the grass isn't too tough, or the going too rough, and where only an average finish is required.

You cannot cut closely to the edges of some lawns with certain mowers, because the wheels tend to slip off.

Lawn Trimmer

The lawn trimmer (line trimmer) is a mower that has a small engine at one end of a shaft, the cutting head apparatus at the other end, and is carried by the user.

It is used for trimming grass against walls and other areas and uses a nylon cord as a cutter. Be careful not to ring-bark trees when using lawn trimmers.

Read the brochure and manufacturer's instructions, as some have attachments that can be added on.

Electrically operated lawn line trimmers are also available.

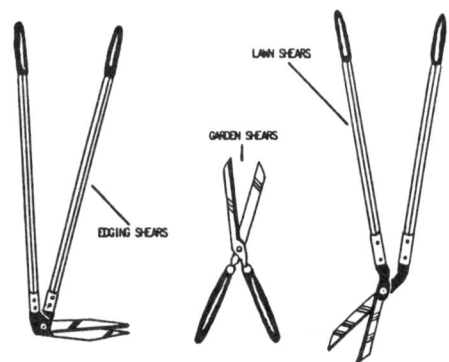

Left to right: long-handled lawn edging shears; garden shears; long-handled lawn shears

Hand Tools

Lawn-grass hand shears are useful for cutting small awkward corners, and if kept sharp the scissor-like blades make a very neat cut. There are also long-handled grass shears, for those who find it awkward to bend down. Also there are long-handled lawn edging shears for keeping grass edges tidy, and one-handed shears for clipping those odd spots. Names of the above may vary between manufacturers.

Grass Cutting Heights

Grass cutting height estimates vary with a particular situation, and are influenced by the use the lawn is to withstand, personal choice and the grass species or cultivar.

My suggested established cutting heights for the home lawn are given here, but if you're not sure of your lawn, then seek local expert opinion on lawn grass height. (The professional greenkeeper will work to his or her own cutting heights.)

If possible, and feasible, cut the lawn in one axis for one complete cut, and then the next time cut the lawn crosswise. For example, if the first cut was north to south—south to north, the second would be east to west—west to east. This helps prevent 'graining', that is the grass growing in one direction.

If you are new to mowing lawns then use the highest height for your grass given below, as you can always gradually lower the cutting height, if you feel so inclined, to a height you are at peace with. Even so the lowest height can only be adhered to if the lawn is level, otherwise grass scalping may occur; also, the correct mower has to be used. Remember, a rotary mower cannot cut as effectively low as the finer cylinder/reel mowers.

Cutting Heights (metric and approximate imperial) (cvs = cultivars)

Grass	Height Millimetres	Inches
Cool-climate Grasses		
Bent Grass (suitable cultivars only)		
Browntop	12-20	½-¾
Creeping	12-20	½-¾
Fescue (suitable cultivars only)		
Chewings	20-50	¾-2
Creeping Red (Slender)	25-50	1-2
Creeping Red (Strong)	20-50	¾-2
Hard	38-64	1½-2½
Tall	38-75	1½-3
Kentucky Bluegrass cvs	20-50	¾-2
Perennial Ryegrass (Fine-leaved) cvs	25-50	1-2
Rough-stalked Meadow Grass cvs	25-38	1-1½
Warm-climate Grasses		
Bahia Grass	38-64	1½-2½
Buffalo (St Augustine) Grass	30-64	1¼-2½
Carpet Grass	20-38	¾-1½
Couch (Bermuda) Grass cvs	12-25	½-1
Hybrid Couch Grass cvs	12-25	½-1
Kikuyu Grass	20-38	¾-1½
Queensland Blue Couch	10-25	⅖-1
Saltwater Paspalum	12-25	½-1
Zoysia Grass	12-38	½-1½

Mow your lawn regularly. Do not remove more than one-third of the leaf at any one cut. The lower the cut the more frequently you have to mow the lawn. The lower the cut, then usually the shallower is the root system, and a shallow root system makes the grass more susceptible to damage in dry periods.

Raising the Cutting Height

In cool climates raise the cutting height a little as the cutting season draws to an end. This is done to leave a sensible cushion of grass to cope with the winter. But don't let the grass height get out of hand.

Be warned that a recently heavily cut lawn attacked by frost can look shocking for a long, long time.

Taking machinery, or walking, on frosty lawns can injure the grasses.

As a general rule, do not cut lawns in cold, windy conditions, or hot windy conditions, as both can cause leaf-tip scorching of one sort or another.

Warm-climate grasses that are dormant in winter will not need mowing during the dormant season except, of course, to keep any winter weeds at bay.

Cool-climate grasses growing in warm areas will need cutting regularly throughout the winter, and local conditions will determine how often and at what height.

Hefty Cutting

If the grass has grown too long then do not cut it down to normal cutting height in one hefty cut; particularly if done in summer, as this results in badly scorched grass that may take several weeks to recover. At any time of the year, it is better to reduce the height of the grass a little at each cutting, until the normal height of cut is reached.

Lawn Grasses Under Trees

Avoid cutting lawn grasses that are growing under trees too low; that is, of course, if you feel that such an operation is practical and fits in with the rest of your lawn scheme, as the longer grass cushions raindrops falling from branches, helping to prevent the lawn soil from being pounded, and presents more grass leaf area to manufacture plant food to help compete with the tree roots.

Methods of Mowing the Lawn

Perhaps you want those dark-green and light-green stripes on your lawn. To achieve this effect you would use a suitable cylinder-reel mower with back and front rollers, plus grass catcher.

On a rectangular or square lawn, begin by cutting out two 'headland' mowing strips, at the top and bottom of the lawn. This allows you to turn at each end without scuffing uncut grass. You can start by mowing left to right, or from right to left, or whatever direction is suitable for your particular lawn and/or mower. Common sense here. (Not all lawn owners would agree with this method as some feel that the taller grass will absorb more

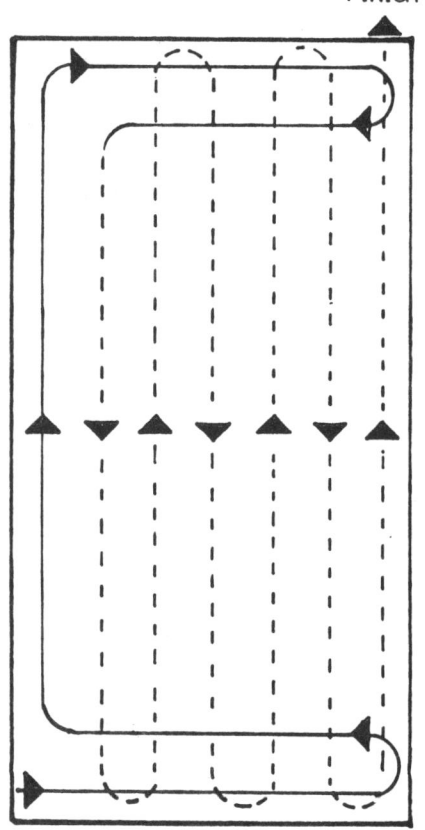

FINISH

1st.
CUT

One method of mowing a formal lawn to get dark-green and light-green stripes using a roller cylinder-reel mower. You may need, or prefer, to start from right to left. Not every gardener agrees with cutting out headlands first.

punishment, and the headlands can be trimmed after the rest of the lawn has been mown.)

The depth of the headlands depends on conditions that exist on site, therefore always allow yourself plenty of room to turn easily when using the mower. Do not turn too sharply at the ends of each run as you may grind out the grass with the back roller of the mower.

Each strip is cut in a different direction to the strip next to it. You mow one strip, say for example north to south, then turn and mow the next strip south to north, and so on until you have finished. It is important to keep each cut as straight as possible; as in most things, practice makes perfect.

If you want the 'chessboard effect' then mow the lawn say for argument's sake north to south, and when you have finished mow the lawn again, this time east to west.

If using a mower powered by electricity then,

because of the trailing electrical cord, the above method of mowing may not be practical or advisable.

You can mow the lawn using wider mowing strips. However, these strips must not be too wide or you will travel over a particular section of grass more times than necessary.

It may be possible when using a rotary mower that you can come off the lawn on to a hard surface, then turn into the next strip. This is all right provided: (a) you do not mess up the hard surface; (b) transport unwanted materials back onto the lawn; (c) in any way damage the mower, blades etc.; or (d) break down the lawn edges.

There are other methods of mowing a lawn. It all depends on a particular gardener's approach, and if the lawn has obstacles within its boundaries such as trees, seats and the like. Be aware that low tree branches can present a mowing hazard.

If you use a ride-on mower then what you can achieve depends on the mower, as some ride-on mowers require larger turning circles than others. The manufacturer's instructions should point this out.

Mower Strip

'Mower strip' is the name given to a 150 mm (6 in) or wider (the width of the mower strip depends on the type of mower you use), strip of concrete (or other paving) set just below lawn height on lawn areas that abut, for example, walls. This means that the mower can cut the grass without knocking into the wall, and the concrete being just below mower height means the mower blades do not catch the concrete. Mowing strips also help keep your knuckles away from any wall.

A mower strip can be used as a buffer zone between the lawn and garden rocks, loose stone, grit etc.

Rectangular paving set in grass

Catching Grass

Should the clippings be collected in the grass box, and possibly composted? Or should the clippings be allowed to fly on to the lawn surface, where they can rot down? There are points for and against.

Points for are: (a) a certain amount of nutrients is returned to the soil and will feed the lawn; (b) there's no need to remove the clippings to another site to dispose of them.

Points against are: (a) rotting clippings can lead to a thatch build up in such grasses as Kikuyu Grass, Couch (Bermuda) Grass, Hybrid Couch Grass and Creeping Bent Grass; (b) too thick a layer of clippings can smother grasses; (c) clippings drying on the lawn surface can make the lawn look very untidy.

If you are catching the grass then it can be useful to have a barrow handy, or something equally suitable, so that you can empty the catcher, carry on mowing, and then cart off the clippings when you have finished with the mower.

Remember that grass clippings can get very hot when stacked. Rotting grass may also give off an objectionable smell. Clippings from stolon (runner) lawns (Couch (Bermuda) Grass, Hybrid Couch and others) may contain stolon nodes that may root if used as a mulch, or used in a compost heap. Fresh grass clippings used as a mulch can generate too much heat around susceptible plants. Refer to suitable books on composting lawn clippings.

Grass clippings from lawns which have recently been treated with selective herbicide should not be used as a mulch, as they may still contain active herbicide, which could damage, or even kill, susceptible plants.

Mower Safety Suggestions

1. It is crucial, because safety is a prime concern, that you always read the lawn mower manufacturer's instructions on how to operate, maintain and store a particular mower. Always keep such manuals handy and in good condition.

2. Remember, a mower that is well maintained and is operated correctly will produce the most satisfactory results.

3. Carefully inspect and remove all debris from the lawn area before mowing. Be aware that the blades in a rotary mower revolve at incredibly high speeds and can sling-shot hard, sharp or blunt objects at dangerously high speeds. Cylinder mower blades can be wrecked by stones, gravel and such.

4. Keep children, pets, and adults for that matter, away from the grass area being mowed. Well away so as not to be in direct line with the mower, in all directions.

5. Do not let others joy-ride while operating a ride-on mower.

6. Do not mow wet grass as it can be slippery and dangerous, particularly when using a mains electric mower. Also it could be bad for the lawn grasses.

7. Mow the lawn when there is sufficient light to see exactly where you are going, and exactly what you are doing.

8. When using a mower wear suitable clothing such as shoes or boots, long trousers and so on. Protect your eyes from missiles thrown by the mower, using suitable eye protection, and so on.

9. Before working on a mower, disconnect the mower spark plug lead, and tie it back securely, making sure that the vital electrical impulse part is not in contact with anything, particularly the plug and petrol tank. Some people remove the plug once the engine is cold. Precautions must be taken to prevent the mower from being started accidentally.

10. Touching the ignition system of a running mower engine, or a mower engine being started up can cause shock, even severe shock, and in certain cases much worse.

11. Check the mower blades, bolts and mowing assemblage before starting the mower to make sure all parts are in good repair.

12. Regularly check mower nuts, bolts and screws before starting the mower to make sure that none of them have worked loose.

13. Do not start a mower in an enclosed space as the fumes emitted from petrol engines are poisonous.

14. Never fill a petrol tank while the engine is running.

15. Fill the tank with enough petrol, or whatever correct fuel, before you start so that the mower doesn't run out of petrol unnecessarily before you have finished mowing.

16. Do not fill the mower's petrol tank on the lawn to avoid petrol spills scorching and killing the grasses.

17. Make sure your feet are in a safe place when starting the mower. Read the manufacturer's instructions on how to start the mower.

18. Do not use a mower with the manufacturer's safeguards removed.

19. It is exceedingly dangerous to pull a working rotary mower, or a similar action mower, backwards

close towards your feet, as the spinning blades could be pulled over your feet.

20. It is exceedingly dangerous to lift a working mower.

21. Do not allow small children to operate a mower.

22. Ensure that you know how to stop the mowing machine safely and quickly, particularly in an emergency.

23. Remember, a recently used mower has a dangerously hot engine, hot exhaust and other parts.

24. Never leave a mower unattended while its engine is still running.

25. Never be away long enough from an immobile mower for children, and others, to tamper with it.

26. Most gardeners are aware that mains electricity can be a force of the most potentially hazardous kind when used in the garden, therefore check the manufacturer's safety instructions concerning mains electrically operated mowers. Make sure that all safety precautions are in place before using a mains electric mower, and if in doubt check with a qualified licensed electrician. Check electrical cords for cracks, breaks and dangerous wearing *before* you plug in. Work sensibly and methodically.

27. I repeat, have the manufacturer's operating and safety instructions conveniently to hand at all times. Also read any safety instructions and warning stickers the manufacturer may have affixed to the machine.

There are many suggestions concerning the safe use of mowers. Above all, use common sense.

11. Feeding the Grass Lawn

Why do we fertilize a grass lawn? What do we want a grass lawn fertilizer to do?

1. To provide a lawn of good colour, and influence the grass growth to produce a consistent lawn surface which complements the garden.

2. To supply the correct balance of nutrients which will help provide a vigorous lawn that resists the invasion of weeds, weed grasses and diseases.

3. To help provide a lawn surface that will take reasonable wear and tear, according to the type of grasses in the sward, and help the grasses to recover after use.

Suitable lawn fertilizer, applied at the correct time and at the correct rate, will greatly enhance a lawn, provided all else in the lawn soil is as it should be.

Regular observation of the lawn grasses for the presence of healthy, or not so healthy, lawn turf is a good way to ascertain whether or not a lawn needs feeding.

Stay with suitable, reputable grass lawn fertilizers, correctly nutritionally balanced for given lawn situations and lawn grasses. Nevertheless, most importantly, do not overfeed the lawn.

Soil Test

You may wish to have your lawn soil tested for its nutrient content. Contact your local Department of Agriculture, Primary Industries or Primary Production for the names of recognized, reputable laboratory soil analysis services; also check out the cost.

Read the Fertilizer Pack Label

Read the label to see, among other things, what nutrients the fertilizer contains, times of application, and rates of application. Is it a 'complete' fertilizer, i.e. does it contain nitrogen, phosphorus (phosphate), potassium (potash)? Is it recommended for your lawn grasses?

Note: The essential elements carbon, hydrogen and oxygen (carbohydrates) are supplied naturally by atmospheric carbon dioxide and water.

Essential Elements (Nitrogen, Phosphorus, Potassium)

On a proprietary, well-balanced, 'complete' lawn fertilizer pack you may see reference made to NPK. The N stands for nitrogen, the P stands for phosphorus, and the K for kalium (Latin for potassium).

Nitrogen is essential for the production of green leaves, amino acids (proteins) and more.

Sulphate of ammonia (ammonium sulphate) is a rapid-release nitrogen fertilizer. Dried blood is an organic nitrogen fertilizer and is reasonably quick acting. Finely ground hoof and horn meal is a slow-acting nitrogen fertilizer, which also contains a little phosphorus. Blood and bone fertilizer contains nitrogen and phosphorus.

Urea formaldehyde contains much nitrogen and is known as a 'slow-release' fertilizer. Isobutylidene diurea (IBDU) is a slowly soluble, slow-release fertilizer which contains much nitrogen.

Phosphorus improves root vigour, transports and stores plant energy, and increases the resistance of grasses to drought.

The most popular of the phosphatic fertilizers is superphosphate. Bone meal is a slow-acting phosphatic fertilizer which also contains a small percentage of nitrogen.

Potassium has various and complicated roles to play and is associated, via the green leaf, with the manufacture of carbohydrates, plant enzymes, protein synthesis, resistance to fungus diseases and overall vigour.

Sulphate of potash (potassium sulphate) is well known and is used on grass lawns.

The gardener is expected to apply nitrogen, phosphorus and potassium in amounts suitable for his or her lawn grasses.

Nitrogen is not necessarily wanted on clover lawns as clover has the facility of manufacturing (or 'fixing') its own organic nitrogen, which also becomes readily available for the grasses. You will see fertilizers specifically compounded for use on clover lawns.

Other Essential Elements

Lawn grasses need other essential elements to flourish and these are calcium, magnesium and sulphur. Usually, these are available in the soil and should not be applied unless needed, as an excess of calcium may depress the uptake of iron. These elements may be supplied as by-products of other fertilizer ingredients.

Trace Elements

Minor elements (trace elements) such as iron, zinc, copper and manganese are also needed by the plant in minute quantities. Again these are usually already available in the soil, although there are certain soils in Australia which are known to have an iron deficiency. Applying trace elements willy-nilly without recourse to professional laboratory soil analysis could lead to very serious soil problems.

Also acid rain could deposit, and might have already deposited, various trace elements on to your garden.

Types of Fertilizer

For convenience we shall place grass lawn fertilizers into two categories—organic and inorganic

Organic Fertilizers

Organic plant and soil nutrients are the residues of plant or animal life. Examples include seaweed, vegetable compost, dried blood, hoof and horn, blood and bone, bone meal, bone dust and fish meal. Some gardeners do not like to use animal products in case they attracts cats and dogs to the area.

One overseas fertilizer firm is producing 'ethically organic' poultry manure pellets for use on lawns.

Inorganic Fertilizer

Inorganic fertilizers, such as sulphate of ammonia, superphosphate and sulphate of potash are much used in horticulture. Their action is reasonably predictable, and by using suitable, small applications of inorganic fertilizer during the growing season, one can control lawn grass growth very effectively. However, if used in excess, or during hot weather, they can scorch, kill, or at the very least, give the lawn grasses problems.

Slow-release Nitrogen Fertilizers

Some forms of fertilizer are coated with substances to extend their fertilizing life, e.g. urea-formaldehyde and IBDU.

Urea formaldehyde and IBDU contain considerable nitrogen and are referred to in general terms as 'slow-release' or 'extended phased release' nitrogen fertilizers, i.e. they release their nitrogen content over a longer period of time than rapid-release soluble inorganic fertilizers.

Liquid Fertilizer

Suitable liquid fertilizers are used on lawns. Both organic and inorganic forms are available. Liquid *organic* fertilizers for use on lawns may be slower acting. Read the label and apply as recommended by the manufacturer.

Be aware that some lawn liquid fertilizers contain selective herbicides such as MCPA, mecoprop or dicamba, and extra care must be taken when using such chemical combinations, because of possible 'off-target' damage to susceptible plants. Read the label before you buy, and use selective herbicides safely.

Fertilizing Periods and Rates

One fertilizer firm, on their bag of (NPK) lawn fertilizer, outlines the differing rates of distribution for light soil, medium soil and heavy soil, and the times to apply the fertilizer, and goes on to point out that the optimum results are obtained by light, frequent fertilizer applications.

Another well known brand name gives a reduced rate of application on their (NPK) fertilizer pack, this reduced rate to be applied every six to eight weeks during the growing season.

There are complete lawn fertilizers that contain rapid-release nitrogen, which is available for the grasses at the beginning of the growing season, plus slow-release nitrogen, which is released slowly during the growing season. The two combined supply both immediate and ongoing needs, and are applied, say, only once a year at the beginning of the growing season.

The fertilizers used for the above 'essential' times must be suitable—balanced for use on lawn grasses—and complete enough to supply the basic needs of the lawn.

Fertilizer-Selective Herbicide

Note that there are also fertilizers which contain selective herbicide in their make up and are used to weed and feed the lawn (not to be confused with Lawn Sand, which is usually a suitable mix of sulphate of iron and sulphate of ammonia, which also weeds and feeds), and those fertilizers that contain selective herbicide should be applied as the manufacturer recommends on the label. Remember any 'off-target' application may kill or injure susceptible plants, so take care not to inadvertently apply it to any garden beds bordering on the lawn.

Straight Fertilizer

You may see references to a 'straight' fertilizer. A straight fertilizer is used to supply a 'principal' ingredient. For example, sulphate of ammonia supplies the principal ingredient nitrogen, superphosphate the principal ingredient phosphorus, and sulphate of potash the principal ingredient potassium.

Your Lawn

It is difficult, if not impossible, for an outsider to give firm fertilizer recommendations for your particular grass lawn soil, as lawns can vary considerably from area to area.

Your particular lawn soil is peculiar to your part of the word. The type and amount of lawn fertilizer for you to use on your lawn depends on local soil, weather and other factors, e.g. humidity, rainfall, seasonal drought, sandy or clay subsoil, the types of grasses in your lawn, the use it receives, the quality of lawn you want, the frequency and height of mowing, and the amount of fertilizer nutrients that already exists in the soil.

You could contact your local Department of Agriculture, Primary Industries or Primary Production, or Botanic Garden, or local experts on lawns and lawn fertilizers for their recommendations concerning the correct sort of fertilizer to use on your lawn and when to use it. Emphasize the type of lawn grasses you have, as fertilizer suggestions for different types of lawns may vary.

Also remember what has been said above concerning having your lawn soil tested for its nutrient content.

Sensible Fertilizing

A lawn needs regular, but sensible fertilizing to keep it in good health, as usually a reasonable quantity of nutrients is lost from the soil each year (principally nitrogen, phosphorus and potassium) by the gardener removing grass clippings, and by water leaching out nutrients from the soil, and by fertilizer gases escaping into the atmosphere.

Leaving the grass clippings on the lawn reduces the loss of nutrients, but the amount of nutrients contained in the grass clippings may not be as much as one anticipates, since nitrogen is lost as atmospheric gas. Leaving grass clippings on the lawn may lead to a build up of thatch among certain grass species, and if in too heavy a layer these clippings will lay on top of the lawn and smother the grasses underneath.

Also, the lawn may not look too attractive with dead, drying grass clippings laying on the surface.

Cool-climate Grass Lawns Growing in Cool Climates

Many gardeners who grow cool-climate grass lawns in cool climates fertilize their lawns once a year, or at most twice a year. They use a reputable brand of complete (NPK) spring and summer lawn fertilizer, and a complete (NPK) autumn lawn feed, applied at the manufacturer's recommended rates and suggested times.

Such a spring and summer fertilizer dressing may be a traditional, complete, organic-inorganic lawn fertilizer.

Some gardeners apply a suitable complete spring and summer lawn fertilizer dressing containing say rapid-release nitrogen, and a slow-release nitrogen, such as urea formaldehyde. This is to provide a suitable early boost to the grasses, and then an extended phased release of nitrogen over the growing period. Suitable phosphate and potash lawn fertilizer is also included.

This fertilizer is applied in spring (September–October–November) at the manufacturer's recommended rates and times, during the so-called grass growing spurt, but only if the air and soil temperatures have increased sufficiently and remain constant, and the soil is moist with the lawn grasses growing actively.

Some gardeners like to use a 'traditional', complete, inorganic spring and summer lawn fertilizer. This traditional fertilizer does not, I repeat, *does not*, contain slow-acting organic, or slow-release nitrogen, or other slow-release organic materials. This spring and summer fertilizer is applied as the manufacturer recommends.

Then possibly, and if necessary, gardeners fertilize the lawn again in autumn (March–April), but using a suitable complete NPK fertilizer that contains a much lower percentage of nitrogen, and the nitrogen content is slow acting, to prevent a nitrogen surge that could result in lush grasses being severely damaged during winter. But again this is applied only when the soil is warm and moist and the lawn grasses are growing well.

Cool-climate Grasses Growing in Warm-climate Areas

Under these conditions a complete spring lawn fertilizer dressing, which includes a rapid-release nitrogen fertilizer and a slow-release nitrogen fertilizer, is applied as the manufacturer recommends, thus giving the lawn a nitrogen surge followed by an extended phase nitrogen release.

Then a suitable complete nitrogen-phosphorus-potassium autumn feed is applied in say April, as the manufacturer recommends (or perhaps a nitrogen-potassium autumn feed if adequate phosphates are available in the lawn soil).

But there are gardeners who like to use a 'traditional', complete, inorganic spring lawn fertilizer dressing, which does not contain slow-release nitrogen, for the spring active growing months. Then, if necessary gardeners apply a suitable autumn feed.

Air-soil temperature and moisture conditions have to be suitable for an early autumn fertilizer dressing. In some areas, such as metropolitan Adelaide, very hot, droughty conditions may prevail in early to mid March and *you do not apply fertilizer to a lawn during a drought period if it is going to place the lawn under stress.*

Cool-climate grasses growing in warm climates such as Adelaide's tend to thrive reasonably well over the autumn-winter-spring seasons. However, it must also be stated that Adelaide's summer temperatures are not kind to certain of the cool-climate grasses.

Warm-climate Grasses

Be aware that all warm-climate grasses, with the occasional exception, originate in parts of the world other than Australia, and possibly each in a different place. A hybrid grass such as Hybrid Couch Grass *(Cynodon dactylon × Cynodon transvaalensis)*, has separate species parents. All may have differing nutrient requirements.

Their winter colour can vary from one area to another (from the tropics-subtropics to southern South Australia), with the greenness depending on the clemency of the winter. Some grasses can brown right off, e.g. Couch (Bermuda) Grass and Hybrid Couch, in the cooler of the warm-climate grass areas.

Some, under specific maintenance circumstances in certain cooler parts of the warm-climate areas, may stay reasonably green, e.g. certain Couch (Bermuda) Grass cultivars and certain Hybrid Couch Grasses; others stay rich green in some microclimates, but are apt to fade in others, e.g. Kikuyu Grass.

Warm-climate grasses in the cooler of the warm-climate areas can be fertilized during spring, say September-October, that is as soon as the grass begins the growth spurt after the winter dormancy period, using a suitable complete lawn fertilizer dressing that includes rapid-release nitrogen and slow-release nitrogen, applied as the manufacturer instructs.

This nitrogen supply may last for a few months during the active growing period. Check the manufacturer's label. An active growing period for warm-climate grasses is usually spring-summer.

Again, some gardeners like to use a 'traditional', complete, inorganic spring and summer lawn fertilizer dressing, which does not contain slow-release nitrogen. This is also applied as the manufacturer instructs.

Whether a warm-climate grass lawn growing in the cooler of the warm-climate areas needs fertilizing in autumn (say April) is determined area by area, as there is considerable variability between local climate areas and, of course, the warm climate grasses may be heading towards the winter dormant state. Seek expert advice locally from those qualified to advise on lawns, as nitrogen and/or phosphates (or any fertilizer) may not be required.

Tropical lawns, because of the wet season-dry season, have their own particular fertilizing needs. Suggested fertilizer applications for tropical lawns may be available from your local Department of Agriculture, Primary Industries or Primary Production.

Grass Lawn Fertilizer Spreader

Although well-balanced fertilizers are essential for a healthy lawn, the application of lawn fertilizer by inexperienced (and possibly experienced) lawn owners has caused more problems via burning-scorching than most other lawn operations.

Applying fertilizer that dehydrates grasses during hot weather can also cause serious damage to lawn grasses.

Fertilizers come in different-sized particles—granular, fine granular and fairly fine powder.

A hand-pushed fertilizer spreader (distributor) has to be calibrated to the person using it. Experiment using an empty fertilizer spreader to

Calibrating fertilizer on wide strip of plastic. Note tape measure (right) and fine strings at intervals

achieve a suitable, sensible, reasonable, but an easy to repeat, walking pace. Once established, then this walking pace should be used by you when calibrating fertilizer, and when applying the fertilizer to the lawn. Common sense here.

Some manually operated spreaders, under the pull of gravity, drop fertilizer from the hopper on to the lawn.

When using a spreader/distributor make sure that it is clean and thoroughly dry, and working properly before using. Check bolts and screws to make sure none have worked loose.

Always load fertilizer into the hopper in a suitable place away from the lawn to avoid spilt fertilizer burning or scorching the lawn, and to avoid staining concrete surfaces and the like.

Remember that certain fertilizer ingredients, such as sulphate of iron, may heavily stain or mark concrete and clothes. Even sulphate of iron that has been applied to the lawn, if accidentally walked back onto surrounding concrete or paving, may result in staining.

You have to determine that the correct amount of fertilizer is distributed over the lawn. There are various methods of calibrating fertilizer.

One method, using a drop spreader, is to lay suitably wide-enough sheets of, e.g. strong brown paper or plastic on top of the ground. Choose a suitable flat surface away from the lawn, in calm conditions, when it is dry, with the paper or plastic secured against being blown away. Then apply the fertilizer over a correctly measured area.

Bear in mind that plastic, or any shiny surface, can be slippery to walk over, and plastic can get extremely hot in hot sunlight. Also remember that

Calibrating a fertilizer spreader using brown paper. Note scale and tape measure (right).

if you lay plastic over a grass surface, the heat generated under the plastic could be great enough to kill, or damage, the grass.

It is important to choose an area where any fertilizer that does accidentally blow away will not cause problems, such as staining paving or scorching desirable plants.

Let us assume that you have measured out a linear run of four metres on the brown paper (I repeat a linear run of four metres and *not* four square metres). Prepare to apply the fertilizer.

Measure the width to which your fertilizer spreader will distribute fertilizer. Let us assume it is 500 mm.

Apply the fertilizer down the run, sweep it up carefully and weigh it. You may find, for example, that you have applied 200 grams, therefore every half a square metre has received 50 grams of fertilizer (200 grams divided by 4 m linear run). Therefore, a square metre will receive 100 grams.

Always check the width of a drop fertilizer spreader as it is possible that certain fertilizer spreaders are in imperial measurements; e.g. 18 in (457 mm).

The snag comes when a fertilizer is recommended by the manufacturer in metric quantities for the square metre, but your fertilizer spreader-distributor is in imperial measurements. It can be worked out, but if in any doubt, then get a competent mathematician to work it out for you.

Using the above linear distance run and application:

Multiply 4 metres by 0.457 m (457 mm i.e. 18 inches) = 1.828 square metres

Divide 200 grams by 1.828 = 109 grams per square metre

(Obviously 18 inches is close to half a metre.)

If you have a *clean*, smooth concrete surface where any staining of the concrete does not matter, and are using granular fertilizer, and your spreader is 500 mm (half a metre) wide then you can mark off an area of, say, four square metres (I repeat four *square* metres).

Let us assume it is recommended that you apply fertilizer at 100 grams per square metre to the lawn. Add 400 grams of fertilizer to the hopper, plus an extra kilogram to act as a control. Treat the four square metres of concrete as though you were treating the lawn, then carefully sweep up the fertilizer and weigh it. Then weigh what is left in the hopper and compare. Theoretically, there should

be a kilogram still left in the hopper; if not recalibrate the spread to get the correct distribution. (The amount you use as the fertilizer control in the hopper is what is sensible and practical for your spreader.)

Be aware that cracks in the concrete may hold fertilizer, and when sweeping up the fertilizer, that if sand and dirt are picked up these will be excess weight. Common sense and observation here.

As a control for the above methods, you can mark out one square metre on brown paper (or whatever) secured against blowing away. Let us assume that the manufacturer recommends 100 grams per square metre. Weigh out 100 grams of fertilizer exactly. Carefully and exactly spread the fertilizer evenly over the square metre. This gives you an indication of how much 100 grams per square metre looks like for comparison.

There are other methods of checking fertilizer calibration.

Check and recheck fertilizer calibration. Record the calibration mark, or whatever, when you are sure it is accurate; also be alert that different particle size fertilizers needs recalibrating, and that different users need to calibrate the fertilizer spreader to the way they operate.

Spreader working parts such as wheels, delivery ports may wear out, and recalibration at regular intervals, to help avoid over-fertilizing the lawn, is a good idea.

Be aware that certain fertilizer ingredients can be caustic, and you should protect your eyes, nose, mouth, and hands from contact with these chemicals. Do not, I repeat *not* test garden chemicals in confined spaces.

Keep a set of scales only for garden work, and do not use them for any other purpose as you are using possibly toxic materials. And don't let anybody borrow your garden scales because of this.

Another form of spreader is the 'broadcast' or 'spinner' type. The broadcast pattern varies and some have a spread pattern as wide as 1.22 to 1.8 m (4 to 6 ft). Check the manufacturer's data.

If you intend using a 'broadcast' or 'spinner' spreader then you must find out the exact broadcast diameter to avoid over application, and 'off-target' application problems, and for a small garden this presents a major problem as you have to find a suitable area where such a machine can be calibrated.

One method of calibration consists of weighing

a given amount of fertilizer, placing it in the hopper, treating a correctly measured area, and then weighing the fertilizer left in the hopper. As stated, this method may not be practical for your garden. Consider such problems before you purchase a spreader.

It is also easy to over-apply fertilizer using a drop spreader if the wheels are allowed to overlap too far. However, the wheel track of the previous application has to be overlapped, because the hopper is usually contained inside the wheels, otherwise you end up with thin strips of unfertilized lawn which look unsightly until the grass grows over. However, avoid unnecessary overlap when using the previous application's wheelmark as a guide line. If you cannot see the wheelmarks on your lawn then it may be prudent to mark out the runs to avoid overlap.

Some gardeners divide the manufacturer's recommended amount of fertilizer dressing in half. They apply one half of the recommended amount in one direction, say for arguments sake north to south—south to north, and the other half is spread crosswise east to west—west to east.

When fertilizing a lawn, you may be able to come off the lawn at both ends on to a hard surface. As stated previously certain fertilizer ingredients can heavily stain concrete and the like. You may have to protect this hard surface before turning, so that no surplus fertilizer falls on to the concrete, or whatever, to prevent staining it.

Do not let the fertilizer spreader 'bump' off the lawn, or 'bump' on to the lawn when returning, as this may cause the spreader to deposit more fertilizer than is required and scorch the lawn ends. Ensure that the spreader moves smoothly off the lawn, and also turns and moves back onto the lawn smoothly.

If you cannot achieve the above and you still want to use a spreader, then treat the two lawn headland areas first, say two fertilizer strips, and fertilize the rest of the lawn, up and down side by side, switching off the hopper to avoid any excess fertilizer falling on to the already treated headlands.

This method can be fraught with problems because of possible over-application, particularly when switching off, turning, and switching on the hopper to do the next strip. Therefore, you must check and re-check the switching off, turning, and switching on procedure in a suitable area away from the lawn, well before you fertilize the lawn.

Before you get anywhere near the lawn check to see how long it takes the spreader to actually deposit

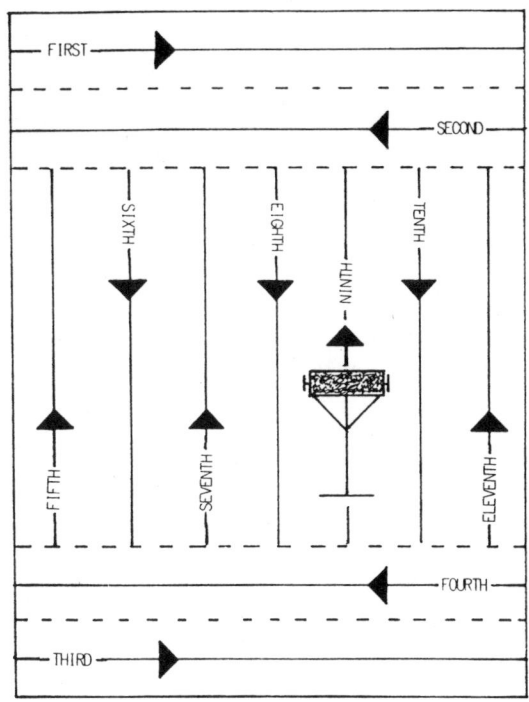

One method of fertilizing a lawn. Switch off hopper at end of row to avoid overdose and spillage

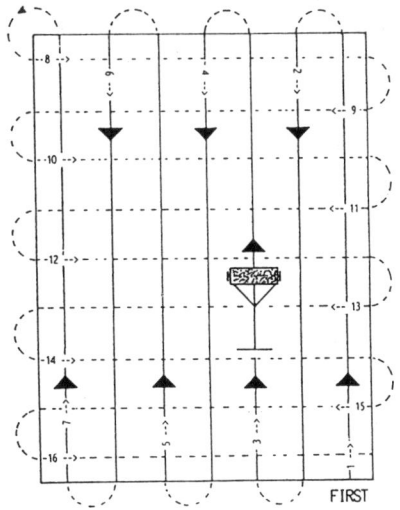

Another method of fertilizing a lawn. To help achieve even distribution when fertilizing a lawn spread half the fertilizer amount in one direction, and then spread the other half in a crosswise direction. Switch off hopper at the end of each run to avoid overdose and spillage. You can sow grass seed in the same fashion. Be aware fertilizer may stain paving.

fertilizer from starting. It is possible, when starting up, that a certain type of spreader may deliver more fertilizer than the recommended amount, which would cause 'lawn end' scorching.

It is sensible to water the lawn, provided sufficient rain hasn't fallen, well before applying the fertilizer so that the soil is moist enough to accept the fertilizer. However, the grass blades must be thoroughly dry before applying the fertilizer. If the grass blades are wet the fertilizer sticks to them, sucking out large quantities of moisture, like blotting paper soaks up ink, thus scorching and possibly killing the grass blades.

Carefully, but generously, water in the fertilizer soon after you have applied it to wash the chemicals off the leaves and onto the lawn soil. Do not over-water and wash the fertilizer off the lawn. If you have deposited little heaps of fertilizer accidentally then, if feasible, remove the excess and then flood the area with water to help lessen grass scorching, but don't be surprised if the grass dies from over-concentration of fertilizer.

Note: If you are using fertilizer that contains selective herbicide then you have to be guided by the manufacturer's instructions on the pack as to what you can or cannot do.

Spreader Maintenance

It is important to look after the fertilizer spreader once you have finished with it. It should be kept clean and dry, as any moisture will turn fertilizer into salts, which could corrode parts of the machine. The instructions that come with a new fertilizer spreader may outline its maintenance.

Spreading Fertilizer by Hand

Grass lawn fertilizer can be distributed by hand. However, it is important that the correct distribution is obtained otherwise the lawn could end up with scorched patches, or yellow and green half-moons. Granular-pelleted fertilizers make application easier, and if done correctly then hand fertilizer distribution can give excellent results.

Remember that fertilizer dust can float up so protect your eyes, nose and mouth, as well as your hands, from contact with these chemicals. Some fertilizer ingredients stain clothes, therefore you should wear old clothes or protective clothing.

Some gardeners, once they have worked out how much fertilizer is needed for a given area, mix clean, fine, dry, lime-free sand, or weed-free, dry sandy soil, with the fertilizer as an aid to more even distribution. For example, they may use 200 grams (7 ounces), or approximately two handfuls of sand/dry soil, with each square metre amount of fertilizer to help facilitate an even spread. But check the product pack to see if the manufacturer comments on this. Notwithstanding, the sand or dry soil carrier has to be suitable otherwise it may not mix evenly and carrier-fertilizer separation will occur, which could lead to uneven, possibly damaging, distribution.

You can divide the lawn up into square metres, using strings as 'railway lines' and place canes, or similar, at one metre intervals as 'sleepers', and apply the correct amount of fertilizer individually to each square metre. Divide the correct amount of fertilizer in half and apply one half, say for argument's sake, north to south and the other half crosswise east to west.

Note: When using fertilizers that contain selective herbicide in their make up, refer to the label instructions on the product pack in case any additions by the gardener interfere with the efficiency of such a mix. Read the label before you buy or use a combined fertilizer-selective herbicide, and use the product safely.

Soil pH

Acid rain has been around since coal was used for combustion, and sulphur plus numerous other ingredients, including trace elements, are transported by wind and rain and washed into the soil.

Occasionally, check the soil's pH and if the soil is too acid for your particular lawn grasses, causing them to thin out, then consider liming the lawn.

If necessary treat the lawn with ground limestone. Before you buy or use the product, check the label to see if it is recommended for use on home lawns. If so then apply at the manufacturer's recommended rates for lawns. Carefully wash the lime through the turf grasses down to lawn surface level.

Too heavy-handed an application of lime can give the lawn soil 'heartburn', encourage coarses grasses to predominate and favour the appearance of worms, none of which is wanted in a fine grass lawn.

Do not use hydrated lime as it has a caustic action on the grass blades.

12. Watering

Golden Rule Number One

When you water the lawn, you water it well. A good, deep flooding getting adequate moisture infiltrating and wetting to a depth of 150 mm (6 in) and more. Then let the lawn get on with its life until it needs another good drink.

Moisture from light sprinklings is contained in the soil surface and the grass roots move up to the surface after it, where they can be decimated by hot sunlight or lose out to successful lawn invaders such as surface rooting Summer Crabgrass and Annual Meadow Grass.

Supplying Sufficient Water

To grow a lawn successfully you have to supply sufficient water to satisfy the evaporation of moisture and the transpiration of the grass plant, plus sufficient to maintain the correct level of soil water.

An arbitrary figure of 25 mm to 37 mm (1 to 1½ in) of water a week is used as the amount of water needed during dry periods to keep a lawn growing actively, but this is only a guide as so many variables come into lawn irrigation, including suitability of lawn grass species or cultivars. Very much more water can be needed in hot inland areas, and perhaps less in cool climates.

It all boils down to what has been worked out professionally for your locality, and a qualified local irrigation expert should know about how much irrigation is needed for local lawns.

You could contact the relevant section of your State/Territory Department of Agriculture, Primary Industries or Primary Production or local Botanic Garden Home Advisory Service to see if they offer charts on the weekly rainfall, or the irrigation needed in your particular area to maintain an actively growing lawn.

The CSIRO Division of Soils (in association with Rellim Technical Publications) publication *When should I water?* gives information on lawn water needs for various Australian places; the Northern Territory Department of Primary Production *Agnote* (March 1983) also gives information on lawn irrigation for various Northern Territory centres.

Soil Types

Sandy soil can be coarse textured, texture being dependent on the amount of sand or loam it contains. Water intake can be high to very high. Water retention can be low to very low. It also has low erosion and good drainage.

Loamy soil can be:

1. Moderately coarse with moderately high water intake, moderately low water retention, low erosion and good drainage.

2. Medium texture with medium water intake, moderately high water retention and moderate drainage.

3. Moderately fine with moderately low water intake, high water retention and correspondingly poorer drainage.

Clay soils are fine textured, and depending on the clay content have low to very low water intake, high to very high water retention, poor drainage plus erosion.

Thatch and Compaction

Moisture has to penetrate deeply into the lawn soil to be effective, but this penetration can be inhibited by lawn soil compaction or by thatch build up. Compaction may be alleviated by aeration, and thatch by dethatching.

Wilting

You have watered your lawn copiously and still it wilts. Apart from thatch it could be that the roots are shallow and suffer during hot sunshine, or fungus disease may be attacking the grasses.

Dry Patch (aversion to water) is where copious water is applied to the soil but the soil is so cemented, most likely by funguses, that water will not penetrate and therefore the grass roots cannot take up water. Aerating the patches and/or using a suitable lawn wetting agent to aid water penetration may help. Lawn wetting agents are generally available in most nurseries, but do read the label. Dry Patch attacks all lawns, particularly fine grass lawns that are under constant stress.

The type of lawn grass will also determine the need for water as some grasses are more tolerant of drought conditions than others, grasses such as Couch (Bermuda) Grass *(Cynodon dactylon)*, Hybrid Couches *(Cynodon dactylon × Cynodon transvaalensis)*, Queensland Blue Couch *(Digitaria didactyla)* and Kikuyu Grass *(Pennisetum clandestinum)*.

Don't be misled by the expression 'drought-tolerant' as the above grasses need adequate moisture to be successful lawns.

Grasses such as cool-climate Browntop Bent *(Agrostis tenuis)* and Creeping Bent *(Agrostis stolonifera;* also known as *A. palustris* and *A. stolonifera* var. *palustris)*, need much more water to survive in warmer climates (if they survive at all!).

Certain cool-climate grass species such as Chewings Fescue *(Festuca rubra commutata)* and Tall Fescue *(Festuca arundinacea)* are more tolerant of droughty conditions in the cooler of the warmer areas, e.g. Adelaide, than those other cool-climate grasses mentioned above, but they also need an adequate supply of water during warm conditions to remain successful as lawns. Tall Fescue would be more drought tolerant than Chewings Fescue, but it still requires sufficient water.

How Green a Lawn?

A lawn that has been watered just sufficiently to keep it green but has been forced to send its roots deep down into the soil after moisture between waterings, will retain a better grass sward.

If the lawn is kept permanently saturated and waterlogged then lawn grasses will not flourish as the roots become stifled and poorly developed.

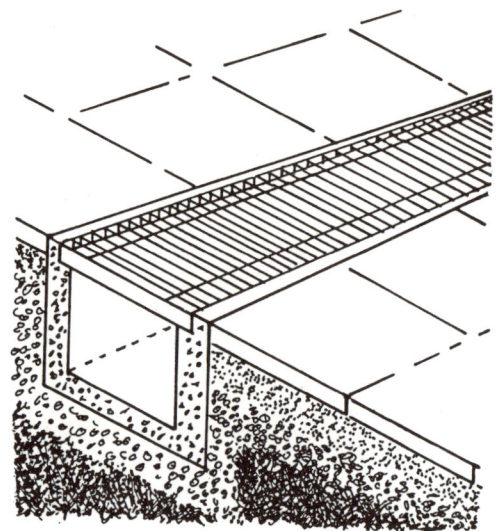

A concrete surface drain to take away surplus water

Moss, algae or fungal problems may occur in such areas.

A balance of air and water is needed and in a well-drained lawn is accomplished automatically as the grasses will take up water, and any surplus moisture will drain away. This is provided *you* don't deliberately keep the lawn permanently saturated.

How Often to Water

When should a lawn be watered? When the lawn has just begun to show stress, or footmarks show clearly on the lawn surface and remain pressed down, it is time to give it a copious watering.

When a lawn begins to look sick, the leaves turn a bluish-green, wilt slightly, and 'footprinting' is obvious then it is time to water the lawn immediately.

Footprinting occurs when you walk over a dry lawn during hot weather and soon afterwards dead-grass footprints appear on the lawn surface, and one could swear that some careless person had wiped his shoes in non-selective herbicide and then taken a stroll across the lawn. A lawn should not be allowed to get to the 'footprinting' stage.

You can remove 150 mm (6 in) 'panatella cigar' cores from the lawn, at different locations, to see if the soil is damp enough. Some gardeners keep a suitable soil auger in the shed for this purpose. Observation of these plugs will help determine if your lawn needs watering. Is the soil dry, crumbles when squeezed, and obviously needs watering? Or

Fine turf laid out, and irrigated, to prevent drying out in stack

A newly turfed Creeping Bent Grass lawn plus top dressing

Using hose to obtain a curve

Hybrid Couch Grass turves

Hybrid Couch Grass turves separated into rooted portions

Hybrid Couch Grass turf divided into plugs for planting

Planting plugs of Hybrid Couch Grass

pH Test. Adding indicator liquid

pH Test. Adding indicator powder

pH Test. Comparing soil colour against colour chart

Perennial Amenity Ryegrass showing various nutrients plant received: (a) 'O' plant nutrients; (b) NPK plus certain trace elements; (c) NPK; (d) nitrogen (N) only; (e) phosphorus (P) (phosphates) only; (f) potassium (K) (potash) only

is it wet? Does it look damp? Is it cool and sticky when squeezed?

Some gardeners insert a screwdriver into the lawn soil to ascertain whether or not there is moisture in the lawn soil, i.e. ease of penetration and dampness on the screwdriver's metal shaft when withdrawn.

Of course, you have to use your common sense when it comes to watering your lawn, because only you know what is happening on site.

Be aware of the location of water pipes, irrigation pipes, electrical cables etc., when poking around in the lawn to avoid accidents.

Best Times to Water a Grass Lawn

When is the best time to water a lawn? Perhaps you don't have a choice and have to water when you can. However, watering a lawn during hot sunlight can be wasteful because of extreme evaporation.

If you have just seeded, planted runners, rooted runners etc., or turfed a lawn and the weather turns hot, then usually you have no choice but to water during hot weather just to keep the plants alive. Common sense is needed here to ascertain when irrigation is needed.

Some grasses are more tolerant of saline conditions than others, but it is possible that saline water plus hot sunlight could cause damage to susceptible plants. Check with local experts on water salinity in your area.

Try not to have shallow pools of surface water lying around for any length of time on the lawn in hot sunlight as it may lead to a phenomenon known as 'scald' (brownish, scorched-looking grasses).

If you can water the lawn before sun-up then this gives the lawn time to absorb the moisture and harden off before the sun evaporates most of it.

If you can begin watering at early dawn then this gives you the advantage of being able to see what is happening, and a reasonable amount of moisture will be absorbed by the grasses before the sun gets too hot.

Watering at evening-night is usually good for moisture penetration. However, humid night-time conditions coupled with high nitrogen fertility can also be ideal for funguses to thrive and attack. Be aware that some sprinklers are much noisier than others when operating and may cause noise problems between neighbours. Check with your lawn irrigation expert. Some councils might ban night watering and some might ban the installation of automatic sprinkler systems.

Traditional Lawn Sprinklers

You can use lawn sprinklers that have been used since reticulated water first reached most houses, i.e. the sprinkler that is connected via the garden hose to the tap and is moved from place to place by you.

These sprinklers can also be controlled by a timer that is attached to the tap and then the garden hose is attached to the timer. The timer cuts off the water supply at a pre-set time. Instructions on how to use these timers are supplied by the manufacturer.

Static sprinklers have no working parts and water in pre-determined patterns such as a circle, half circle or quarter circle, or as determined by the manufacturer.

Oscillating sprinklers have moving parts that oscillate (swing) a fan of water left then right—backwards and forwards—and usually produce a rectangular water pattern.

Rotary sprinklers have arms that spin around creating a circular spray of water. Some have 'butterfly' spinners.

Impact sprinklers, usually, can be regulated to water in circles or part circles. The water from the hose is 'knocked' by the sprinkler impacting on it to produce an even spray cover.

Turret sprinklers can have various head watering patterns.

Soaker hoses are long ribbon-strips of perforated plastic tubing which water reasonably large strips in a very gentle fashion.

Travelling sprinklers (wheeled-mobile) for the home garden are mostly rotating sprinklers which use water pressure to drive themselves along the hose in a watering pattern pre-determined by you. Some

Travelling sprinkler

are designed to stop automatically, but be on hand when using this type of sprinkler in case somebody decides to remove the sprinkler stop.

With all sprinklers, ensure that water droplets are large enough to fall on to the lawn and not so finely misted by water pressure that most of the water evaporates before reaching the ground.

Quick-coupling Sprinklers

Quick-coupling sprinklers are not much used by the home gardener but are used extensively by the professional. Water pipes are laid underground. Valves are situated along the pipes below turf level and spaced at the correct distances apart to give proper coverage. This spacing has to be worked out carefully to make sure that the water pressure and flow rate will provide adequate coverage.

Into these valves a sprinkler, usually with a bayonet fitting, is inserted. The water is turned on and the area watered for a given time. Then the water is turned off and the quick-coupling sprinkler removed. The valves usually have covers to keep out dirt and the like.

Quick-coupling sprinkler

Golden Rule Number Two

When choosing a sprinkler, or sprinkler system, ensure that your water pressure will work it, and conversely that the water pressure is not too high for the sprinkler, causing. excessively wasteful misting, and possibly damaging the sprinkler.

Automatically Controlled Watering Systems

If you are having somebody design your irrigation system then make sure beyond any reasonable doubt that he or she is expertly qualified to do so.

If you are planning to use pop-up sprinklers to irrigate your lawn then the correct spacing of these sprinklers is critical.

One type of pop-up sprinkler

An automatically operated sprinkler system does need some maintenance, and this has to be compared with the labour and possible inconvenience needed to maintain a manually operated irrigation system.

Windy, hilly or sloping lawn sites present their own particular problems. If your lawn is in such a situation discuss the problem with the lawn irrigation expert.

Tall grass could inhibit sprinkler throw, therefore you must ensure that the grass is kept low enough so that when the sprinkler jets rise, water is sprayed correctly over the lawn.

Solenoid Valves

Put simply, and somewhat naively, a solenoid activated (automatic) valve is worked by suitable electrical stimulus, and when a suitable electric stimulus from the automatic sprinkler controller (timer) reaches the valve, the valve allows water to flow through to the sprinklers.

The solenoid valve allows water to flow until the electrical stimulus cuts off.

There are various types of solenoid valves, and certain manufacturers may refer to solenoid valves by a different name.

Sprinkler Types

Types of sprinkler used for automatically watering lawns are pop-up spray type or pop-up impact-knockabout type or pop-up gear-driven type.

The working parts of some are more complicated than others. Some are considered to be more vandal-proof than others. Some tend to be less conspicuous in the lawn than others. Some sprinklers are noisier than others.

Interchangeable Nozzles

Certain firms offer pop-up sprinklers with a series of interchangeable nozzles, for example, full circle, half circle, three-quarter circle, two-thirds circle, one-third circle and quarter circle. They also have nozzles which they refer to as square, centre strip, end strip and side strip which may be useful for those awkward sections and corners.

Once installed, an automatic watering system's sprinklers have to be inspected regularly when operating to see if everything is working correctly.

Grasses should not be allowed to grow over the sprinkler head and stop or impede the rising sprinkler action. If grasses are not impeding the sprinkler action but the spray isn't working correctly, then check to see if the nozzle is blocked. Grit and dirt around the sprinkler head may also cause problems to the sprinkler guides.

Most important: Do not buy an expensive irrigation system that has been designed to work off a high-pressure, high-flow-rate supply but when installed in your lawn only spits at the grass because of lack of pressure and flow rate. Discuss this with the lawn irrigation design expert.

Manually Operated Pop-up Sprinklers

There are gardeners who prefer to have a row (or rows) of pop-up sprinklers which they can control manually by turning a valve on and off.

Trees

Remember that trees in a lawn will compete for any water you apply to the lawn, and therefore you will have to supply sufficient water for both trees and grasses.

Be aware of the damage that can be done by trees by digging irrigation trenches close to them.

Underground Services

Before you even think about physically installing an underground watering system check to see where any services run, such as gas, electricity, telephone, water and so on. You obviously don't want to damage any of these. And don't forget to include those services that have been installed by you or by previous occupants. Cutting through an electric cable could prove fatal.

Keep in mind where the water pipes and valve cables are located once you install an underground sprinkler system, as aerating a lawn with a fork and so on, could easily damage a sprinkler system.

Keep in a safe place a detailed plan of the irrigation system design. This plan should show *exactly* where the pipes, sprinklers etc. are located.

Check for any restrictions your local water board authority may have in force concerning the need for check valves to prevent backflow.

Tapping into the mains water supply should be done by a qualified master plumber, registered/licensed for this type of work.

To Start

Begin by drawing the measurements of your garden on graph paper. Graph paper is often provided free of charge by irrigation suppliers. If not it is cheap enough to buy from a local stationer.

Establish a scale, for example 1 m on the ground equals 1 cm on the plan, or 1 yard on the ground equals 1 in on the plan. This scale may have to be varied according to the size of your garden.

If you only intend to irrigate a lawn then mark in abutting buildings, flower beds, trees and shrubs, footpaths, driveways, the position of the house and the domestic mains water service.

Locate and then mark on the plan the meter location and any water supply source which originates from the domestic mains supply. For example, the position of the water supply source closest to the water meter and position of any water sources close to the proposed lawn area.

If you intend to use an automatic controller then mark on the plan the nearest *suitable* electrical power source.

Locate and mark on the plan services such as electricity cables, gas and telephone. It's vital to know where any services are *before* you start digging holes and trenches.

Ask your local lawn irrigation design expert before you buy the necessary equipment, if he or she will plan the irrigation system free of charge. Or how much they charge for this service.

Pressure and Flow

Your designer will need to know the exact pressure and flow rate from the water point source you are going to use.

You can ask the irrigation supplier if you can borrow a flow/pressure testing apparatus. Some suppliers may hire these out. You may be given an instruction sheet on how to work the testing apparatus. The sheet may ask you to read and record a number of important facts including the static water pressure and flow rate at your water source. Carry out the subsequent water measurements and record them with the utmost precision and care.

You may consider it expensive to employ a qualified master plumber to do this work for you, but if anything goes wrong, which can happen with older, or for that matter, new water-pipe fittings, then you have the expert on hand to sort out the problem.

You may not want to take the irrigation system from a water source near the proposed lawn area, but want to go directly from a water source close to the water meter to ensure maximum flow rate and pressure.

Discuss your intentions with the properly qualified lawn irrigation designer or with a qualified master plumber as this operation can become complicated.

It is imperative that you record the correct pressure and flow details of the water supply source your irrigation system is to operate from.

The pressure gauge should measure in kiloPascals (kPa), but some older pressure gauges may measure pounds per square inch (psi).

Ensure that all garden water supply sources apart from the water supply source you are testing are off. Also make sure that no water is running in the house, including the toilet, but before you turn off or divert any water check that none is currently being used for a vital or specific task, e.g. somebody taking a shower. Common sense is imperative here to avoid injury to persons or damage to equipment or both.

Do you use an air-conditioner that uses water to cool down hot air inside the house? Will this be working when your irrigation system is working? If so how much water does it use per minute?

Ensure that the water supply source is fully open when taking the readings and take several readings throughout the day. Turn off the water supply source after each reading. You would list and record all the readings, plus the time of day at which they were taken, plus the date and the weather conditions.

Checking the Water Flow

Also discuss the below carefully with an expert lawn irrigation designer.

When checking the flow remove any connections from the water supply source as any connection would restrict flow resulting in an inaccurate reading. Make sure that no other water is running in the garden or house. Then take a reading of exactly how long it takes to fill, for example, a 9 litre (2 gallon) bucket.

To work out how much water flows per minute using a 9 litre (2 gallon) bucket is easy and the literature from the irrigation firms tells you how. For example if it took 90 seconds to fill a nine litre bucket the flow is six litres per minute.

You would also take this test at the time you anticipate using the sprinkler system. You may want it to come on at 9 o'clock at night or 6 o'clock in the morning. It is also possible that you may want it to come on again, say at mid-day or six o'clock in the evening.

It is important to log the date, time of day and weather conditions when testing a water flow for your lawn irrigation system. Designing a system using, say, the highest flow rate and pressure in winter could possibly lead to a system that doesn't cover a sufficient area in summer, which results in a lawn that looks tatty.

Conversely, an irrigation system which is under greater pressure than it needs to work properly can have sprinkler problems and misting.

If you have more than one outside water supply source then, if feasible, check all of them and record the information. Why? It is possible that the water supply source nearest the future lawn, the supply you intend using, has corroded pipes.

Water pressure and flow rate may vary with seasons as perhaps more gardeners would be using lawn sprinklers and other water outlets during the summer.

I make the point, discuss the above with an expert lawn irrigation designer.

Stretching the System

Do not scrimp when designing an irrigation system by what I know as stretching. Stretching means trying to design a system based on cost and not on practical design. A sprinkler system that doesn't quite cover leaving a series of green circles surrounded by unsightly yellow patches makes for a distressing looking lawn.

Check the manufacturer's recommendations and see the margin to be allowed for sprinkler overlap.

At first glance it may seem wasteful, but not as 'wasteful' as over-stretching the system.

Lawns sprinklers are usually arranged in square, rectangular or triangular spacing. Various factors determine which system is used.

How Much Water Falls on to the Lawn?

One method of testing how much water falls on a given spot within the sprinkler's throw is to place sensible-sized, straight-sided tins (cans), or similar containers, with no obstructions around the inside top rims, at regular distances from the sprinkler centre out on all sides, and record how much water is received in each tin after, say, one hour's irrigation.

After the hour has elapsed the amount of irrigation water in each tin is measured with a rule to get the exact depth of water.

I set out to water an area of 23.45 m². It was an awkward-shaped lawn; approximately 7 m × 3.35 m. I placed 25 large tins at set distances over the lawn surface. The time was 8.45 am, on 9 January (Australian summer). The daytime temperature rose to 38°C (100°F). No other taps were on.

There are various types of water meters used world-wide (imperial/American/metric). The one I used is metric and read 2428067 litres. The area was watered for one hour and after this time the meter reading was 2429163. Therefore, 2429163 minus 2428067 = 1096 litres.

The area was watered by four quarter-circle sprinklers, one in each corner of the lawn, and two half-circle sprinklers, one either side approximately in the middle of the lawn.

Next we need to calculate the depth of water applied. Since one litre of water over 1 m² equals 1 mm, if the amount of water used is divided by the area we should get the depth of water applied, i.e. 1096 litres divided by 23.45 m², which equals 46.7.

Therefore, according to the meter, I should have applied approximately 47 mm. However, this does not take into consideration any evaporation that occurs from the time the water leaves the meter to the time it lands in the tins, the evaporation before the depth of water in the tins is recorded, or water not landing on the lawn area.

The readings of each tin were as follows.

```
QCS --*32 mm ---*34 mm ---*30 mm-QCS
      |
      |   *30 mm    *35 mm    *37 mm  |
30 mm*                                *40 mm
      |   *33 mm    *33 mm    *36 mm  |
      |
 HCS     *60 mm    *58 mm    *55 mm-HCS
      |
      |   *38 mm    *38 mm    *36 mm  |
41 mm*                                *40 mm
      |   *38 mm    *38 mm    *33 mm  |
      |
QCS --*38 mm ---*35 mm ---*30 mm-QCS
```

Prevailing wind is diagonally from top right-hand corner to bottom left-hand corner.

A total of 948 mm of water was collected in the tins, which if divided by 25 (the number of tins) equals approximately 38 mm.

Observe that the centre row has more sprinkler overlap.

The point being, just because the water meter stated that approximately 47 mm should have been applied over the lawn as a whole doesn't mean that this amount has been applied exactly to each square metre.

This is where checking the area similar to the above and visual observation of how deeply the moisture has penetrated into the soil is most useful. The time of day, wind, etc. could influence how much water falls.

If you suspect the meter's accuracy then check with your local water authority.

The professional irrigation designer, when measuring and checking sprinkler pattern, delivery uniformity on large lawns or playing fields, may use tins as outlined above. He or she may also employ a method known as Christiansen's uniformity coefficient.

To check the amount of water delivered by a spinning, circle sprinkler having a radius of, e.g. 3 m you can use the following.

The area of a circle = pi radius squared (pi = 3.14 approximately)

3.14 × 3 × 3 = 28.26 m²

The 28.26 square metres is divided into the amount of water delivered by the spinkler, which is recorded by reading the meter before and after an hour's watering. No other water outlets should be on when checking the sprinkler's output. Assume the reading was 520 litres.

520 divided by 28.26 = 18.4.

Therefore, theoretically, 18.4 mm was applied to the area, but again this does not take into consideration evaporation, wind effect etc. It only records the amount of water that has passed through the meter.

Heavy Duty Pipe

You must use the correct heavy duty class of pipe that is to be attached to the main line water supply from the meter as this pipe, like the water that is supplied to your house, will be under constant pressure from the mains water supply.

Discuss with a qualified irrigation designer or plumber the correct heavy duty pipe to use and where to use it. Use a qualified master plumber to connect pipes to the mains water supply.

Automatic Controllers—Station Timers

Automatic irrigation controlled by an automatic sprinkler controller (timer) allows you to set the time when you want water on the lawn.

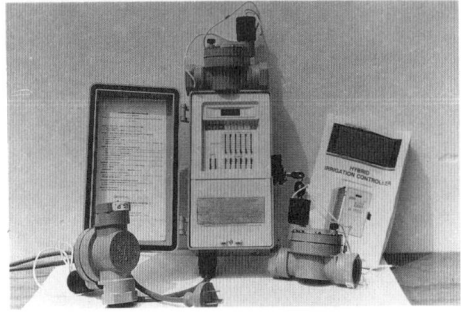

Automatic irrigation controller and solenoid valves

The solenoid valve, which controls a row of sprinklers, is in turn controlled by a suitable automatic controller. An automatic controller can appear complicated to operate when first seen, but it is not all that complicated once the expert has explained its operating procedures.

Automatic controllers are many and varied, expensive or reasonably affordable, sophisticated and not so sophisticated.

For example, you can have a reasonably inexpensive automatic controller controlling six solenoid valves with each solenoid valve controlling a row of sprinklers.

One automatic controller, at least, can have a water duration per station for a period of a few minutes to 60 minutes. Discuss this with the lawn irrigation expert.

Depending on the sophistication of the automatic controller you can irrigate your lawn twice in one day. Or if you are not satisfied with the amount of water the lawn has received, perhaps because of droughty conditions, you may be able to press a button, or similar, and repeat the watering cycle.

You may not want a six-station controller for your lawn as you only need three solenoid valves for three rows of sprinklers. Depending on the automatic controller you may be able to use the other stations for watering a different part of the garden. Do not mix sprinklers having different pressures/flow rates on the same line. Check with the lawn irrigation expert concerning this.

There are various station controllers such as four-station controllers, six-station controllers, nine-station controllers, twelve-station controllers and possibly more. Read the manufacturer's data.

Pipe Freezing

Gardeners who live in areas where water in pipes can freeze in winter should check with their local water authority, or qualified master plumber, on the depth you need to go with your pipe to prevent water from freezing in the pipes, and the various means of draining water out of irrigation pipes for the winter.

Electricity

The electrical power to the controller has to be installed by a qualified electrician licensed for this type of work as you are dealing with the full force of electrical current. Also discuss with the electrician the need for a transformer, earth leakage circuit breakers, and installing the wiring from the controller out to the solenoid valves. The electrician should point out the most suitable position to house the controller. The manual should also cover this point. Read the manual that comes with the automatic controller very carefully.

Keep in mind that electricity in the garden is a very powerful factor and can be easily overlooked as a potent force of the most dangerous kind.

Draw up a plan of where any electrical cables run and keep it in a safe place so that you can refer to it quickly at any time in the future. You may also wish to indicate, with a sign on the ground, where the electrical cables run underground.

Piping

A master shut-off valve can be fitted to the line so that when anything goes wrong with the irrigation system the water supply can be cut off to allow for repairs, without the need to turn off the mains, so that water is still allowed to feed the various household conveniences.

Irrigation pipes are easy to install with the advent of suitable semi-rigid PVC irrigation pipe and polythene tubing (manufacturers may have different names for this type of piping). Make sure you get the correct piping for your irrigation, pipe that will withstand the pressure of the water. These pipes are usually readily available at your irrigation supplier. The PVC pipe comes in long, but easy to handle lengths, and is easily cut using a hacksaw. The flexible polythene tubing that comes in long coils is also reasonably easy to handle, and is also easy to cut.

Although both are easy to install some consider the flexible polythene tubing is easier, but it is a matter of opinion.

PVC and polythene tubing fittings are many and varied and permit the gardener to achieve irrigation wonders. It should be noted that various manufacturers may have their own names for their own particular pipe fittings: read the manufacturer's literature.

You Have Your Plan

You have your plan and you have had it checked by the local irrigation expert. You know where and how to avoid any services that run underground. The tools you need to install irrigation lines are basically simple. From herein you refer to your irrigation design plan which will be unique to your lawn. You can also refer to the literature issued by the irrigation equipment manufacturer.

New Lawns

If you intend seeding or turfing a new lawn, and are going to install an automatic watering system then, before you start, discuss this aspect of lawn irrigation installation with the expert irrigation designer.

Remember that the sprinkler jet has to rise above the seeded lawn or turf at the correct height to perform properly.

If the spinkler housing is too high above the lawn

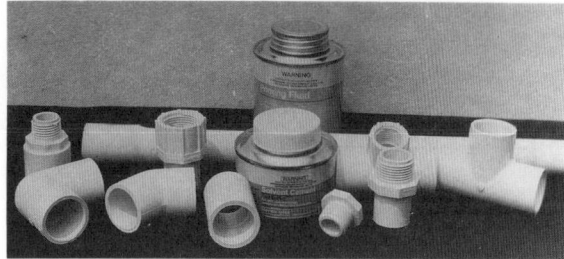

Various components used in one form of lawn irrigation

Polypipe T-joint coupling

Selection of black polythene tubing fittings; plus sprinklers used for lawn irrigation

Adjusting a rachet clip

surface it could be damaged or even cut off by the mower. You can also trip over sprinklers that are too high. Manufacturers usually provide instructions on where their sprinklers are to be positioned in relation to the lawn surface.

Protect sprinklers during installation, to avoid their being adversely affected by dirt and sand.

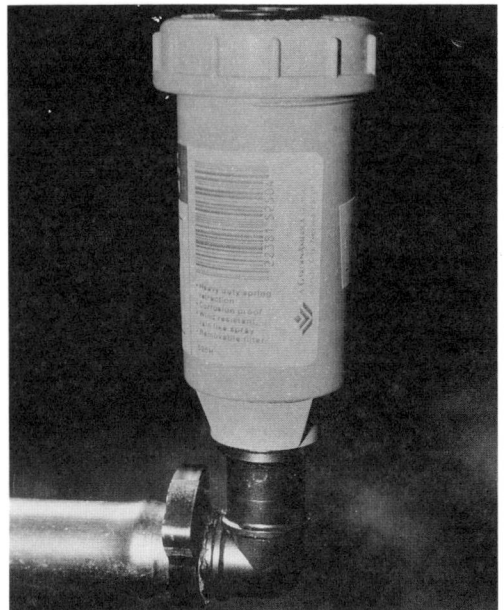

Sprinkler attached to threaded elbow

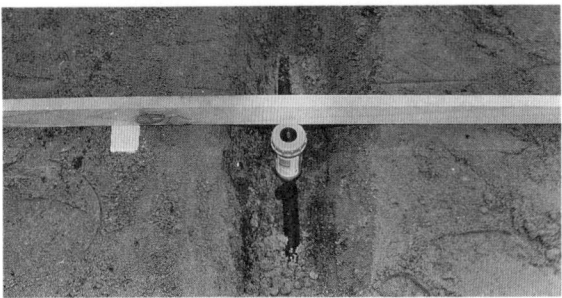

Checking height of sprinkler with that of surrounding ground

Sharp sand can wreak havoc on a sprinkler guide.

It is possible that dirt, sand and grit may have got into the pipes during installation. Flush out the pipes without the sprinklers attached to get rid of this muck. Use your common sense on how you go about this, because if you're not careful you can end up with more sand and grit in the pipes than before you started, as it can get sucked back in.

Irrigation Contractors

Perhaps you can hire a firm to design and install your irrigation system. Make sure that they are properly qualified for this type of work, registered/licensed and properly insured before you contemplate letting them work on your lawn area.

Finally

To conserve moisture and help the grass to survive drought conditions you can cut the lawn as high as the particular type of grass permits, but you have to allow for the automatic irrigation to spray properly. More grass blades equals more food for the roots. It also means that the grass blades protect the soil and this equals less evaporation.

13. Top Dressing

Top dressing lawns is a practice that is frequently carried out incorrectly. It is vital that any top dressing be spread thinly to avoid smothering the grass bases and to avoid cleavage and perching.

Why Use Lawn Top Dressing?

1. Usually top dressing has little value as a manure, but it does add a reasonable amount of bulk to the lawn.

2. It encourages grasses to spread and tiller.

3. It helps to obtain a level lawn surface.

4. It may, I repeat may, help improve the physical texture of the lawn soil.

5. It may help combat thatch, and more.

Notwithstanding, a level lawn which is healthy and adequately fertilized is in little need of top dressing. Indeed, your lawn may be so perfectly level that it does not need top dressing at all.

Compatible Soils

It is important, when using soil as a top dressing, that it be compatible with the existing lawn soil to avoid layering.

It is also important never to use top dressing containing fine clay and fine sand material that will cause drainage problems by blocking existing soil pore spaces.

Top dressings should be free of weed seeds, weeds and weed grasses, particularly rooting stolon and rhizome sections.

Mixes of suitable weed-free soil or sterilized soil, plus suitable sand and finely ground or granulated acid peat are used on garden lawns. Also used is suitably friable sandy loam on its own, or suitable sand on its own, particularly for a heavy lawn soil.

Compost

Well-rotted compost is sometimes suggested as an ingredient of a lawn top dressing.

Well-rotted acid compost that has been screened (sieved) to be free from lumps that would upset the lawn level, and mixed in, say, equal proportions with suitable soil and sand can be used provided: it has been made properly; it is completely, guaranteed, weed-free, including from portions of weed grass rhizomes and stolons that can root; it was made without too much clay in its soil-layer structures; and you can guarantee supplying a similar compost quality for future top dressings.

Avoid inhalation of dust, and wash thoroughly after using soil and/or composts.

Hollow Tining

Hollow-tining, i.e. taking out small cigar-sized cores of turf using a tubular fork, before top dressing, can be useful in so far as the top dressing will trickle into the core holes and improve aeration, drainage and root growth.

When to Apply Top Dressings

Top dressing is applied when the grass is growing actively, that is when the basal leaves can grow above the top dressing layer with ease, usually spring or early autumn for cool-climate grasses, and usually spring for warm-climate grasses, depending on local climatic conditions. The grass bases could be partly smothered if top dressing is applied during the dormant season, or even too close to the dormant season.

Top dressing should not be applied to a cool climate grass lawn during high summer as the dark-coloured dressing can absorb much heat, which is then transferred to the susceptible grass bases putting them under stress, particularly those grasses that spread by overground (stoloniferous) runners.

Soil Quality

The quality of any soil or loam used in a lawn top dressing is of paramount importance as soil that is limy, silty, salty, contains clay and sand fines, or is full of weeds or weed grasses, will damage the lawn.

The soil should be screened (sieved) to be free from lumps which would upset the lawn surface, and small stones and grit that could damage the mower and lawn users.

Some soils are very suitable sandy loams that can be used on their own. Also such soils, if used as an ingredient in a top dressing, may make it unnecessary to add any more sand.

Sterilized Soil

Soil can be treated by the supplier to provide what is sometimes known as sterilized soil, where all the unwanted soil organisms and weeds have been killed. It is vital that you check that this soil is suitable for use on lawns and will not harm the lawn grasses.

Sand

The texture of the sand you use, which must be clean washed, inert, lime free and salt free, depends on who is going to use the lawn.

Coarse sharp sand can cause injury to the exposed skin, or get picked up in between animal paws, and large gritty pieces of sand can damage the bottom blades of the finer mowers. Possibly you want to play lawn games, and large sand particles could upset the run of the ball.

Some sands to be found in suppliers' yards are not suitable for lawns, as they may contain clay, among other ingredients, and, indeed, can be entirely counter-productive.

Be aware that sea sand may contain much lime in its bulk brought about by the accumulation of calcium carbonate deposits.

It can be a good idea to inspect the sand at the local yard before ordering.

Particle Size

Keep in mind that for your lawn you want a sand that is open enough to allow for adequate drainage, but not so sharp as to cause injury or disturbance to users, and possibly damage some mowers.

Also bear in mind that some fine sands can bind and form water-repellent layers.

Peat

Suitable peat for lawns is finely ground or granulated peat that will form a 'soil' when mixed with sand and loam.

Peat is usually sedge or sphagnum. Both are usually acidic, but, as a precaution, always check the pH just in case. Acid peat is often used in a lawn top dressing, but not often on its own.

Suitable acid sedge peat is used extensively in lawn composts, as usually it has a reasonable pH, has high humic quantities, and can be finely ground to form organic particles which are easy to apply and quick to break down. Finely ground moss peat is also used. Peat is usually mixed with sand and soil. If you use peat then make sure it is moist, not wet, before application.

Any peat, whether it be sedge or sphagnum, applied on its own to the lawn surface could form peat layers that can dry out rapidly, and can eventually be impervious to water. If finely ground sedge peat is used on its own then it is applied as a very thin layer, 250 grams of *moist* peat per square metre (approximately 8 ounces per square yard), and worked well into the grass. The same goes for finely ground moist sphagnum peat. But better still mix the peat with an equal portion of suitable sand and apply.

Mixes

Depending on the nature of the loam, i.e. whether it is sandy or medium loam, a conventional suitable sand:medium loam:peat mix top dressing ratio is 5:3:2. All parts are by volume and not by weight.

five parts (e.g. buckets) of suitable sand

three parts (e.g. buckets) of suitable, good quality loam-soil

two parts (e.g. buckets) suitable acid granulated peat

Top dressing ingredients have to be mixed thoroughly.

Use top dressings containing more sand for existing clayish lawn soils, and top dressings containing more peat/organic material for existing sandy lawn soils.

It is possible that reputable garden suppliers have suitable lawn top dressings already mixed. Seek professional advice on likely sources.

Sand Top Dressing

You don't have to use soil or peat in a lawn top dressing, but can use suitable sand on its own, particularly if your lawn soil is on the heavy side. Always make sure that you use only thin layers of sand, say 1.5 mm ($\frac{1}{16}$ in) depth, as thick layers of sand can stifle grass, and cause what is known as 'cleavage', a condition where the sand-grass root layer separates eventually from the soil base.

Leaf Mould

Be watchful about using leaf mould in your top dressing, as some leaf moulds may be alkaline.

Amount of Top Dressing

Although a 1.5 mm ($\frac{1}{16}$ in) depth was stated above, the amount of top dressing to use varies, and is influenced by various factors such as lawn level, height of grasses, types of grasses, and so on.

On a home lawn as little as 1.5 mm ($\frac{1}{16}$ in) depth could be used, or a maximum of 6 mm ($\frac{1}{4}$ in), but no thicker than this depth. Indeed, a depth of 6 mm ($\frac{1}{4}$ in) top dressing could be too great for fine grasses of the bowling green quality, but may be suitable for coarser grasses.

The difference in soil quantity needed to apply 1.5 mm ($\frac{1}{16}$ in) and 6 mm ($\frac{1}{4}$ in) depth of top dressing, for say a 10 m² lawn, may surprise you, especially when it is dumped in one heap in your yard. Work it out, or get somebody to work it out for you.

Decide on the exact depth of top dressing your lawn requires and will accept *before* you order. I emphasize, decide on the exact depth of top dressing your lawn requires, and is able to take without the grass bases being smothered.

Correcting Uneven Spots

Small hollows will be filled in automatically when top dressing is applied and worked into the lawn surface. For small, but deeper hollows, the turf can be slit across the centre and up the sides of the hollow, and peeled back by carefully cutting underneath, say at 25 mm (1 in) depth, thus making two sections of turf, with the end of each section still attached to the lawn. Leaving one end of the cut turf attached to the lawn means that the lifted section of turf should recover more quickly. These flap sections are rolled back. Soil is then placed underneath to bring up the level, the turf is replaced, levelled, seeded if necessary, flooded with water and then kept moist until the turf roots have struck into the soil.

You may need to slit the hollow into a cross, similar to slicing a sandwich into four triangles, and roll back the four sections, but still leaving the base of each triangular section attached to the lawn. Or you may need to take out whole turves. After a suitable amount of soil has been added to the depression, the turves are replaced, correctly levelled with a straight edge, flooded with water and then kept moist until the roots have struck into the soil.

For bumps in the lawn you would use the same techniques as above but, of course, remove soil.

You may need to insert a whole turf on a badly worn section. Lay the new turf on top of the badly worn section, cut around the outside of the new turf and move it out of the way. Lift the badly worn section with a spade, prepare the soil to receive the new turf, lay the new turf, level it, and keep it well watered.

Broadcasting the Top Dressing

You can broadcast the top dressing over a lawn in the same fashion a roadworker fans sand from a shovel over the road.

Broadcasting top dressing over lawn using a shovel

The more effectively you spread the top dressing the easier it is to work into the lawn. Great blobs of top dressing can badly upset the lawn level.

Work the top dressing well into the lawn grass surface, leaving the grasses standing out above it. Work, for argument's sake, north to south and then east to west.

You can rub the top dressing into the grass using a 'lute', which can be like a very wide wooden rake

Luting in the top dressing

Using a lawn rake to ensure grasses remain above top dressing

without teeth. Or you can use the back of the garden rake, but this is not as successful. It's obvious that a wide toothless wooden rake, say 1 to 1.5 m (3¼ to 5 ft) wide, would level out an area of lawn more satisfactorily than the back of a smallish garden rake.

You can make a wooden lute, but remember that shifting large quantities of top dressing with a wide wooden lute can be very taxing on the muscles.

Manufacturers have designed and made lutes specifically for top dressing lawns. Enquire at your local nursery.

Remember, the grass blades and grass crowns (bases) must stand out above any top dressing to avoid being smothered.

Using a stiff brush to ensure grasses are above top dressing

The weather is a factor to consider when top dressing, as both hot and cold conditions could badly affect the grasses. If top dressing is carried out during mild weather, however, the grass blades should be able to grow away above the top dressing, avoiding the crowns being stifled, or scorched, which could cause susceptibility to disease.

Once the top dressing has been applied and has been luted and brushed in, it is time to water the lawn copiously, but sensibly, to wash any top dressing from the grass blades, and from above the grass crowns, down on to the lawn soil surface.

One hour after top dressing has been applied; plus irrigation

14. Pests and Diseases

Grass lawns can be attacked by a host of insects, but the principal pests are black beetles, various grubs, mole crickets and ants. However, some locations have a lawn pest peculiar to that part of the country.

There are basically three groups of grass lawn insects.

1. The root eaters. These attack and eat underground roots which result in dead patches on the lawn. Sometimes the leaves can be easily lifted off from the roots, exposing the insects. Or the plant fails even though it is receiving adequate care. The lawn level is upset by burrowing insects which also devour lawn grass roots.

2. The grass blade-stem leaf suckers. The grass blades die or yellow, or even whiten.

3. The grass blade chewers and eaters. The grass is grazed in circular patches or dead patches appear in trails.

Some people consider earthworms a pest, particularly in fine grass lawns.

Not so obvious lawn pests, although their activities on the lawn are obvious, are moles, bandicoots and rabbits. Birds may literally tear up turf to get at the insects in a lawn.

The home lawn owner may not realize an insect attack is taking place until considerable damage has been done to the lawn.

The first step is to isolate the insect that is damaging the lawn turf as subsequent treatment depends on the type of insect. If you cannot identify it, then check with an expert who can. Discuss control in home garden lawns with your local botanic garden's entomologist, or the Department of Agriculture, Primary Industries or Primary Production.

Insecticides

An insecticide is a chemical that kills insects. Specifically labelled insecticides for treating lawn pests are available in your local garden shop or nursery. Read the label on the product carefully to ensure that the insecticide (or nematicide or fungicide) you intend using is suitable for the job you have in mind.

Note: Also ensure that the label on the product refers to treatment of home garden lawns and also make sure that it refers to the insect that is causing the problem in your lawn.

Below is a selection of lawn insecticides seen recently in one State's local gardening shops.

1. A lawn beetle product containing chlorpyrifos for controlling lawn beetles, mole crickets, ants, millipedes, earwigs and slaters.

2. A lawn grub killer containing trichlorfon for controlling lawn caterpillars and lawn armyworms.

3. Lawn beetle killer granules containing fenamiphos.

4. A lawn grub control containing diazinon.

5. A blackheaded cockchafer control containing carbaryl.

The action of an insecticide depends on the particular active constituent, and may be: (a) systemic—translocated through the plant tissue and when absorbed by the pest attacks the pest's nervous system; (b) a stomach poison; (c) contact action; (d) affects the pest's nervous system.

Only treat the lawn for insects if they are in large enough proportions to cause continuing problems.

African black beetle *(Heteronychus arator)*

This is a shiny black beetle approximately 10 to 12 mm (½ in) long. The whitish-creamy larvae grow to about 25 mm (1 in) long and 6 mm (¼ in) in width, and when resting curl into a 'C' shape.

Root-eating black beetles

The larvae are active on lawns late spring to early summer-autumn although times of extreme activity for both larvae and adults vary between localities. If in considerable enough numbers the larvae can cause major turf problems.

The adults are active spring to late summer-early autumn, and can be a problem in the lawn but not necessarily as bad a problem as the voracious later-stage larvae. The beetles become dormant in winter, then mate and lay eggs in spring.

A bad attack by the larvae can be ascertained by the appearance of brown or dead patches, the size of the patches expanding rapidly. Rolling back a spade-width of turf will usually expose the culprits.

Black beetle grubs are not such a problem on thick, well-managed lawns as they are on patchy lawns, therefore keeping the grass thickened up helps prevent infestation.

Armyworms (*Spodoptera mauritia, Spodoptera spp.*)

The effects of lawn armyworms when in full assault are dramatic. They feed voraciously on the grass blades, particularly lawns in certain parts of northern-central coastal New South Wales. They attack on various fronts like soldiers (hence the name armyworm), and sometimes devastate the entire lawn.

New South Wales gardeners may be able to obtain a Department of Agriculture *Agfact* on armyworm caterpillars.

Armyworms—and cutworms *(Noctuidae)*—are important pests in the Northern Territory during March-April and October-November. A Department of Primary Production technical bulletin *Insect Pests of the Home Garden*, may be available to Northern Territory gardeners.

The caterpillars, which are members of the moth family, are greenish-greyish, brown to black. Some have longitudinal stripes running down their bodies and are approximately 30 to 45 mm (1¼ to 1¾ in) long.

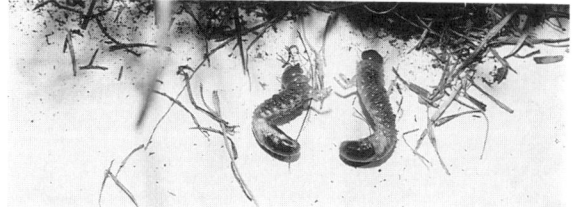

Lawn grubs attacking Hybrid Couch Grass

Blackheaded Pasture Cockchafers

These are the larvae of the beetle *Aphodius tasmaniae*. The greyish, 15 mm (½ to ¾ in) larvae live in tunnel-like burrows and are usually distinguished by their black heads.

The adults are often seen in swarms around street lights etc. in mid to late summer. Eggs are usually laid in areas where grasses are shortest or thinnest.

They are farming insects in that following rain they surface, harvest the grass blades and take them back to their burrows. However, they also graze at ground level. They are noticeable summer-autumn-winter.

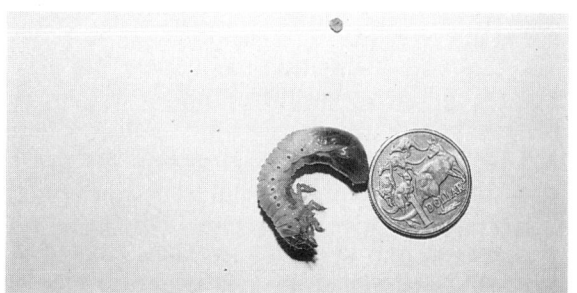

Mature white curl grub compared to a dollar coin

Cockchafer Grubs

The larvae of scarab-cockchafer *(Scarabaeidae)* beetles, also called curl grubs or white curl grubs, are whitish grubs with distinctive brown heads. Some can become quite large. Their bodies look soft. Some can live in the ground for up to two years, feeding on various roots, and may include grass roots in their diet.

Scarab grubs are an important pest found in Canberra lawns late summer-early autumn. Canberra gardeners may be able to obtain a fact sheet on lawns, which includes a section on pests and diseases, from the relevant local authority.

Mining ants

Funnel Ants *(Aphaenogaster pythia)*

These are a nuisance in that they create small mounds of soil at the entrance to their nests on the lawn surface. These mounds become slippery, cause problems for the mower and operator and may disrupt the lawn level. The ants bite if disturbed.

Mole Crickets *(Gryllotalpa spp.)*

These are distinctive, brownish, chirruping (in summer after rain), winged insects approximately 30 to 40 mm (1¼ to 1½ in) long, with modified spade-like front feet which they use to burrow into the ground to construct permanent residences. They feed on the grass roots, causing the grasses to die eventually. However, they mainly tend to 'spoil' lawns by upsetting the lawn surface levels.

Sod Webworms *(Herpetogramma licarsisalis)*

Also known as grass caterpillars, they are approximately 18 to 25 mm (¾ to 1 in) in length. The caterpillars can be green-brown-grey with dark-blackish circular spots on their bodies.

They are night feeders and concentrate on new shoots, some of which they drag into their silk-lined tunnels as a food store. If in heavy enough infestations these caterpillars can do considerable damage to the lawn. Birds will flock to areas heavily infested with sod webworms.

Earthworms

There is much controversy concerning earthworms and their presence in the lawn. An acid soil helps keep the worms at bay as worms don't seem to like an acidic soil. Collecting the grass cuttings in the catcher when mowing and disposing of them off the lawn means that there is less food for the worms.

Not all worms cast on the surface, indeed few do.

However, these few cause problems for the rest of the worm population.

Worms do have their good points. By burrowing in the soil they improve aeration and drainage. Their casts are superb soils which, if raked or brushed into the lawn surface and allowed to dry prior to mowing, act as a top dressing.

Worms also have their bad points. Their casts are ideal sites for lawn weeds. Their casts can become slippery and dangerous when you are using the mower. They can also mess up the mower. Their casts, when flattened, can smother fine grasses.

If your lawn has a severe worm infestation and you cannot use the lawn, then you have to consider getting rid of the worms.

Diseases

Note: The names of fungus diseases may change from time to time. I have used names commonly associated with the particular disease.

Grasses can be attacked by many funguses but only a few are savage.

Careful management, i.e. correct watering, adequate drainage, correct insect control, fertilizer application and mowing, general care and sensible use will keep your lawn in a much stronger position to repel or recover from fungus attack.

Top dressing that smothers the grass crowns leads to a weakening of fine grasses and encourages fungus attack. Brushing early morning dew from the lawn surface, using a clean brush, helps eliminate a suitable microclimate for funguses.

Tree, shrub and flower borders that inhibit air-flow over the lawn, air which evaporates moisture from the lawn surface, may also inadvertently provide ideal conditions for fungal attack.

Air and water pollution can contribute to lawn diseases but usually these are outside the control of the home lawn owner.

Fine Grass Lawns

If you want a fine grass lawn like a golf or bowling green, then your lawn will be beset with the lawn fungal problems associated with such lawns.

Firstly, try to control fungus diseases by correct cultural methods, but if this fails then use suitable lawn fungicides registered in your State or Territory for use on home garden lawns.

Fungicides

A fungicide is a chemical which kills fungus, fungal spores and fungal mycelium. Various fungicides are sold in nurseries and garden shops to treat home lawns. Refer to the label.

Some fungicides are systemic and are absorbed into the plant's system. Some help protect the leaves of plants from fungus attack. Some are systemic but also protect the plant's surfaces, acting as a preventative.

Below is a selection of lawn fungicides seen recently in one State's local gardening shops and nurseries.

1. Benomyl for treating dollar spot and fusarium patch.
2. Chlorothalonil for treating brown patch and dollar spot.
3. Mancozeb for treating brown patch *(Rhizoctonia, Helminthosporium)* and dollar spot.
4. Triadimefon for treating dollar spot.

Fungus Identification

Having seen many lawn diseases I can identify a few major diseases by their appearance, for example the vicious bleached-reddy-brown, irregular patch appearance of fusarium patch *(Fusarium nivale)* particularly on Browntop-Red Fescue greens, and especially when accompanied by tinges of pinkish-whitish pus-like, cotton-wool bud mould. Or the American silver dollar patches of dollar spot.

In my opinion for the home gardener to identify lawn fungus diseases is difficult. Spores can only be identified under a microscope, or by culture, by a plant pathologist.

Check with your local botanic garden or Department of Agriculture, Primary Industries or Primary Production expert, and seek information concerning lawn fungus diseases and their treatment, if fungus diseases are a problem on your lawn, as grass lawn diseases can be complicated.

Your local Department of Agriculture, Primary Industries or Primary Production may also offer fact sheets or *Agnotes* on lawn pests and diseases.

Do not confuse lawn fungus attack with damage caused by bitch urine scald, fertilizer burns, petrol drips, mower scarring, lack of water, lack of soil fertility, saline irrigation water, grass old-age where the blades are dying naturally, or the effect of cold weather on Couch (Bermuda) Grass and Hybrid Couch Grass.

Some diseases are prevalent on cool-climate grasses while others are prevalent on warm-climate grasses, and some are prevalent on both.

You may see nitrogen fertilizer recommended to combat a particular disease, but also be warned that too much nitrogen fertilizer can encourage a more insidious disease, and acidifying fertilizers, such as sulphate of ammonia, can lower the soil pH to a level where desirable grasses become weak, debilitated and wide open to fungus attack. Conversely, a limy soil (high pH) will encourage fungus diseases that thrive in such soil conditions.

The finer grasses such as Chewings Fescue, Creeping Red Fescue, Browntop Bent, Creeping Bent and to a slightly lesser extent Kentucky Bluegrass, seem to be particularly susceptible to fungus attack. Tougher grasses, such as Fine-leaved Perennial Ryegrasses, Kikuyu Grass, Tall Fescue, Common Couch (Bermuda) Grass and Buffalo Grass (St Augustine) seem better able to withstand lawn fungus depredations. However, they are not immune to all fungus diseases, particularly when growing in inhospitable environments.

Important Grass Lawn Diseases

Brown Patch (*Rhizoctonia* spp.)
Also known as smoke ring, this causes small purplish-green patches which become large, brown, splotch-patches with a 'smoke-ring' outer halo. It attacks Bents, some Fescues and has been known to occur on Bluegrasses (Meadow Grasses), Zoysia Grass and Buffalo Grass (St Augustine).

Corticium (*Corticium fuciforme; Laetisaria fuciformis*)
Synonyms are autumn rust, red thread and pink patch. At first, irregular large spots to dinner-plate sized patches of bleached grass appear, accompanied in dry weather by brittle pink needles, or pink 'jelly' and spidery mycelium in damp weather.

Corticium can form an incredibly beautiful pink carpet when it spreads across large expanses of turf. It is, however, very tiring for the grasses. It attacks Red Fescues but will also attack Fine-leaved Perennial Ryegrass, Browntop and Creeping Bents, and Kentucky Bluegrass (Smooth-stalked Meadow Grass).

Corticium is usually indicative of a suitable nitrogen fertilizer shortage, but be prudent when

Sheep's Sorrel   Ribwort Plantain   Cat's-ear

Dandelion   Creeping Oxalis

Capeweed   English Daisy

Greater Plantain   Jo Jo   Nutgrass

Paterson's Curse (Salvation Jane)   Caltrop

Annual Meadow Grass   Summer Weed Grass

applying a nitrogen fertilizer, such as sulphate of ammonia, as this could favour fusarium patch.

Damping-off Disease
(*Pythium* and *Fusarium* funguses)
This occurs mainly on young grass seedlings, causing them to collapse. When the soil is moist and cold the fungus thrives, but the seedlings do not. Seedlings can also collapse during high temperatures and this can often be brought about by one of the *Fusarium* organisms.

Even when seedlings have developed and are growing well they can be attacked by a second stage damping-off disease.

Using the correct pre-seeding fertilizer, plus proper drainage, will help the young grass seedlings to germinate freely and survive.

Dollar Spot *(Sclerotinia homeocarpa)*
As the name suggests, this disease forms circular brown, or bleached, silver-dollar sized 25 to 50 mm (1 to 2 in), spotty patches over the lawn. These patches can sometimes join to form much larger patches. It is found particularly on Red Fescues but will attack Creeping Bent and Browntop Bent. Sometimes it will attack Perennial Ryegrass, Zoysia Grass and Bluegrass lawns.

Dry Patch
Dry patch is where copious water is applied to the soil but the soil is so cemented, possibly by funguses, that water will not penetrate and therefore grass roots cannot take up water. Treat by aerating the patches and/or using a suitable lawn wetting agent to aid water penetration. Dry patch attacks all lawns, particularly fine grass lawns that are under constant stress.

Fairy Ring *(Marasmius oreades)*
The fairy ring fungus mycelium breaks down organic material which stimulates the outer ring of grass, causing it to turn a rich green. Then the fungus cements this same area of soil and kills the green ring of grass.

Toadstools appear in due season in fairy rings on the lawn. The fungus spreads outwards like a stone ripples water.

Marasmius oreades is extremely difficult to eradicate although aerating, plus treating with a suitable lawn wetting agent to further water penetration, may help.

Occasionally these fairy rings disappear without obvious reason. Sometimes they spread seemingly for ever, unless they hit impenetrable obstacles such as buildings, or when the rings join together.

There are many different types of fairy rings that appear on lawns, some of them innocuous, but the above is the most problematic.

Fusarium Patch Disease *(Fusarium nivale)*
Fusarium patch is a vicious fungus disease that seems to prefer overcast, moist mild conditions and a 5 to 16°C (40 to 60°F) temperature. However, there is a form that seems to thrive under lower temperature conditions, indeed it seems to appear following snow-melt.

Small, wettish, yellow irregular patches appear throughout the lawn, coalesce to form larger patches, and then collapse to form saucers of infected areas. These patches are sometimes accompanied by pinkish white, cotton-wool bud mould (mycelium).

Fusarium nivale is prevalent on the finer Bent Grasses and Annual Meadow Grass *(Poa annua)*, but will attack other fine grasses. However, it is not so obvious on coarser grasses.

Do not use quick-acting nitrogenous fertilizers in cool climate areas late in the season. Do not smother grasses with autumn top dressing. Both these encourage the incidence of fusarium patch on fine Bent Grass.

Ophiobolus Patch *(Ophiobolus graminis; O. graminis* var. *avenae; Gaeumannomyces graminis)*
Also known as take all, these yellow, bleached, bronzed, circular patches, which are small and saucer-shaped to begin, can join together to develop into some extremely wide patches.

It usually attacks Bent Grasses, indeed it has been known to attack Bent Grasses leaving Fescues and weeds unscathed in the centre of the attack. Usually, but not necessarily, it is associated with moist, humid conditions and limy, high pH soils.

Good lawn maintenance plus a slightly acid soil may help prevent its occurrence.

Using Poisons

Three Golden Rules

1. Do not use any insecticide, fungicide or nematicide unless you have to.

2. Use the least toxic material that will do the job you have in mind.

3. Read the manufacturer's label *before* you buy the product and *before* you use it, and use the product safely.

Be careful and use your common sense.

Other Rules You May Find Useful

Keep herbicides, insecticides and nematicides and fungicides well separated from one another, as it is frighteningly easy to grab a herbicide spray and begin to use it before you realize that you had meant to use a fungicide.

The lawn, usually more than any other part of the garden, is the province of young children, adults and animals. Therefore, if you treat a lawn with any chemical, make sure that sufficient time has elapsed before people and animals are allowed to use the lawn. Remember, dogs will lick lawns and sometimes eat grass. Dogs and cats lap pools of moisture. Children will play on lawns and lick their fingers.

Keep the concentrated pesticide in the manufacturer's container in a safe place, also ensuring that it doesn't get smashed accidentally.

Use the least toxic substance that will do the job, and protect yourself with suitable clothing.

Keep children, pets and onlookers well out of the way of any spray. Do not spray areas of lawn if childrens' toys, food, etc. are lying around. Remove or dispense with these objects.

Certain plants are intolerant of certain insecticides, pesticides and fungicides.

Do not spray the lawn with pesticides if it is too hot or windy. Do not spray if the spray is being blown back on to you.

Certain pesticides are flammable. *Read the label.*

Some pesticides are volatile and will drift. Off-target damage can be considerable. Choose a cool, windless day, when no rain is expected, to use the spray and use the least volatile spray to reduce spray drift. If feasible use a coarse nozzle to help reduce spray drift.

Certain pesticides will kill fish, or may poison bees. Some pesticides are toxic to animals and birds.

Do not feed chickens or other animals with grass clippings from treated areas.

Read the label to ascertain and observe directions concerning the protection of the environment.

Some garden chemicals can cause irritation to the nose, mouth and eyes. Read the label.

Certain pesticides should not be used anywhere near edible crops, especially at harvest time.

Do not smoke or eat while using garden chemicals.

Do not spray or mix chemicals in confined spaces.

Never, I repeat *never*, when using chemicals in the garden, lose sight of them, or leave them laying around for children to pick up. Lock up the chemicals after use in a safe, sensible spot that is outside the house, and is out of the reach of children, but not so high that the chemicals will fall into your eyes, face and mouth when you reach for them. Keep the key in a safe place.

Discuss with local relevant safety-health authorities the various types of suitable clothing and other protective equipment. Wash exposed parts of the body thoroughly after using chemicals.

There are more safety precautions. Using your common sense is imperative.

Do not use garden chemicals unless you have to. Remember the pest's natural predators will substantially control the pest.

Always have the proper Poisons Information Centre (or whatever the equivalent is where you live) phone number readily to hand, before you open or use pesticides.

Note: The information contained in this book on garden chemicals and their uses is, to the best of my experience, complete and true. But all suggestions and recommendations are given without any guarantees. It is the responsibility of the reader to check the details of these chemicals, and their effect on people, animals and plants. I emphasize the point that the purchase and use of gardening chemicals in the user's garden is the user's responsibility.

15. Weeds

A dense stand of vigorous lawn grasses is the best defence against the infiltration of lawn weeds.

The pH of the soil will sometimes decide which particular weed will dominate. For example, a very low pH will support acid soil loving weeds, such as sheep's sorrel *(Rumex acetosella)*. Conversely, a neutral to alkaline pH will favour weeds such as clover and certain coarse grasses.

Common Lawn Weeds and Weed Grasses

Weeds can be annual (live, flower and die in one year), biennial (grow vegetatively for the first year, then in the second year produce flowers, seeds and die), or perennial (live for two years and longer). Of the three annual and perennial are the most troublesome.

It is usually best to treat weeds before they set and scatter seeds.

Weed Grasses

Annual Meadow Grass, synonym Annual Bluegrass *(Poa annua)*
Paspalum *(Paspalum dilatatum* and *P. distichum)*
Crabgrass *(Digitaria sanguinalis)*
Yorkshire Fog *(Holcus lanatus)*
Cock's-foot *(Dactylis glomerata)*

The deeper-rooting grasses such as Yorkshire Fog and Cock's-foot are hard to control and are usually dug out, or spot treated by using the non-selective herbicide glyphosate. Remember, if the glyphosate herbicide touches desirable grasses they also will be killed.

Grass-like Weeds

Nutgrass (sedge) *(Cyperus rotundus)*
Golden Nutgrass (sedge) *(Cyperus esculentus)*

Field Woodrush *(Luzula campestris)*
Toadrush *(Juncus bufonius)*

The above sedges and rushes look like grasses and are fairly resistant to selective weedkillers. Nutgrass *(Cyperus rotundus)* presents a major problem in Australian grass lawns as it is very resistant to selective herbicide and spreads vigorously from its copious production of underground nut-like bulbs. The non-selective herbicide glyphosate can be used to spot treat nutgrasses *(Cyperus rotundus; C. esculentus)*. However, if the glyphosate herbicide touches desirable grasses they also will be killed.

Rosette Weeds

Capeweed *(Arctotheca calendula;* synonym *Cryptostemma calendula)*
Cat's-ear *(Hypochoeris radicata)*
Common English daisy *(Bellis perennis)*
Creeping buttercup *(Ranunculus repens)*
Dandelion *(Taraxacum officinale)*
Greater plantain *(Plantago major)*
Hawk's beard *(Crepis virens,* synonym *C. capillaris)*
Hoary plantain *(Plantago media)*
Paterson's curse, synonym Salvation Jane *(Echium plantagineum)*
Ribwort plantain *(Plantago lanceolata)*
Sea plantain *(Plantago maritima)*

These weeds can be dug out by hand or they may be killed using 2,4-D or MCPA. Remember, certain selective herbicides can adversely affect certain lawn grasses.

Other Lawn Weeds

Bird's-foot trefoil *(Lotus corniculatus)*
Caltrop *(Tribulus terrestris)*
Creeping oxalis *(Oxalis corniculata)*
Crow foot buttercup *(Ranunculus acris)*
Dove's-foot cranesbill *(Geranium molle)*
Jo-Jo *(Soliva pterosperma,* synonym *S. sessilis)*

Mouse-ear(ed) chickweed *(Cerastium vulgatum, C. fontanum)*
Pearlwort *(Sagina procumbens)*
Self heal *(Prunella vulgaris)*
Shepherd's purse *(Capsella bursa-pastoris)*
Thistles *(Cirsium* species*)*
Three-cornered Jack *(Emex australis)*
White clover *(Trifolium repens) and other clovers (Trifolium* species)
Yarrow *(Achillea millefolium)*

Dig these weeds out by hand-weeding if possible. Some are easy to kill with 2,4-D or MCPA, whereas for others you may need to use a suitable selective herbicide that also contains mecoprop, dicamba or bromoxynil. Check the label on the product.

Moss and Algae

Moss and algae in grass lawns can be controlled by lawn moss killers. However, this will only be of a temporary measure, as the cause of moss forming is usually dampness, excessive shade, waterlogging and possibly too acid a soil. Establish the reason why moss is forming, and if possible correct it.

Read the label on the grass lawn moss killer carefully to make sure that the product is suitable for your lawn grasses, and the method of application. Also check to see which grass species, and other plant species, it should *not* be used on.

Some of these products contain sulphate of iron, which may stain paving, clothes, etc.

Selective Herbicides

It is important that you find out the correct name of the weed in your lawn before you treat it to make sure that the selective herbicide you use is suitable for killing this weed.

I feel that there are fine grass lawns in various parts of the world that have never been treated with selective herbicide, the weeds being removed by hand. If feasible, hand weeding is preferable.

What is a selective herbicide for use on grass lawns?

A selective herbicide (sometimes referred to as a selective weedkiller) for use on grass lawns, if used at the recommended rate, using the correct method of application in suitable climatic and soil conditions, is a product that will not harm a specified group of plants (e.g. certain lawn grasses), but will damage unwanted, and susceptible, plants (e.g. lawn weeds).

Take note, those of you who are using clover as part of your lawn alternative sward, that selective herbicide for grass lawns will consider clover, and other 'dicot' plants as weeds. Read the label.

What is the 'active constituent' as seen on a label?

An active constituent (some countries refer to this as active ingredient) is the active chemical material included in the product, as distinct from other material(s) such as dilutents, carriers, surfactants and so on.

The two best known selective herbicides for use on grass lawns are MCPA and 2,4-D (MCPA and 2,4-D are active constituents). They are growth-regulating chemical substances, which if applied and used correctly will kill certain lawn weeds by causing them to become internally erratic.

Plants affected by the selective herbicide's active constituent usually show a characteristic twisting and curling.

Why aren't grasses killed by selective herbicide?

Herbicide selectivity is an extremely complicated subject involving plant cell membranes and plant nucleic acids.

Nevertheless, certain grass species and cultivars will be damaged from using certain selective herbicides for use on grass lawns.

Buffalo (St Augustine) Grass, Centipede Grass, Bahia Grass, Kikuyu Grass, Carpet Grass, Rough-stalked Meadow Grass (syn. Rough Bluegrass), Bent Grasses, and possibly more, are susceptible to injury from certain selective herbicides such as certain formulations of 2,4-D.

Also under certain climatic conditions at least one combination MCPA/dicamba selective herbicide may injure Kikuyu and Buffalo (St Augustine) Grass.

Young grass seedlings can be very much adversely affected by particular selective herbicides, as can newly laid turves. And grasses growing in the shade seem to be more susceptible to damage from selective herbicides.

However, over-application, incorrect rate and the wrong timing of selective herbicides for grass lawns cause toxicity, as does too frequent use. Always ensure that you leave enough time between one application and the next when using a selective herbicide.

Off-target Damage

The misuse of selective herbicide has the potential to create major problems. Off-target damage is damage caused by the selective herbicide drifting onto, or moving to, susceptible plants which are nearby, or even far away from, the target area of weeds that is currently being treated.

Glasshouse/greenhouse crops, grapevines, tomato crops, chrysanthemum crops, cabbage crops, cucumber family crops, pea crops and more, including ornamental plants and trees, have been damaged or destroyed by the misuse of selective herbicides.

I suspect that many problems between neighbours have occurred because of damage caused by off-target herbicide application.

Vapour Drift

Selective herbicides for use on grass lawns come in various formulations, such as amine salt, sodium salt or low volatility or high volatility ester forms.

Ester forms of selective herbicides may vaporize as gas from the area recently sprayed when the air temperature rises and drift considerable distances; possibly many kilometres. The volatility and drift of even low volatility esters, once the temperature rises, gives cause for much concern.

There are those who feel that 2,4-D ester selective herbicides are too highly volatile and should *not* be used in home gardens.

Be aware that although low volatility or high volatility esters usually evaporate rapidly, *all* selective herbicides under specific climatic conditions will vaporize and drift.

Bulbs in Lawn

Many gardeners grow bulbs in grass lawns, particularly in cool-climate areas where the grass dies back during winter. Be aware that selective herbicides can adversely affect bulb shoots.

MCPA and 2,4-D

MCPA and 2,4-D selective herbicides were invented over forty years ago and are still used to control weeds in grass lawns.

MCPA is absorbed mainly through the foliage and is circulated throughout the plant to the growing points, where it interferes with the growing cells. 2,4-D is absorbed mainly through the plant's foliage and stems, and is circulated throughout the plant, also interfering with the growing cells.

Many broad-leaved weeds are susceptible to MCPA and 2,4-D selective herbicides.

Mecoprop

Selective herbicides for use on grass lawns from a slightly different organic grouping were produced that had more effect on certain more resistant weeds, and one of the first was mecoprop. Mecoprop has some contact action, is absorbed through the leaves and circulated throughout the system to the plant's growing points.

Dicamba

Dicamba, from a different organic grouping to those mentioned above, is also used for killing 'harder-to-kill' lawn weeds. It is absorbed into the foliage and translocated also through the plant shoots, and effects cell elongation. Dicamba can also be absorbed by 'off-target' plant roots. The persistence of this herbicide in the soil can be a problem as the roots of desirable plants, such as shrubs, that find their way into the lawn can be damaged or killed by dicamba.

This information is important for those gardeners who grow grass lawns under trees where obviously tree roots are growing in the lawn area, or have tree, shrub or flower bed islands in the lawn.

Be aware that the grass clippings may still contain the active constituent dicamba, and as a precaution the clippings should not be used for garden compost or mulch.

Indeed, the clippings from a grass lawn recently treated with selective herbicide should never, I repeat, never, be used as a mulch around plants.

Bromoxynil

Bromoxynil, from a different organic grouping to all those mentioned above, is used as a selective herbicide. There is relatively little translocation once the material is absorbed by the plant, but the active constituent does inhibit respiration and photosynthesis. It is moderately toxic.

Cautions

All the selective herbicides listed above may damage or kill susceptible plants in off-target areas.

Mecoprop and certain other selective herbicides

may stay active on the top of the soil for several weeks, preventing the emergence of new seedlings, for example lawn grass seeding that is done too soon after lawn renovation-weed spraying.

Certain chemical manufacturers professionally mix various selective herbicides as indicated on the label, for example mecoprop plus 2,4-D plus dicamba, or MCPA plus dicamba, or bromoxynil plus MCPA, for use in a given situation.

Read the Label

There is a wealth of important information given on the manufacturer's product label. Always read the label before you buy and before you use selective herbicide for use on grass lawns, and check all cautions and safety directions. Also be aware that certain herbicides are poisonous.

'Lawn Sand'

Certain grass lawn weeds may be killed or checked by using a suitable so-called 'lawn sand' herbicide.

The title lawn sand can be confusing as lawn sand may contain a suitable mixture of sulphate of ammonia, sulphate of iron, plus a suitable carrier, which first 'weeds then feeds' the lawn.

This mixture has a burning, dehydrating effect on weeds, particularly the flat rosette type, which hold the lawn sand like a plate. Certain proprietary brand names may be available. Read the label.

Such a concentration of chemicals can cause scorching and blackening of the lawn grasses, but if applied correctly the grass will recover and the weeds may die or be severely checked.

Do not walk over, or allow others to walk over, the treated lawn when the lawn sand is laying over the weeds. No rain should be expected, but nor should the lawn be in the grip of a drought.

Very carefully check the manufacturer's instructions on the label concerning application, cautions etc. Over-application of lawn sand can be disastrous for the lawn grasses.

Lawn sand can also heavily stain concrete, slate, bricks, and also clothes, therefore avoid spillages and wear suitable protective clothing. Also avoid walking the lawn sand onto a path under your shoes.

Do not use lawn sand on Dichondra, Lippia, Clover and other types of dicotyledon lawns which the lawn sand would consider as weeds. The manufacturer's label should explain this.

After the recommended time irrigate the lawn.

Following irrigation the properly applied lawn sand turns into a lawn fertilizer.

Applying Selective Herbicides

There are various 'spot-treatment' selective herbicide products, such as hand-operated (trigger-operated) sprays that are pre-packed with correctly diluted selective herbicide.

For the home gardener spraying may be restricted to smaller hand-operated, specially designed selective herbicide sprays, or suitable watering-cans with sprinkle-dribble bars for applying selective herbicide, or a suitable fine-rose watering-can.

A sprinkle-dribble bar attachment is a hollow tube, with sealed ends, with fine, specially designed perforations along its length, which is properly fixed by the operator to the spout of a suitable watering-can. The sprinkle-dribble bar is held parallel to the lawn surface at the correct height. The solution trickles-dribbles on to the weeds currently being treated.

It is possible that even a small hand-operated, specially designed selective herbicide spray cannot be used in the home garden, because of the proximity of susceptible plants, and the potential movement in the air of the droplets produced by such sprays on to these plants. Even a fine rose or sprinkle-dribble bar on a watering-can may present application problems.

However, all selective herbicide spray equipment has to be operated with great care to prevent drift, splash, run-off, over-concentration of the selective herbicide, and off-target damage.

You can carry out dummy runs using only clean water, before you first attempt to apply selective herbicide to a lawn using the above methods, to get the hang of using the equipment. You would also keep the sprinkle-dribble bar (refer to manufacturer's instructions), or rose, or spray nozzles sensibly, correctly, reasonably close to the ground to help prevent drift, splash, run-off, dribble or trickle from reaching surrounding susceptible plants. Make sure the trickle-dribble bar or fine rose is properly, securely fixed to the watering-can spout to prevent accidental over-application. (Let this clean water, if applied to the lawn grasses, dry out before applying selective herbicide.)

Make sure the spray jets are working properly and the spray nozzles are calibrated correctly. (Do refer to the manufacturer's instructions.) It is pointless having a container full of selective herbicide if the spray isn't going to work.

Always use clean water as dirty water could cause problems such as blocking spray holes or jets.

Marking Out the Area

You could mark out the area in strips like railway tracks at whatever width you decide and is suitable, so that you know where you are to spray and where you have sprayed. Take sufficient care to make sure that the area to be sprayed is marked correctly to avoid overlapping and over-application.

If you use strings as guides then remember the strings will become saturated with the herbicide, so handle them with due care.

Powder Herbicides

There are some selective herbicides that come as a powder. Remember that under certain circumstances, for example windy conditions, powder will drift on to other susceptible plants.

Fertilizer/Selective Herbicide

There are fertilizers that include selective herbicide for use on grass lawns in their make up, such as granules that weed and feed (not necessarily available in Australia), and are spread over the lawn using a fertilizer spreader or similar. Read the label on the pack and use the product safely.

When Using Herbicides

Don't use selective herbicide unless you have to. If feasible, dig out weeds by hand, particularly if the lawn is surrounded by precious plants. Seek alternative treatments if, because of susceptible plants and potential drift hazard, selective herbicides cannot be used on your lawn.

It is most important, when using selective herbicides for use on grass lawns, that you read and heed the manufacturer's instructions given on the product pack, following cautions given and safety directions.

Check the active constituent on the label to make sure it is the one you require for the specific task you have in mind. Remember, there may be more than one active constituent in a container of herbicide, and perhaps one of these active constituents could have disastrous consequences if used on your lawn.

Always take the utmost care to preserve the manufacturer's instruction label, for the obvious reason of being able to read it.

Keep the concentrated selective herbicide in the manufacturer's container in a safe place, also ensuring that it can't fall and smash.

Weeds are more susceptible to selective herbicides when they are young and growing actively, and this is usually combined with ample rainfall, adequate soil fertility and suitable growing temperatures.

The temperature should be moderate without extremes of cold or heat. In cold weather certain weeds become relatively inactive. In hot weather, even too warm weather, a selective herbicide's volatile vapour can easily drift on to susceptible plants.

Calm weather conditions should prevail. Windy conditions, even a slight breeze, will transport selective herbicide on to susceptible off-target plants.

No rain should be expected for a day or so following spraying as rain may wash the selective herbicide off the grass blades before it is absorbed; check the manufacturer's instructions. Don't spray if the weeds are wet.

If suitable spraying conditions do not prevail, then delay any spraying until the correct weather conditions for spraying grass lawns with selective herbicide do prevail.

Read the label on the product to see whether the manufacturer recommends cutting the lawn before applying the selective herbicide, and when to cut it after application.

Use the least powerful, the least volatile selective herbicide that will do the job. If necessary, have an expert on grass lawns identify the lawn weed(s) you wish to kill so that you can use the correct herbicide.

Only buy as much selective herbicide as you need and can use, as you don't want to have surplus quantities of selective herbicide hanging around unnecessarily.

Only mix as much selective herbicide as you can use at one spraying. Never leave a bottle or pack of concentrated selective herbicide open when spraying. Screw the cap back on, or reseal it and store in a safe place out of harm's way and then commence spraying. Make sure you never lose sight of the spray you've already mixed, to prevent accidental use by others.

Measure out and mix the materials in a safe, sensible place taking great care with the concentrated herbicide. Do not inhale herbicide dust or fumes. Avoid enclosed spaces. Wear suitable protective clothing.

Some weeds are destroyed by one application of selective herbicide whereas other weeds may need more than one application. Don't apply the second application until the manufacturer's recommended time has elapsed between sprayings.

Spray during the early morning under calm conditions, but don't spray selective herbicides when there is dew on the grasses as the dew can evaporate, taking the selective herbicide with it, thus becoming a potentially dangerous drift hazard.

Don't spray on misty or foggy days as the herbicide vapour could be trapped in the mist or fog and drift onto desirable plants.

Don't spray if the weeds or lawn are under stress from drought.

Don't spray if the soil has a low fertility.

Don't spray if the lawn is under stress from frost or waterlogging.

Don't overuse selective herbicide. You may do more harm than good by scorching the weed and still leave the weed root intact to regenerate. You may also damage, even kill, desirable grasses.

Don't keep selective herbicide or weed spraying equipment in areas where sensitive plants, including bulbs and seeds, are stored as the herbicide vapour could drift on to these.

Use separate spraying and measuring equipment for selective herbicide for use on grass lawns. Mark this equipment, loudly proclaiming that this equipment is to be used for selective herbicide only, and do not use this equipment for any other gardening purpose.

Store all chemicals and equipment in a safe, sensible place outside the house securely locked away from the prying hands and mouths of children, and also from the curiosity of animals.

Keep children, pets and adults well out of contact when using selective herbicide. Dogs and cats will lap at pools of moisture.

Dispose of used herbicide containers safely.

Wear suitable clothing when using herbicide chemicals. Check with relevant State/Territory health and safety officials where suitable protective clothing and equipment can be obtained.

Don't smoke or eat when using herbicides. Wash yourself after using herbicide.

Don't use clippings from recently treated grass lawns as a mulch around plants in case the active constituent is still active.

Don't use dicamba where desirable shrubs, trees and flower roots can absorb the active constituent.

Remember, a healthy lawn goes a long way to keeping weeds at bay.

Other Herbicides

Weed Grasses

There are weed grasses that can infest grass lawns, weed grasses such as Crabgrass *(Digitalis sanguinalis)* and Annual Meadow Grass *(Poa annua)*.

How can you kill grasses that are weeds in a grass lawn? It is difficult and the simplest way is to dig them out by hand.

You could also slash the plant root of the tougher weed grasses such as Paspalum Grass and Cock's-foot *(Dactylis glomerata)* with a sharp knife taking care to protect your hands. This type of treatment can be an ongoing thing.

You could spot treat the weed grass with a non-selective herbicide known as glyphosate. However, both the beauty and the drawback with glyphosate is that the herbicide is translocated throughout the plant and will kill any grass it touches, including desirable grasses.

There are products available in nurseries that can be used to control Annual Meadow Grass *(Poa annua)* in certain grass species/cultivar lawns—they can *only* be used on *specific* species/cultivar grass lawns. They cannot be used on certain soils. If you consider Annual Meadow Grass to be a problem in your lawn then check out these products, and carefully, thoroughly, read the manufacturer's label.

Disodium methylarsonate (DSMA)

DSMA is a selective post-emergent herbicide used for the control of Paspalum, Crabgrass, and more, on specific grass species/cultivar lawns only. Read the label on the pack for details, including application restraints.

Check the label for the States/Territories where the use of DSMA is suggested, and the various State/Territory application rates for each grass.

Be aware that DSMA is poisonous and should be handled with extreme caution.

Soil Fumigants

Bowling green surfaces are sometimes treated with methyl bromide to kill all life that exists in the playing area of the green, before being planted with new grasses. This treatment is generally not appropriate for home lawns.

Methyl bromide is a dangerous poison and its application should only be carried out by firms licensed by governments to undertake this type of work.

Methyl bromide kills all plant and animal life in the soil. Bowling greens do not have tree roots, shrubs and flower roots which have spread under the green, but your lawn area may contain the roots of plants which will be adversely affected by the methyl bromide.

Non-selective Herbicides

A non-selective herbicide is a product that, usually, will kill or damage any plant it comes into contact with, whether it be an undesirable or a desirable plant, including your precious lawn. Some of these chemicals last for a short time in the soil, while others last for years in the soil, so be wary.

Glyphosate

Glyphosate is a non-selective herbicide that kills plants by translocation of the active constituent to the plant's growing points. It is used to control weeds in the garden as it does break down reasonably quickly in the soil. It can take three to fourteen days for the effects to be readily visible, but may take even longer in certain climatic conditions.

Note: The information contained above on garden chemicals, equipment etc. and their uses is to the best of my experience complete and true, but all suggestions and recommendations are given without any guarantees. It is the responsibility of the user to check the details of these chemicals and their effect on people, animals and plants, and check on current registrations that apply. I emphasize the point that the purchase and subsequent use of gardening chemicals is the user's responsibility.

16. Renovating an Existing Lawn

Safety is paramount before attempting to renovate an existing lawn—you never know what hazards lie hidden in an overgrown lawn.

You have moved into a house and the grass lawn is overgrown, full of weeds, thick with wormcasts and generally in a sorry state. Ask yourself, 'Is such a grass lawn worth renovating?' You examine the lawn thoroughly, and finally decide that the lawn may be worth renovating.

Depending on how tall the grass is, and after carefully checking for and removing from the area any mowing hazards, mow the lawn using a rotary mower, and again examine the lawn thoroughly. If the grass is too tall then you may have to use other methods of cutting the grass.

Check to see if any services such as water, gas, electricity and telephone, run under the lawn as you don't want to harm these—or be harmed by them.

Weeds

It is possible that the grasses are suitable lawn grasses, but are in danger of being over-run by weeds.

If so, ascertain the sort of weed(s) that are inhibiting the grasses as this will determine the correct selective herbicide to use. Is moss a problem? Is drainage a problem? Are the existing lawn levels suitable?

The lawn has to be sprayed for weeds at the

correct time, and in the correct weather conditions. Check the manufacturer's label on the selective herbicide pack, and Chapter 15 for further information on using selective herbicide.

Remember that certain selective herbicides can remain active in the soil for several weeks and inhibit the germination/growth of grass seed/seedlings. Be aware that certain selective herbicides can harm, or even kill, trees and shrubs whose roots inhabit the grass lawn.

Be mindful that selective herbicides for use on grass lawns cannot be used on certain grasses.

Is it Still Worthwhile?

You have sprayed the lawn correctly, the weeds have died, or are well on their way to dying. Inspect the lawn again, or get a lawn expert to have a look, to ascertain whether it is still feasible to continue renovation work. Thus far you haven't spent much time, effort or money, so if you feel that you should cut your losses and re-do the whole lawn from scratch then do so, but if you're sure, or are advised, that your lawn grasses will form a decent lawn then continue renovating the lawn.

Thatch

De-thatching should only be done when weather conditions are suitable and the grasses are active enough to grow after treatment.

Mow the lawn. Then, using a sharp-pointed rake, rake out any thatch that exists to allow the lawn surface to 'breathe', so that you can just make out the soil surface between the grass roots. Don't be too savage. It's pointless pulling out roots that could help form the new lawn. Carefully, you have to provide sufficient tilth to take any new seeds.

You can hire a contractor to de-thatch your lawn with a specially designed, power-operated machine. The blades slash vertically at the grass similar to you slashing the grasses with a sharp knife. Ensure that the contractor is properly qualified, licensed, and insured.

This operator has to know what he or she's about as a heavy hand could chop out too much or all of your suitable grasses. And you could do the same if you hire such a machine and don't know how to use it.

Rake up any thatch and dispose of it.

Hollow Tining

You can take out cores of turf, like small cigars, using a hollow-tined fork, leaving the lawn covered with a series of small cigar-sized holes, or you could hire a contractor to hollow tine the lawn using a machine. Hollow tining is best done when the lawn grasses are growing vigorously.

GRASSES —
THATCH —
MAT —
SOIL —
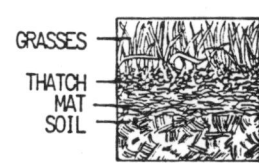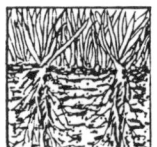

The effects of hollow tining. *Left to right* shows: thatch, mat and consolidated soil; cores of turf removed; roots colonizing core holes

Rake up the cores of turf and dispose of them sensibly. These cores may be suitable for future top dressings.

You can top dress the lawn using suitable, clean (i.e. inert, lime and salt free) sand, but not too sharp or too fine, rubbing and brushing it into the holes to help facilitate drainage. Ascertain the quality of sand as sand that is too sharp may not be suitable when children, or animals with sensitive paws, use the lawn. Coarse sand with large gritty pieces can damage the bottom blades of certain mowers. Too fine sand could cause drainage problems.

It's possible that your lawn doesn't need hollow tining.

Seeding Up

Does the lawn need mowing to accept the following operations? If so then mow it. Remember that you've already created a tilth on the existing lawn surface bare patches, which will take seed.

Spot Treatment

Remember to allow sufficient time between treatment with selective herbicide and seeding, or the seeds may not germinate. A utility method of renovation is as follows. Fertilize the entire lawn and carefully wash in the fertilizer. Allow the soil to dry out. You can use the tine of a garden fork to scarify awkward small patches. Spot-treat the bare patches with seed and top dressing.

Spread the seed over the bare patches, and then lightly sprinkle suitable top dressing over the seed. When using very fine seeds, top dress the bare

  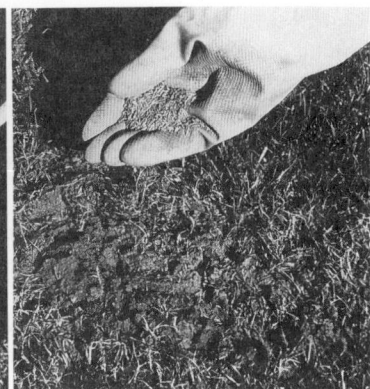

Lawn aerating tools: (left) garden fork; (right) hollow-tine fork   Pricking bare patches in lawn using garden fork   Seeding up bare patches

patches and then sow the seed on top. A suitable seedbed has to be provided to accept the seed.

The lawn can look ugly after spot treatment, but it's surprising how soon, given suitable follow-up treatment, these patches grow over.

If possible, try to keep children, and others, off the lawn until the lawn has become established enough to take more use.

Levelling

You can top dress the whole lawn surface with suitable lawn top dressing to bring up the levels. Be sparing with top dressing say 6 mm (¼ in) would be the maximum, and this would depend on the types of grasses being top dressed.

Carefully rub the top dressing into the lawn surface with a wooden lute or back of a garden rake, making sure that the grass blades are above the top dressing otherwise the blades will be stifled, and open to fungus attack.

After luting you can sensibly brush in the top dressing with a stiff broom to get the blades to stand up above the top dressing.

Overseeding the Entire Lawn

When overseeding the entire lawn you can use a grass seed mixture, or a seed blend, or a single variety or cultivar of seed, all of which have to complement the existing lawn grasses.

Divide the amount of grass seed needed into halves, and spread the seed evenly in opposite directions, say, half the amount north to south and the other half east to west. Tumble-rake the seeds into the lawn surface. Re-level the lawn, if necessary, but it shouldn't be necessary if you're careful.

Roll the lawn using a light roller, if the lawn is not too wet.

Does the lawn need mowing again? Then mow the lawn once the existing grasses are standing up.

Now, if you have not already, add a suitable, reputable brand of lawn fertilizer at the manufacturer's recommended rates, and water it in well.

Keep the seeds well watered to aid germination and growth.

Keep the existing lawn grasses cut at a suitable height, but not too low, as this could pull out the young grass seedlings. The seeded grasses should slowly catch up and thicken the lawn sward.

Carry out normal lawn maintenance, bearing in mind that you are caring for young grass seedlings.

Sprigging Up

It is possible that your lawn is composed of, say, Couch (Bermuda) Grass, and rather than sow seed you want to sprig the lawn using suitable Couch (Bermuda) Grass sprigs. Choose the correct time to do so, and see Chapter 8 for further details.

Finally

Lawn renovation is best done at the correct time of the year and under suitable weather conditions to prevent unnecessary damage being inflicted on to the lawn grasses. By seeking local expert opinion you should be able to ascertain when that time is.

Don't let naivety or cupidity cloud your logic, so that you end up spending more time and money renovating a lawn than it is worth, when it would have been cheaper and better to have created a new lawn from scratch.

17. Grass and Other Lawns in New Zealand

Cool-climate (cool-season) grasses used for fine lawns are selected cultivars of Browntop *(Agrostis tenuis)*, Chewings Fescue *(Festuca rubra commutata)*, Slender Creeping Red Fescue *(Festuca rubra litoralis)*, and suitable Creeping Bent *(Agrostis stolonifera; syn. A. palustris; syn. A. s. var. palustris)* cultivars.

For less fine lawns Fine-leaved Perennial Ryegrass *(Lolium perenne)* or Kentucky Bluegrass *(Poa pratensis)* cultivars are used. Make sure the Perennial Ryegrass is a fine-leaved cultivar suitable for lawns, as there are Perennial Ryegrass cultivars that are not suitable.

It is also possible that modern suitable cultivars of Tall Fescue *(Festuca arundinacea)* may find their way into mixtures, or be used on their own, for hard-wearing lawns in reasonably hot, dryish areas.

Crested Dogstail *(Cynosurus cristatus)* is similar in appearance to Perennial Ryegrass, but is slower growing.

Other cool-climate grasses are used for lawns for specific reasons.

A mixture of suitable Chewings Fescue and Browntop cultivars is used to produce a bowling green type lawn. Suitable Browntop cultivars are used on their own for the same purpose.

Make sure it is really Browntop *(Agrostis tenuis)* and not Dryland Bent *(Agrostis castellana)*, as the two have been linked in the past as *Agrostis tenuis*. Find out the name of the Browntop *(Agrostis tenuis)* cultivar.

The finer cultivars of Creeping Bent *(Agrostis stolonifera, syn. A. palustris, A. stolonifera var. palustris)* are also used to produce a golf green lawn. However, the maintenance of fine-leaved Creeping Bent cultivars is very demanding, because of the stoloniferous nature of the plant and the stolon thatch build up.

Creeping Red Fescue for lawns can be Strong or Slender Creeping Red Fescue. For the finest lawns Slender Creeping Red Fescue *(Festuca rubra litoralis)* is used.

Deal with reputable firms and use only the best, suitable, certified grass lawn seed cultivars available.

Although cool-climate (cool-season) grasses seem to predominate throughout much of New Zealand, certain areas do use warm-climate grasses; grasses such as the rank, invasive Kikuyu Grass *(Pennisetum clandestinum)*; Couch (Bermuda) Grass, also known as Indian Doab *(Cynodon dactylon)* cultivars; Transvaal Doab, also known as Germiston Couch and South African Couch *(Cynodon transvaalensis)*; and Hybrid Bermuda Grass also known as Hybrid Couch *(Cynodon dactylon × Cynodon transvaalensis)*; and possibly certain suitable *Paspalum* species.

Consult an expert before contemplating making a grass lawn to ensure that your climate is suitable for a particular species or cultivar of grass.

Grass Lawn Weeds, Pests and Diseases

Check with your relevant local Department of Agriculture expert as to where and how to obtain an authoritative reference work on the content and use of garden chemicals. Also read the information given elsewhere in this book on weeds, insect pests and diseases.

Grass Lawn Weeds

European weeds are prevalent in New Zealand grass lawns, although native and other weeds are also found.

There are more weeds that will attack grass lawns. Some are easy to control with selective herbicides, others more difficult. *Always read the label on any*

Botanical Name	Common Name
Achillea millefolium	Yarrow
Arctotheca calendula	Capeweed
Cerastium (vulgatum) fontanum	Mouse-eared Chickweed
Crepis (virens) capillaris	Hawk's-beard
Erodium cicutarium	Storkbill (Common Erodium)
Geranium molle	Dove's-foot (Geranium) Crane's-bill
Hieracium pilosella	Mouse-eared Hawkweed
Hypochoeris radicata	Cat's-ear
Leontodon taraxacoides	Hawkbit
Leontodon autumnalis	Hawkbit
Oxalis exilis	Creeping Oxalis
Oxalis pes-caprae	Bermuda Buttercup (Soursob)
Plantago coronopus	Bucks-horn Plantain
Plantago lanceolata	Narrow-leaved (Ribwort) Plantain
Plantago major	Broad-leaved Plantain
Prunella vulgaris	Selfheal
Ranunculus repens	Creeping Buttercup
Rumex acetosella	Sheep's Sorrel
Sagina procumbens	Pearlwort
Soliva sessilis (pterosperma)	Onehunga Weed
Taraxacum officinale	Dandelion
Trifolium species	Various Clovers
Veronica arvensis	Field (Wall) Speedwell

selective herbicide before you buy it and before you use it, and ensure that it is registered for use on home grass lawns, and then use the product safely.

Some chemicals used to control various weeds, pests, insects and funguses are poisonous, or cause off-target damage if used incorrectly. Remember, off-target damage can sometimes be frightening. Also remember that weeds can be dug out by hand, and this may be the better alternative. See Chapter 15 for more information on weeds and weed control.

Be aware, those of you who are using clover as part of your lawn sward, that selective herbicide will consider clover, and other dicotyledons as weeds. Also certain grasses can be affected.

Rushes and Sedges

Various rushes and sedges will invade grass lawns. Toadrush *(Juncus bufonius)* is found, as is Field Woodrush *(Luzula campestris).* The sedge Nutgrass *(Cyperus rotundus)* is very common in warm-climate (warm-season) areas. Indeed, this sedge is among the top 20 world's worst weeds.

Weed Grasses in Fine Grass Lawns

There are weed grasses that will proliferate in New Zealand grass lawns, some being more regional than others.

Botanical Name	Common Name
Cynodon dactylon	Couch (Bermuda) Grass (Indian Doab)
Digitaria sanguinalis	Crabgrass
Holcus lanatus	Yorkshire Fog
Holcus mollis	Creeping Soft Grass
Paspalum species	
Pennisetum clandestinum	Kikuyu Grass
Poa annua	Annual Meadow Grass

Weed grasses, being of the same family as the lawn grasses, are usually difficult to eradicate. Therefore, if you have such a problem seek local expert advice on grass lawns.

Insects

New Zealand grass lawns are invaded by a number of important insect pests, some being more damaging to the lawn grasses than others. These insects include: Grass Grub *(Costelytra zealandica)*; Porina Caterpillar *(Wiseana cervinata)*; Tasmanian Grass Grub (Blackheaded Pasture Cockchafer) larvae of the beetle *Aphodius tasmaniae*; and Black Beetle *(Heteronychus arator)*.

Other insects that attack New Zealand grass lawns are the Black Field Cricket, Army Caterpillars, weevils, possibly nematodes, ants and earthworms, although ants and earthworms are more disruptive than predatory. And of course birds will tear into turf areas where large infestations of insects occur to get at the insects.

For more specific information consult relevant journals and books on grass lawn insects in the home garden. Check with your relevant local Department of Agriculture officials concerning up-to-date information and safety recommendations when using chemicals and the like, as garden chemicals are not to be treated casually or lightly. Remember that some insecticides/pesticides are 'deadly poisons', some are 'dangerous poisons', some are 'poisons', some are 'harmful substances'.

Diseases

New Zealand turf grasses are afflicted by many of the turf diseases mentioned previously in this book. These diseases include: Anthracnose; Brown Patch (synonym Rhizoctonia Brown Patch, Smoke Ring); Corticium (Red Thread); Damping-off Diseases; Dollar Spot; Fairy Rings; Fusarium Patch; Leaf Spots and Melting Out; Ophiobolus Patch (Take All); Rust (Crown Rust); and Slime Moulds.

Correct identification of the fungus disease is important as some fungicides are specific for a particular fungal disease.

Cotula Lawns

There are only a few *Cotula* species used for bowling green lawns; one is *Cotula maniototo* (synonym *Leptinella maniototo*) and another is *Cotula dioica* (synonym *Leptinella dioica*).

Cotula greens can take close mowing, but are bothered by weed grasses and *Hydrocotyle* species.

Cotula being a dicotyledon—it is a creeping button weed of the daisy family (*Asteraceae* synonym *Compositae*)—as opposed to grass which is a monocotyledon, demands a special type of expert maintenance, and for the home lawn owner may be perhaps a bit too demanding.

Some gardeners may know *Cotula* as *Leptinella* Many years ago the genus name *Leptinella* was dropped in favour of the genus name *Cotula*. In a recent New Zealand journal I noticed that the genus name for Button Daisies *(Cotula)* is now considered to be *Leptinella*.

Controlling weeds in a *Cotula* species bowling-green type lawn is too specialized to be discussed here, and you would seek suitable professional advice. Remember, *Cotula* species are dicotyledon plants, and not monocotyledon plants.

Dichondra Species

Dichondra species (for example, *Dichondra repens*, also called Kidney Weed, because of its leaf shape, or Mercury Bay Weed) are used by some as a lawn grass alternative. The seed and plugs may be expensive to buy and such a lawn is difficult to maintain. It is also vulnerable in colder areas. Selective herbicides used for controlling weeds in grass lawns will consider *Dichondra* a weed.

Carefully check instructions given on the seed pack and seek local, expert, professional advice on suitable *Dichondra* species lawns for your area.

Preparing for a Lawn

First measure your proposed lawn area correctly, and find out how much seed or turf is needed, and the cost thereof. Preparation for a lawn is covered in Chapter 4.

Sowing Grass Seed for Lawns

When to sow lawn grass seeds depends on various factors such as a soil warm enough to promote germination and growth, and adequate moisture to sustain this growth until the grasses are in a strong position to cope with any weather vagaries.

Cool-climate grass seeds can be sown in early-mid autumn, provided a drought is not in progress, and spring as both times usually provide suitable conditions for subsequent germination and growth.

Autumn sown seed has the added benefit of a soil warmed from the previous summer, which will help seed germinate and establish before the onset of winter, and be in a good position to combat weed invasion. In certain areas, however, the damage to young seedlings from severe frosts may negate any gains made from an autumn sowing, and therefore often the sowing is delayed until the soil warms up in spring.

If the seed is sown and no rain has fallen then you would have to water the seedlings to get them established.

Seed can also be sown provided artificial irrigation can be supplied in sufficient quantities, and more importantly, at the correct intervals during the day, as a lawn full of recently germinated seedlings may be wiped out on a hot day between the time you go to work and the time you return.

Certain areas of the North Island are different from certain areas of the South Island and need their own specialized treatment as to when to sow lawn grass seed.

Often spring (September) sowings are supplemented by artificial irrigation to establish the grass sward before summer. But, of course, summer rainfall can be adequate over parts of the South Island.

The point is common sense must be used to determine if the seedlings need a gentle watering or not, the important factor being that the seedlings must never be allowed to dry out. By that I don't mean that they should be in a constant state of flood. Just provide a warm, moist soil, and a gentle saturation. Often this is provided in these early stages by watering by hand using a garden hose with a fine watering rose attached so that the water falls gently, but copiously, on to the surface. (Heavy-handed watering will gouge out the seedlings and redistribute them causing a patchy lawn.)

You may not be able to use such a watering system, or prefer to use sprinklers. You may have installed an automatic watering system and don't feel obliged to pamper the grass. In this case do the best you can, but be aware that seedlings are easily washed out of the soil.

It is a good idea to seek professional advice on sowing grass seeds or starting grasses vegetatively in your area as it is difficult to pontificate on regional climates and local microclimates.

Runners, Rooted Portions, Blocks, Plugs and Turves

Warm-climate grasses, such as Indian Doab, synonym Couch (Bermuda) Grass *(Cynodon dactylon)* cultivars; Transvaal Doab, synonyms Germiston Couch, South African Couch *(Cynodon transvaalensis)*, Hybrid Bermuda Grass, synonym Hybrid Couch *(Cynodon dactylon × Cynodon transvaalensis)* and the rampant, invasive Kikuyu Grass *(Pennisetum clandestinum)*, are used in certain areas of the North Island.

Usually these grasses are planted vegetatively, i.e. using runners, rooted portions, blocks of rooted turf, plugs of rooted turf or possibly whole turves, after the winter period and once the soil has warmed up sufficiently to bring about the subsequent growth of the young plants.

These types of warm-climate grasses are restricted to those areas that will provide the warmth necessary to sustain such grasses. Winters that are too cold will kill off warm-climate grass, or at best savage it, even if the summers are warm enough to sustain growth.

With turves you get immediate cover, but you have to have the lawn grass mixture the supplier grows. Therefore you must find out what grasses the turf contains before you buy and thus ensure that the turf sward is what you want for your lawn.

Deal with a supplier who has a reputation for supplying the right quality turf.

Cool-climate Grass Turf

Usually turf is laid in autumn, winter and spring when cooler weather and rain is anticipated to establish the turf, and thus allow for the roots to strike and stabilize. Obviously drought and severe frosts may damage new turf. The best time for turf laying for lawns in your area calls for local knowledge.

Turf is notorious for drying out rapidly during hot weather, during windy conditions, and even relatively mild conditions. Remember, you are laying plants that have been severed from the bulk of their moisture-seeking roots, and therefore if turf is laid without sufficient rainfall or sufficient artificial irrigation it will inevitably dry out and die.

Even if the roots have struck into the soil it is feasible that the joints haven't knitted together, and as a consequence will open much wider during drought.

More information on turfing a lawn is contained in Chapter 9.

Summary

Find out which grasses will make the lawn of your choice in the area in which you live. Find out the problems associated with such lawns. Talk it over with grass lawn experts, and I do mean grass lawn experts. For Cotula and other lawns discuss their upkeep etc. with suitably qualified experts.

Work on suitable lawn grasses and *Cotula* species (i.e. species, varieties or cultivars for given areas) is being carried out in New Zealand.

18. The Lawn Year in the United Kingdom

January

Not much work can be done on the lawn. Plans for new lawns can be worked out. Brochures from lawn specialists can be studied. Wet periods can be used to check drainage and if waterlogging occurs, and persists, suitable drainage can be contemplated. However, keep off the lawn if possible to prevent unnecessary damage. Aeration may be carried out if feasible. Fungus disease may occur after snow melt. Grasses generally do not need mowing, therefore mowers can be checked and, if necessary, sent away for overhaul to be ready for when the grass does begin growing.

Check to see if HMSO or similar organizations, issue booklets, etc. on the use of garden chemicals for the home gardener-lawn owner.

February

Frosts may continue. Occasional mild spells may occur. Worm cast may appear and in suitable dry conditions their casts are brushed off the lawn. Continue aeration if conditions are suitable. Towards the end of the month consider top dressing the lawn if necessary. Also towards the end of the month treat any areas for moss using a suitable proprietary lawn moss killer, also checking for causes of moss. Work seed beds for spring lawns if feasible, breaking down any clods from previous lawn preparations.

March

A sudden flush of growth may occur but do not cut the grass too closely as frost accompanied by cold winds may return causing severe damage to the grasses. Only tip the grasses if necessary to keep them in check. Any turf lifted by frost can be lightly rolled in suitably dry conditions to settle it. Renovations can be carried out. Aeration can be carried out. Lawns can be dewormed if the infestation warrants it. Areas for new lawns can be prepared towards the end of the month. Check for leatherjacket grub (larvae of the daddy longlegs) attack. Seed sowing can begin at the end of the month. Grass seed for lawns must be suitable lawn cultivars and mixed professionally. See section concerning cool-climate (season) grasses.

Turfing can be carried out. Lawn mosskiller may be applied. Read the label on the pack.

April

Mowing can continue on a regular basis provided weather conditions are suitable, but do not cut too low. Lightly roll if necessary. Spring and summer lawn fertilizer can be applied mid-late April if not already applied; allow fertilizer to properly stimulate grasses and weeds before applying selective herbicide. Insect control, such as for leatherjacket grubs, can be effected. Selective herbicides may be applied mid-April on, provided the weather and soil conditions are suitable and the grasses and weeds are growing vigorously. Fusarium patch (*Fusarium nivale*) may appear and may need to be treated. In warm areas seedlings and turfing can commence.

May

Mow frequently, gradually reducing the cutting height aiming towards the established summer height. New lawn areas can be prepared and seed sowing can be done during this month in most areas, and their subsequent maintenance is covered elsewhere in this book. If needed, apply selective herbicides on established turf provided the weather conditions are suitable and the grasses and weeds are growing vigorously. If drought conditions occur then water lawns. Dollar spot fungus disease may appear, treat with suitable fungicide.

Effect of selective herbicide on lawn weeds

One half of grass (left) untreated. Other half (right) treated with the non-selective herbicide glyphosate

Winter colour of Hybrid Couch Grass lawn

Secondary damping-off disease on Browntop Bent eight weeks after sowing

Fungus disease, possibly brown patch, attacking cool-climate grasses in summer

Fungus disease on Creeping Bent cv., possibly dollar spot attack

Brachycome multifida   *Grevillea laurifolia*

Helichrysum bracteatum   *Hemiandra pungens*

Myoporoum parvifolium (nearest)—effective use of ground covers

June

Regular mowing at summer height, possibly aerating and watering can take place. Dry weather may mean that the cutting height has to be raised a little.

Selective herbicides may be applied provided weather and growing conditions are suitable. Corticium and dollar spot fungus disease may occur. A suitable dressing of sulphate of ammonia can be applied if needed in late June, and is watered in well.

July

Irrigate lawn before drought conditions are obvious. Check for fusarium patch and corticium fungus disease. Cut the lawn just before you go away on holiday. Daddy longlegs may be appearing on the lawn area and if in sufficient numbers may indicate a future leatherjacket attack on the lawn.

August

Seeding new lawns after mid-August can be completed provided irrigation is available during any drought period. Selective herbicides may be applied, but only if weather, soil and growing conditions permit. Fusarium patch, dollar spot, ophiobolus patch, and red corticum-thread may appear, particularly during muggy, close weather. You can give the lawn its slow-acting autumn fertilizer dressing at the end of August if weather conditions permit. Do not use sulphate of ammonia or lawn moss killers containing sulphate of ammonia to avoid encouraging lush growth and possible fungus attack.

September

In warm areas seeding a new lawn can be carried out. Damping-off disease can be a problem on the new lawn seedlings, and if necessary treat with suitable fungicide. Aerating the lawn can be carried out using a hollow-tined fork. At the end of the month scarifying the lawn may be carried out if needed. Worn areas can be overseeded or patch-turfed. Apply a light top compost dressing if needed. Mowing continues but the cutting height is raised a little in preparation for winter. Be prepared for worm infestation. Apply a slow-acting autumn lawn fertilizer if not already applied and the grass needs it. Complete areas in preparation for turfing.

October

A light top compost dressing may be applied early in the month. Worming may need to be carried out. Fusarium patch disease may occur. Sweep leaves from the lawn. Aerating can be carried out. New lawn construction can be put into operation including seeding. Turfing may also be carried out provided weather conditions are suitable. Continue mowing regularly at established winter cutting height. The first two weeks in October provide the last chance to apply slow-acting fertilizer.

November

Sweep leaves from the lawn. Check for leatherjacket attack. Turfing should be complete during November. Lawn construction can take place during dry periods. Carry on mowing if and when necessary. Aeration can be carried out. Deworming can also be carried out. The fungus diseases dollar spot and red thread may appear.

December

Check if mower needs sending away for professional overhaul; also check other lawn tools. Prepare for new lawn. Keep an eye on the lawn.

PART 2 - LAWN ALTERNATIVES

1. General Information

There is no real substitute for a grass lawn as grass is the most efficient ground cover. Certain 'lawn plants' will not be as satisfactory as a grass lawn, and generally cannot be used as effectively, or absorb as much punishment, as can lawn grasses. Lawn alternatives cannot be treated with selective herbicides as they are readily damaged or destroyed, eg plants such as dichondra (*Dichondra* sp.), clover (*Trifolium* sp.), lippia (*Phyla* sp.) and many more.

Lawn alternatives may not be readily available commercially, or otherwise. *Dichondra repens* is generally available, usually as seed, but possibly plugs may be available. Lippia *(Phyla nodiflora)*, because of its wide use over the years, may be available in sufficient quantities in certain areas to form a lawn. Clover seed is usually readily available. However, as for the others mentioned below, they may, or may not, be.

Plant Names

Not all that long ago there was only one pea-legume family, the Leguminosae, which was divided into the sub-families Mimosoideae, Caesalpinioideae and Papilionatae. Leguminosae was then separated into three distinct families: Fabaceae; Mimosaceae; and Caesalpiniaceae.

However, not all writers agree that the pea family should be placed into three separate families.

Lobelia and *Pratia* species are referred to in some books as being part of the Campanulaceae family, and in others as part of the Lobeliaceae family. There are more variations.

Botanical nomenclature is in a state of flux, so be aware that it is going on.

Common Names

There is nothing wrong with common names provided everybody knows the plant by such a name, and it is descriptive. Common names that mean different plants to different people may cause major problems. Be aware.

Acacia Leaves

Acacias (wattles) do not usually have adult leaves but have phyllodes, i.e. flat dilated petioles (stalks or leaves) that perform the functions of leaves, and which look like leaves.

2. Lawn Substitutes

The preparation for a lawn alternative-substitute should generally be the same as for a grass lawn as the area is being designed to simulate a grass lawn. However, also see details given further on concerning specific plant fertilizer needs and soil pH.

Anthemis nobilis (now known by some as *Chamaemelum nobile*)

Chamomile is a cool-climate, daisy family, perennial lawn weed, but is used by some gardeners as a lawn substitute. There is a virtually non-flowering form of chamomile, not necessarily available in Australia, which is used in the United Kingdom. Chamomile is a scented, aromatic plant.

Cotula maniototo, C. dioica

Although cotula is used for bowling-green type lawns in New Zealand these fine button daisies, with their tiny fern-like leaves, are not much used, if at all, in Australia. Cool-temperate areas.

Dichondra repens

Dichondra (also known as Kidney Weed; Mercury Bay Weed) is a member of the convolvulus family, and is a decorative, slow-growing plant with small kidney-shaped leaves. However, in the right situation it can grow vigorously and be a ground-hugging plant, which roots at the nodes. It looks vaguely similar to the native violet *Viola hederacea*. Dichondra is found in the wild in Australia and New Zealand (it is relatively popular in New Zealand), and various other parts of the world, and succeeds in an acid to neutral, well-nourished, moist soil. The flowers are insignificant. There are various *Dichondra* species, so make sure you get the one that makes a suitable lawn substitute.

Dichondra is used sometimes to replace grass in areas where traffic is minimal, and where the temperature doesn't fall below zero. Dichondra takes a reasonable amount of sun and shade, but in too deep shade it tends to veer towards scraggliness, and in too hot weather tends to yellow. Frost tolerance is still under scrutiny. It needs sensible feeding to keep it thick and carpet-like. It is usually available as seed or perhaps small blocks, and is expensive to buy.

Ironically, one of the biggest weed problems of Dichondra is grass and/or clover. Dichondra can be difficult to maintain as any selective herbicide that kills lawn weeds would also kill the Dichondra; therefore it needs regular hand weeding only.

Dichondra leaves are also easily scorched by sulphate of ammonia.

Phyla nodiflora (synonym *Lippia nodiflora*)

Lippia, a member of the verbena family, is a hard-wearing, vigorous, prostrate plant. It produces a pretty pinkish 'clover-head' of flowers. In hotter areas it seems to be more carpet-like. Possibly frost resistant.

Trifolium fragiferum

Suitable strawberry clover *(Trifolium fragiferum* var. *fragiferum)*—its name alluding to the fact that the clustered flower heads look like a small strawberry—is a downy-haired, small-leaved plant with prostrate rooting stems, originating from Europe and Western Asia.

Dichondra repens (ground cover)

Suitable strains are used in lawn seed mixtures to give an overall green-lawn appearance, because clover produces nitrates in its roots, and this promotes green leaves. Seeds are usually available at local nurseries; make sure to get a variety suitable for a lawn.

There are periods during the year when the clover goes off, and in my opinion clover on its own does not make for an ideal lawn. It can also stain clothes. Other clovers may be found in grass mixtures—white clover *(Trifolium repens)* is one.

The above flowering lawn alternatives may attract bees, which may cause problems with stings.

Lawn-looking Areas

The following plants can look like a plant lawn, but cannot necessarily take much traffic, if at all, and are used principally for appearance.

Ajuga reptans

Common carpet bugle grows to 100 to 125 mm (4 to 5 in); occasionally taller to 300 mm (12 in).

Flower colour is variable—blue or occasionally white or pink—and it flowers late spring-early summer. Leaves are 38 to 70 mm (1¼ to 2½ in) long

Ajuga reptans (variegated form)

and some cultivars have variegated, or bronzish, or purplish leaves. It can be invasive.

Common carpet bugle is grown in cool-climate areas as an evergreen, creeping, carpeting plant, in good sun, and possibly semi-shaded areas. Also seen in suitable temperate areas. Propagate by divisions. Planting distance: 150 to 500 mm (6 to 20 in).

Montia australasica (low altitude form)

It has been suggested that the low altitude form of Montia australasica (synonyms *Claytonia*

australasica; Neopaxia australasica) can be used as a lawn substitute. It has also been indicated for use in dampish areas. It is a creeping perennial with weakish, but invasive stems, fine, linear (lance-like) leaves and snow-white flowers on long slender stalklets. It is found near southern Murray River swampy areas, and temperate areas of Australia and New Zealand. Reasonably frost resistant.

Festuca ovina glauca (synonym *F. glauca*)

Blue Fescue is a grass related to Sheep's Fescue, discussed elsewhere in this book, and one might consider that it is used as a lawn alternative. However, Blue Fescue is used extensively worldwide as an unmown grass feature in borders and gardens for its beautiful silver-grey-blue, reasonably low growing, needle-like foliage. It is not used as a 'walk-on' lawn because of its tufty habit. Moist temperate to cool climates.

Selliera radicans

A smooth-leaved, perennial plant, with prostrate, creeping stems, to 300 mm (12 in) long, which root at the nodes. Flowers are white, although violet and purple markings have been reported on the outside of the corolla. Leaves can be fleshy, ovalish to oblong. Found growing wild in many parts of southern Australia, New Zealand and elsewhere. Frost tolerance, or otherwise, is still being assessed.

Thymus serpyllum

Use suitable cultivars only. A flat-prostrate to 100 mm (4 in), dark-green evergreen with small aromatic leaves, its branches being covered in due course by a host of pinkish flowers. *Thymus serpyllum* (of gardens) needs a bright sunny position and free drainage soil. Various cultivars have been produced. Most temperate-cool areas.

Viola hederacea (Native Violet)

Height: 150 to 200 mm (6 to 8 in). Spread: 1 to 2 m (3 to 6 ft). Flowers are very small, pansy-violets, usually variegated or slightly blotched violet-lilac or pink-white. It flowers in spring, also frequently throughout the year. Mat plant with creeping runners. Leaves are 8 to 15 mm (approximately half inch), smooth, kidney-shaped or almost circular. It grows in protected, full sun or filtered shade in moist soils. Temperate to cool climates.

3. Growing Ground Covers

I use the term ground covers to include semi-ground covers, mat clump, climbing and creeping plants. These can be conveniently divided into Australian native and exotic plants. Exotic plants are those that originate in other countries. There are so many different plants to choose from, but we shall concentrate on popular species, varieties and cultivars.

Growing Australian native plants separately from exotics gives the garden a unique character and helps increase the incidence of Australian plants.

However, Australian native and exotic plants having the same soil, moisture, fertilizer and climatic requirements can be, and are, mixed to form very pleasing ground cover gardens.

Creeping conifer 'breaks up' edge of kerb. Note stone mulch

Sweet violets *(V. odorata)* colonizing a large area

What do you mean by ground covers, semi-ground covers, mat, clump, creeping and climbing plants?

Ground covers are reasonably quick growing, ornamental plants selected because of their ability to provide a low-growing, dense foliage canopy, and which are effective in forming large area, ground-hugging colonies, leaving much less room for weeds to establish and thrive.

Do not be deluded that ground covers will automatically suppress the appearance of weeds as certain weeds are great ground covers in their own right.

Once established, and if weed invasion is suppressed, then ground covers may need little maintenance, the proviso being that the correct species, varieties or cultivars are chosen. Some ground covers are more suitable and successful as weed suppressors than others, therefore the less competitive need more nurturing until they become mature enough to cater for themselves.

Ground covers are also useful in providing cover for awkward places where grasses would not survive, or cannot be maintained effectively, such as steep banks, shady places and uneven sites.

Semi-ground covers is an expression I use to describe those plants which are low and shrubbish in their growth habit, covering reasonably large areas, but will also grow up to a height of 1 m or slightly taller.

Mat plants form a carpet-like growth, but not necessarily vigorously.

Clump plants, in our context, are reasonably low growing and form small clumps.

Climbing and creeping plants are those plants which travel over the soil and possibly climb obstructions, but here they are used mainly as ground covers. Be aware that climbing plants used as ground covers may overpower any shrub that is placed within their spread.

Pest, Poisonous and Irritating Plants

Remember in Australia that many weeds have become pest plants and what may be a desirable plant for various other parts of the world, or even other parts of the country, may not be suitable, or allowed, in your area. Examples include Salvation Jane (Paterson's Curse), soursob, cactus (in Queensland) and lantana in certain northern areas. Check with your local authority whether a particular plant is suitable, or allowed, in your State or Territory.

Some plants have poisonous berries, or other parts, or may cause allergies or irritations to certain people or animals. You should find out about such plants before buying or planting them. There are books on the subject, or check your local Poisons Information Centre for information they have.

Quarantine/Plant Protection

Each State or Territory Department of Agriculture has a section that deals with plant and seed quarantine. For more information contact the relevant section. There are strict quarantine laws concerning the importation of plants and seeds into Australia. Other countries may have equally strict quarantine laws. There are also rules governing the movement of plants between States and Territories so be aware of this.

Fertilizing Australian Native Plants

Australian native plants, generally, have managed to survive in soils that are low in plant nutrients, particularly phosphorus. Therefore, to apply liberal dressings of superphosphate, blood and bone, bone meal, bone flour and the like, or even composts containing high levels of phosphorus, to these delicately poised plants could cause major problems such as droughting, root scorch, fungal attack and even death.

It has been reported over the years, that the following plants have been checked, or have died, from superphosphate application: *Banksia* species, *Grevillea* species, *Isopogon* species, *Adenanthos* species, *Dryandra* species and *Prostanthera* species.

Many Australian plants, such as members of the Fabaceae-Leguminosae (e.g. peas, certain acacias) have the ability to produce nitrogen from special nodules contained in their roots.

There are slow-release, NPK fertilizers specially compounded for use on Australian native plants. *Read the label* to see if the product is recommended for use on your particular plants, and how it should be applied prior to planting, and if recommended after planting. However, if a plant is growing well in your garden then it may not be necessary to fertilize it. Common sense here.

Properly produced blood and bone organic fertilizer, containing nitrogen and phosphorus, is often recommended as a fertilizer for Australian native plants. Read the label to see what the packet contains, and to see if it is recommended for use on Australian native plants, and if so which Australian plants specifically.

Also be aware that although some fertilizers may contain blood and bone, they also may contain quick-acting inorganic fertilizer ingredients, which are possibly not wanted by your particular plants; indeed may be counter-productive. Hoof and horn fertilizer is also used but this contains principally slow-acting nitrogen, plus a little phosphorus. Animals may be attracted by animal fertilizers.

Fertilizing Exotic Plants

It is exceedingly difficult, if not impossible, to generalize on exotic plant fertilizer requirements as their needs differ so.

Exotic plants are many, varied, chosen for a variety of reasons, and have arrived in Australia from all parts of the globe. Most have their own peculiar nutrient and soil needs. The treatment of such plants is decided plant by plant.

Therefore, fertilizers are used to cater specifically for the species or cultivars you are planting. Again, a reputable brand of slow-release fertilizer may be the way to go. *Read the label* on the manufacturer's product to see if this particular product is recommended for the plants you have in mind.

A trip to the nursery should give an indication of what is available.

Iron Deficiency

Plants growing in limy soils may suffer from iron deficiency which, put simply, is where the calcium knocks iron out of solution and therefore the essential iron is unavailable to the plant. Chelated iron is used to combat iron deficiency, but discuss the problem with an expert as there are other plant deficiencies which also show up in the leaf. Be extra careful when analyzing plant food deficiencies, and the subsequent treatment, to avoid creating other plant nutrient problems.

Pests and Disease

Space does not permit an involved discussion concerning pests and diseases of ground cover plants, therefore suitable books on pests and disease of Australian native plants and exotic plants should be consulted. Some of the more common pests include crusader bug, scale, red spider mite and aphids. Remember, if you use pesticides of any sort then read the manufacturer's label before you buy, and before you use, and use the product safely.

Siting the Plants

There are ground covers that can survive in open, hot sunlight. Those that can survive in the open but not in hot sunlight. Those that can take filtered shade. Those that can take heavier shade. Those that are frost tolerant or resistant. Those that are moderately frost tolerant. Those that are susceptible to frost damage and those that are killed by it.

Frost Tolerance

This is a debatable subject as what can be 'moderately frost resistant' to some may not be so for others.

In the relevant section I have frequently used the expression 'possibly-usually frost resistant' to make people aware that it is a subject that cannot be treated lightly. Many Australians may be surprised just how far north the approximate limit of frost does stretch.

Therefore, in areas where frost is expected, even occasionally, a plant's frost resistance, or otherwise, in that particular locality, has to be ascertained by a plant expert.

Check out books on the Australian weather. Information on your local climate may be published by the Department of Science, Bureau of Meteorology.

The Society for Growing Australian Plants' local knowledge has contributed greatly to the furthering of Australian plants. The National Botanic Garden in Canberra has been diligently recording such information concerning plants.

Furthermore, is your garden a frost trap? If so then frost tender plants would most likely be killed, or severely damaged, whereas just up the hill, for

Crusader bug

Scale encrustation on plant branches (note ants)

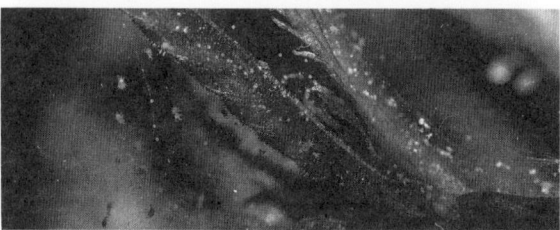

Red spider mite attacking plant

Aphids on shrub shoots

example, out of the frost trap, the same species or cultivars may be succeeding.

To simplify, the question is, 'Is the plant you intend growing frost resistant in *your* garden?' Find out.

Invasive Plants/Vigorous Plants/Weeds

There are native and exotic ground covers that are invasive and vigorous and can quickly dominate areas where such domination is not wanted, and become pernicious weeds. However, these plants may also be useful for problem areas and where such a cover is needed, and would not be considered pernicious weeds in these areas.

Weeds are a problem gardeners will have to address to get their plants established. Hand weeding can be practised, but care has to be taken so as not to damage ground cover plant roots. The non-selective herbicide glyphosate, can be used to individually treat weeds. Be aware that if any herbicide touches a desirable ground cover then that plant may be killed. *Remember to read the label on any herbicide, or any other garden product, before you buy, before you use, and use the product safely.*

How far do you want the plants to spread, as plants placed too closely together can choke out each other? Some plants are so rampant, e.g. *Kennedia rubicunda* that they will crowd out areas and have to be removed. Alternatively, there are plants that are not planted closely enough and the spaces between become colonized by weeds.

Also remember that certain ground cover plants can climb tree trunks and eventually kill the tree. A prime example is ivy, which looks beautiful until it kills the tree, and then it looks ominous. Or such plants can choke out other shrubs. Conversely, these plants may possibly be utilized for steep banks and the like.

When planting shrubs on banks you can use the quincunx method—one spot in the centre and a spot in each corner (like the five spots on dice). Planting shrubs in this fashion may, I repeat may, help prevent water gullying.

You may be told that there is no such plant as an Australian native plant weed. Any plant out of its environment may establish and dominate sensitive, local plant areas whether it be Australian or not.

You could discuss this aspect of Australian native plant ground covers for use in your area with your local botanic garden, home garden advisory service, or expert at your local Society for Growing Australian Plants.

Choosing Ground Covers

You can choose your ground cover for other practical reasons, for evergreen or autumn foliage colour, or flower colour, or berries-fruits, and so forth, so that the whole design results in a pleasing effect. See what others have done and if you like what you see then adapt it, using your own ideas to make it unique.

Choosing Cultivars

There are many cultivars (cultivated varieties) on the market and it can be useful to check them out before ordering or planting to establish if the colour, form etc. is what you want.

Flowering Times

Flowering times of plants are very much governed by local climate, your garden's microclimate or even by various microclimates within your garden. You will see, for example, that a plant is expected to flower in winter and spring but, for example, in your garden it only flowers in spring. Check out local flowering times for particular plants.

Coastal Soil

Do not assume that because certain plants are recommended for use in a sandy soil, they are suitable for coastal sandy soil. You need a particular type of salt resistant, wind resistant plant to withstand the rigours of a coastal environment, whether the soil be sandy or otherwise. Therefore, you must choose plants that can cope with your particular coastal situation.

Indeed, some coastal soils can be very much exposed to sea spray and winds. Others may be protected by coastal shrub barriers or even denser or higher coastal barriers. Some gardeners can create microclimates in their gardens to provide for susceptible shrubs.

Humidity

Many Australian plants grow in harsh or cool conditions and so forth, and if planted in a northern, humid environment may not succeed. If you live in such a climatic region then check that the plants you have in mind will survive, and are suitable for the purpose you have in mind.

Mulches

A mulch can be organic or inorganic and its purpose is to help conserve moisture and help suppress the incidence of weeds, although it would be wishful thinking to consider that this could be one hundred per cent successful. Mulch can also be used to present a pleasing appearance. Suitable mulches may help prevent clay soils cracking. There are those who do not like to use mulches of any kind.

Fire risk areas have to be considered when choosing the type of mulch to use, and a discussion with the local fire-fighting authority could prove interesting.

Any material used must be free from any toxic substances that could destroy or harm the existing plants.

1. *Hardwood sawdust granules*, although of limited use, are occasionally used to provide a pathway through plants, particularly as a soft path through a native plant area. Keep well watered and consolidated to prevent it blowing away and to make the going easier.

2. *Pine bark* is used as a mulch as it has a natural, attractive appearance (although not everyone would agree with this).

3. *Pebbles* are used as mulch, but they are expensive and very difficult to keep free from weeds.

4. *Scoria rock* is popular where it can be obtained reasonably cheaply, although out of its natural environment it may be considered by some as artificial.

5. *Crushed brick* can be used but you have to make sure it is the right colour to complement your garden design. Ensure that it is of a suitable particle size, and also that it is free from chemicals that could injure plants and soil.

6. *Black plastic* has been used extensively as its ability to suppress weeds is good. However, using black plastic has drawbacks such as: preventing air from flowing over the soil; the soil being heated by the sun's rays falling on to the plastic which absorbs the heat; and correct watering of the plants being made difficult. If used, wide circles have to be allowed around plants to allow the roots to breathe, and to help keep the transmitted heat away from sensitive bark and roots. It also has to be covered with a suitable mulch material to make the final appearance attractive and to help stop it from blowing away; although it should be secured separately.

7. *Black plastic weed mat* is used to help suppress weeds. It allows a certain amount of air and moisture to penetrate to the plant roots, but also gets too hot when exposed to hot sunlight. It too is usually covered with suitable mulch material to make it look more attractive and help prevent it blowing away, although it should also be secured separately.

Notes on Height and Spread

You may see, for example, height indicated as prostrate to 600 mm (2 ft) or spread as 1 to 3 m (3 to 10 ft). This is because that particular plant has been observed separately growing to those varying dimensions, and here it is pointed out that local soil, soil nutrients, climatic conditions, local plant form, and more may influence the height and spread of a plant.

It is imperative to check the form, height, spread, flower colour and flowering time of a particular plant before you purchase, or before you plant, to ensure that they are what you require as these features may vary between plants having identical names.

The 'Reflective Pause'

Before you even remotely think of doing any work in your garden have what I call a reflective pause. Ask yourself, 'What will happen if...?' Don't just rip out plants, or move plants, or change the pH of the soil until you have thought it through very carefully. If your soil is acid then why not consider acid soil loving plants, if they are suitable, that could succeed in such a soil? If it is a limy soil then consider plants that would be at home there; again only if they are suitable? Do not claw out a climber only to find that you have exposed your view to the local gasometer, and so on.

It is also a good idea to have some sort of practical design in mind before you start, and know where any services such as electricity, gas, phone, water, sewer and so on are located as you don't want to damage these, or be damaged by them.

Remember even ground cover plants can find their way into sewers, or draw water away from foundations.

Indeed, on certain clay soils certain plants can be so hungry for water that they can cause massive cracking, which in turn affects foundations. If your soil is suspect then discuss the problem with suitable soil engineering experts before you plant.

Establish which areas of the garden are sunny and which are shady. You can, for example, plant suitable sun lovers in open sun, or conversely plant shade-loving shrubs away from the sun. Also find out where the prevailing winds come from as it could be important when it comes to protecting certain shrubs.

Make yourself a simple planting plan. Find out the eventual spread of the plants and plant the ground covers accordingly.

Check whether you need an irrigation plan. You can use irrigation drip feed to water plants, or overhead sprinklers, or sprinklers worked by a timer, either manual or automatically controlled.

Site Preparation

Correct site preparation is imperative and usually should be finished before the plants are ordered.

Irrigation

Irrigation can be accomplished by using a sprinkler on a hose, or even carting buckets of water to each plant when needed, or the popular drip feed watering. This is where drippers are laid by each shrub and the water drips on to the root area of each plant for a given period of time. Drippers can have various delivery rates, for example, four or eight or many more litres per hour. You can use microjets, or other sprays, provided such overhead spraying doesn't harm the plants. A trip to a garden irrigation supplier could prove eye-opening and rewarding. Many irrigation firms issue brochures.

One type of drip irrigation

Drainage

Most ground covers need good drainage to survive, although there are ground covers that will take wetter soil conditions than others. Drainage is discussed elsewhere in this book, but be aware that if using land drains then roots can block pipes. Any drainage work is done prior to planting. Rubble or stone-filled trenches can also be used to catch moisture and redirect it.

Soil

This is discussed in more detail elsewhere, but acid peat and/or well-rotted acid, weed free compost are used and dug in to prepare the immediate planting area prior to planting ground covers. As stated

A method of soaking dry peat

previously peat should always be moist before being applied to the soil so that it absorbs moisture quickly. Peat contributes little or no nutrients to the soil but does aid soil improvement.

Gypsum, *calcium sulphate*, is used to improve certain clay soils, which helps cause the clay particles to clump into groups thus aiding water, air and root penetration. It is applied as the manufacturer instructs.

Adding gypsum to break up clay soil

Sandy soils can be open and free draining, or so filled up with sand fines that they are impervious to water. Either way it may be useful to add acid organic material such as acid peat or well-rotted, weed free acid garden compost to aid moisture retention. Note that the emphasis is on acid as you can always add lime if absolutely necessary.

Clay soils can also be opened up using humus, acid peat or well-rotted, weed free acid compost. Occasionally, clean, coarse, sharp, inert, saline-free sand is suggested, but be aware that such vast quantities are needed that perhaps professional laboratory soil physical analysis should be considered before embarking on such a mammoth project.

Imported soil has to be of the right quality as some soil is full of silt and salt and instead of improving your soil sets like concrete and has to be removed. Check with a local expert authority on suitable topsoil sources.

Space does not permit a detailed study of soils for ground covers, but there are books that go into the problem more deeply.

Checking the soil pH is vital as this will decide which plants are likely to succeed in such a soil. It is exceedingly easy to raise the pH of a soil, but it is difficult to lower the pH of the soil. Follow the instructions on the soil testing kit. You can also get your soil checked by a reputable, professional soil laboratory.

It is important to know your soil pH before ordering plants as there are plants that will survive in only an acid soil, others in a neutral soil, others in an alkaline soil. Whereas others can survive in a slightly acid-neutral-slightly alkaline soil. You could save yourself problems by choosing plants that are at home in your soil and local climatic conditions.

Saline soil conditions call for expert local knowledge as saline soil amelioration can involve complicated treatment.

Pruning

Ground covers, generally, do not need much pruning and any pruning that is done is just to keep the plant in check, or to keep the shape. Savage pruning and hacking should be avoided.

Trees

Suitable trees may prove to be an effective barrier to the prevailing winds and allow sensitive plants to be planted out of the wind. Remember, certain trees can be dangerous when tall and attack sewers, other services, and building foundations.

Varied Height Planting

By planting ground covers, semi-ground covers, clump plants and mat plants of different heights you create more interest. However, while a large expanse of one-height ground cover may look boring to some, it can look perfectly acceptable to others; it is a matter of choice.

Container-grown Plants

Container-grown plants should be chosen carefully before purchasing. Pot-bound plants, in my opinion, never come to much. Common sense is necessary while browsing through a nursery. Does the plant look healthy overall, with healthy foliage? Is it well furnished with foliage? Is it crawling with, or free from, insects and diseases? Don't waste your time and money on rubbish.

Planting

Dig a deep enough hole to take the root adequately. The top of the root ball should be at soil level; if below the surface the plant stem may rot at the base. If too high the root ball can dry out unnecessarily. In certain areas you may need to create soil saucers round the plants to prevent unnecessary water run off.

4. Australian Native Plant Ground Covers

Note: Flowering times can vary between localities as local climates, and even garden microclimates, influence flowering times.

Acacia aculeatissima

Height: prostrate to 250 to 500 mm (10 to 20 in). Spread: 1-2-3 m (3-6-10 ft).

Yellow flower balls in winter-spring; honey scented. Foliage (phyllodes) thinnish, pale green and prickly to thorn-like. Possibly moderately frost resistant, although some doubt about its ability to withstand heavy frost has been expressed. Full sun. Medium-heavy soil, but must have good drainage. Used on banks or for covering large areas.

Acacia amblygona (prostrate form)

Height: prostrate to 300 to 600 mm (1 to 2 ft), sometimes taller. Spread: 1 to 3 m (3 to 10 ft), cascading.

Golden-yellow flower balls on short stalks winter-spring. Lance like to egg-shaped—some almost triangular—phyllodes (leaves). Full sun. Dry, medium to heavy but well drained, moist soil. Frost tolerance still in question.

Acacia ligulata

(Prostrate form of umbrella bush only; available in some States.)
Height: 100 mm (4 in). Spread: 2 m (6 ft).

Yellow flowers winter-spring. Only possibly moderately frost resistant. Reasonable tolerance of slightly acid, neutral and alkaline soil. Soil use: limestone or sandy or second-line coastal soil.

Acacia pravissima

(Use only suitable low-growing forms or cultivars.)
Height: prostrate to 500 to 600 mm (20 to 24 in). Spread: 4 to 5 m (13 to 16 ft).

Yellow flower balls winter-spring; possibly summer. Small egg-shaped, roughly four-sided-trapezium phyllodes (leaves). Full sun, open situation, and light to medium soil with good drainage. Slightly lime tolerant. Moderately to frost resistant.

Ajuga australis

Height: 250 to 300 mm (10 to 12 in).

Flower colour variable from bluish purple to occasional pink and also white; possibly late winter-spring flowering—summer in hilly-mountain areas. Vegetative division is necessary to obtain true colour. A member of the mint family, this Australian bugle is found in various parts of Australia, particularly temperate areas. In hilly-mountain areas it can be procumbent. Like most members of the mint family it will sucker and root invasively in the right growing conditions. Leaves hairy, egg-shaped to oblong, toothed, greyish or dark green, 43 to 120 mm (1¾ to 5 in) long. Possibly frost resistant.

Astroloma humifusum (Native Cranberry, Cranberry Heath)

Height: prostrate to 75 to 100 mm (3 to 4 in) to ascending. Spread: 400 mm to 1 m (16 to 36 in). (Various forms; check for height.)

Red, narrow, tubular, 10 mm (½ in) flowers in autumn-winter-spring, but depends on local conditions. Tight mat plant, small, involved narrow-linear leaves, pointed and moderately prickly. Open, well drained soil including sandy. Moderately to frost resistant.

Banksia species, varieties and cultivars

Note: The frost susceptibility of banksias depends on species, varieties or cultivars as some are definitely frost tender and can be killed by frost.

Banksia petiolaris

Height: prostrate to 300 to 400 mm (12 to 16 in). Spread: 1 to 4 m (3 to 13 ft).

Flowers, 75 to 120 mm (3 to 5 in) long, yellow, often cylindrical, some oblong cylindrical; spring-summer. Sunny, open situation, very well-drained, light to medium soil. Possibly frost resistant.

Banksia repens (Creeping Banksia)

Height: prostrate to 300 to 500 mm (12 to 20 in). Spread: 1 to 4 m (3 to 13 ft).

Flowers cylindrical, yellowish brown, red-brown, bronzy-red; in spring-early summer. Light, well-drained, open soils. Reasonably frost resistant, although I see in one catalogue that B. repens is not classed as frost resistant.

Brachycome melanocarpa

Height: 100 to 450 mm (4 to 18 in). Spread: small clumps.

Flowers daisy-like, 20 mm (less than 1 in) wide, white or purple-blue, depending on form. Branching. Irregular-toothed leaves oblong or circular to wedge shaped. Full sun and a light to medium well-drained soil. Possibly frost resistant.

Brachycome multifida (Cut-leaf Daisy)

Height: 100 to 300 mm (4 to 12 in). Spread: 300 mm to 1.2 m (1 to 4 ft).

Flowers 20 mm (under 1 inch), mauve blue, lilac blue, lilac pink; spring—but frequent depending on area. Finely divided, carroty-looking leaves; compact—often tufted plant. Full sun. Clay soil with good drainage and sandy soil. Possibly frost resistant. Many garden uses. Various varieties and cultivars available.

Brachysema sericeum (various forms)

Height: variable—prostrate to 1 m (3 ft). Spread: variable 1 to 4 m (3 to 13 ft). (Check colour, height, spread, form and flowering time before buying.)

Pea flowers creamy-white, although red to reddish-black are found; as are lime-yellow. Winter-spring flowering. Slightly acid-neutral soil. Clay soil well drained, sandy. Full sun or only reasonably shade tolerant. Frost tolerance not fully assessed.

Correa decumbens

Height: 200 to 400 mm (8 to 16 in). Spread: 1 to 3 m (3 to 10 ft).

Solitary, red, 25 mm (1 in) tubular flower bells; stamens project out like bell-clappers; also yellow or green tipped; depending on form. Dull-green, oblong-blunt leaves. Winter-spring flowering, although occasional flowers do appear at other times. Possibly moderately frost resistant. Clay only if well drained. Full sun or lightly filtered shade. Useful for small gardens. Most areas except too dry-hot; too hot-tropical; too cold.

Correa reflexa (Native Fuchsia)

A prostrate form of this normally tall, red-green bell-flowered plant (also other colours) is available in some States; winter-spring. Possibly frost resistant. Moist or dry situations, but not too dry. Not suitable for tropical-subtropical or too cold conditions.

Cotula coronopifolia

Height: 100 mm (4 in). Spread: 600 mm (2 ft).

Yellow button flowers look like a large common daisy flower without white petals; winter-spring but occasionally much of the year. Smooth-leaved, often coarsely toothed perennial with stout fleshy creeping stems, which root at the nodes. Found naturally in damp or shallow-water spots. Sun or partial shade. Considered frost tender by some.

Dampiera diversifolia

Height: prostrate. Spread: to 1 m (3 ft).

Flowers: dark, bright blue, usually massed on the plant; spring-summer possibly early autumn. Suckering-trailing habit. Open, well-drained, moist light-medium soil. Full sun with extra watering applied when necessary, or lightly filtered sun. Possibly frost resistant; not heavy frost.

Dampiera diversifolia

Dampiera hederacea

Height: 300 to 500 mm (12 to 20 in). Spread: 300 mm to 1 m (1 to 3 ft).

Flowers: bright blue; winter-spring-summer. Suckering habit. Leaves can be heart-shaped, ivyish; slightly hairy. Well-drained soil. Full sun in cooler areas, or lightly filtered partial sun in others. Not fully frost resistant.

Dampiera stricta

Height: 200 to 600 mm (8 to 24 in). Spread: 200 to 600 mm (8 to 24 in).

Flowers: almost star-like, shades of blue to occasional white; winter-spring. Erect, stiffish plant with weak, angular stems; leaves stemless attached to main stem. Light, open well-drained soils. Partial sun. Careful selection needed when choosing plants. Possibly frost resistant.

Disphyma crassifolium (Round-leaved Pigface; Rounded Noon Flower

Synonyms D. australe, D. clavellatum.
Height: prostrate to 100 mm (4 in). Spread: 1 to 2 m (3 to 6 ft).

Flowers: 30 mm (1¼ in); rosy pink-purple; winter-spring-autumn. Succulent foliage. Sandy-coastal, sunny, frost-free areas.

Eremophila biserrata

Height: prostrate to 100 mm (4 in). Spread: 1 to 2 m (3 to 6 ft).

Flowers: 25 mm (1 in) long; green; spring-summer. Branches root at nodes. Sunny situation. Well-drained clay-sandy soil. Possibly frost resistant, but not suitable for cool-cold southern and high areas.

E. densifolia, blue flowered, frost tender to only possibly-moderately frost resistant, and E. serpens, frost tender, green flowered, are used in some States as ground covers. The prostrate form of E. glabra, frost tender, and various other E. glabra forms such as the burgundy-flowered and Roseworthy form are also used.

Frankenia pauciflora

(There are varietal forms being considered and evaluated.)
Height: prostrate to 100 to 150 mm (4 to 6 in). Spread: 300 mm to 1 m (12 to 36 in).

Flowers: stalk-less; star-like; spring-summer-early autumn; pink—rarely white. Moderately-possibly frost resistant. Grows in well-drained limestone, sandy, coastal areas, temperate States. Open, full sun, or very lightly shaded site.

Goodenia lanata

Height: prostrate. Spread: 800 mm to 1 m (32 to 36 in).

Flowers: yellow; spring-summer. Woolly-leaves. Well-drained, moist soil. Full or slightly filtered sun. Possibly frost resistant. Not for hot inland extremes.

G. varia has certain yellow-flowered, prostrate-procumbent forms which are used in some States as ground covers; possibly frost resistant.

Grevillea species, varieties and cultivars

There are many grevillea forms, subspecies, varieties and cultivars used as ground covers. Only a few are mentioned. Grevilleas, as a group, are being totally revised.

A trip to a suitable Australian plant nursery could be enlightening, particularly when the grevilleas are in flower.

Some species or cultivars have been reported as causing allergies in certain persons.

Grevilleas are used in most temperate, mild areas, except too cold southern areas and moister, humid northern areas. Many grevilleas are frost tender or killed out by frost. Local expert authority on grevilleas is important when considering them.

Grevillea alpina (low forms)

The red-yellow, frequent flowering, 'goldfields' procumbent form, and other forms-other colours, are available in some temperate States as a ground cover. Reasonably frost resistant.

Grevillea aquifolium

Height: variable; prostrate to 1 m (3 ft). Spread: variable to 2 m (6 ft).

Flowers: red to red-green 'toothbrushes'—also other colours, forms; late winter-spring-early summer. Holly-like foliage; can be variable. Possibly frost resistant. Well-drained soil. Sun or reasonable shade.

Grevillea biternata

(This plant, also known as G. tridentifera and G.

Grevillea biternata

curviloba, is subject to name change—discuss with a competent Australian native plant nurseryman.) Height: variable; prostrate to 100 mm (4 in); certain erect shoots to 1 m (3 ft) and possibly higher. Spread: 2 m (6 ft)—possibly wider.

Flowers: creamy-white; sweetly scented; in dense communities; winter-spring. Vigorous growth; foliage fine, dissected. Susceptible to frost damage in certain areas. Well-drained light to medium soil. Open site.

Grevillea brownii

(In some books *G. brownii* has been placed under *G. depauperata*.)
Height: 200 to 600 mm (8-24 in). Spread: 1 m (3 ft).

Flowers: orange-red, some gold; frequent winter-spring. Possibly-moderately frost resistant. Well-drained sandy soil; not coastal sands. Full and lightly filtered sun.

Grevillea confertifolia (low-growing form)

Height: 150 to 300 mm (6 to 12 in). Spread: 1 to 2 m (3 to 6 ft).

Flowers: pink-mauve pink; spring. Well-drained sandy (not coastal region) soil, plus sufficient moisture. Not for hot root-baking sites; full sun in cool areas; also filtered sun tolerant. Reasonably frost resistant.

Grevillea diminuta

Height: 300 mm to 1 m (1 to 3 ft). Spread: 1 to 2 m (3 to 6 ft).

Flowers: rusty-red in suspended clusters, can be obvious some time before flowering; spring-summer. Procumbent. Reasonably frost resistant. Well-drained, open sunny site; light to medium soil; also in moderately filtered shade.

Grevillea × gaudichaudii (hybrid)

Height: prostrate. Spread: 2 to 3 m (6 to 10 ft).

Flowers: dark burgundy-red toothbrush form; winter-spring-summer. Oakleaf form foliage. Well-drained soil. Full sun. Reasonably frost resistant.

Grevillea ilicifolia (Holly-leaved or Holly-bush Grevillea)

(Prostrate forms only.)
Height: variable; sometimes procumbent, sometimes up to 1 or 2 m (3 to 6 ft). Only low-growing forms used as ground covers.

Flowers: usually red, possibly some greenish; spring. Holly-like leaves 30 to 60 mm (1¼ to 2½ in) long. Well-drained, sunny site. Possibly frost resistant.

Grevillea laurifolia

Height: prostrate. Spread: to 3 m (10 ft).

Flowers: short, dense; dark-red toothbrushes; spring-summer. Trailing branches, leaves smooth-edged, broad, regular oval-shaped, laurel-like, up to 100 mm (4 in) long. Sunny site, open situation and light to medium well-drained soil. Possibly frost resistant.

Grevillea nana

Height: variable; prostrate to 600 mm (2 ft). Spread: 600 mm to 1 m (2 to 3 ft).

Flowers: loose heads, pink or cream have been reported—check colour; spring-summer. Narrow leaves stiff, deeply cut, segmented. Possibly-moderately frost resistant.

Grevillea nudiflora

(Prostrate forms only.)
Height: prostrate to 200 mm to 1 m (8 to 36 in). Spread: 1 to 3 m (3 to 10 ft).

Flowers: clusters of red, red-yellow reported; spring-summer borne on leafless stems. Spreading plant, narrow, lance-like, stiff leaves. Possibly light frost resistant. Sunny site, sandy.

Grevillea obtusifolia (G. thelemanniana ssp. obtusifolia)

(Prostrate form only.)
Height: 300 mm to 1 m (12 to 36 in). Spread: 1 to 2 m (3 to 6 ft).

Flowers: red, hanging clusters; usually spring; some winter—some summer. Possibly frost resistant. Well drained clay and sandy soil. Open site but filtered shade tolerant.

Grevillea 'Poorinda Royal Mantle' (cultivar)

Height: prostrate. Spread: vigorous.

Flowers: dark-red toothbrush; winter-spring; possibly on. Attractive foliage with burgundyish new growth; leaf margins regular or lobed, even coarsely; to 100 mm (4 in) long. Full sun, well-drained medium to heavy soil. Reasonably frost resistant.

Grevillea steiglitziana

Height: ground-spreading, not prostrate, to 300 mm to 1 m (1 to 3 ft). Spread: 1 to 2.5 m (3 to 8 ft).

Flowers: red, possibly with some green; abundant, hanging clusters; winter-spring, possibly summer. Lobed, holly-like foliage. Sunny, open, well-drained light to medium soil. Reasonably frost resistant.

Grevillea synapheae

Height: 200 to 600 mm (8 to 24 in). Spread: 1 to 2 m (3 to 6 ft).

Flowers: cream, massed, rounded clusters; spring-possibly winter. Leaves divided, greyish-bronzish when young. Well-drained soil, sandy (not coastal) soil. Full sun; filtered shade tolerant. Possibly frost resistant.

Grevillea thelemanniana (prostrate forms)

Height: 300 mm (12 in). Spread: 2 m (6 ft).

Flowers: red; winter-spring. Well-drained soil, sunny site. Frost tolerance not known generally for all forms.

Grevillea thelemanniana (grey-leaved form)

Height: 100 to 300 mm (4 to 12 in). Spread: 1 to 2 m (3 to 6 ft). As above, except that this form has a fine cascading habit.

Check flower/foliage/growth etc. details of *G. thelemanniana* before purchase.

Halgania cyanea (Rough Halgania)

Height: 300 to 400 mm (12 to 16 in). Spread: 1 to 1.5 m (3 to 5 ft).

Flowers: blue or deep purple; spring—frequent

various times of year. Rough small leaves, 5 to 25 mm (¼ to 1 in), long and narrow, often three toothed at summit. Suckering. Limestone-sand soils. Frost resistant. Full sun; partial sun in hot areas.

Hardenbergia species and cultivars

Hardenbergias are climbers but some forms can be used as ground covers. Some spread further than others and some are too upright; discuss ground cover form suitability.

Hardenbergia comptoniana (WA Coral Pea)

Spread-climbing: to 3 m (10 ft).

Flowers: small, drooping, dense clusters; usually purple-bluish; winter-spring. Neutral, well-drained clay, sandy soils. Full sun and filtered shade. Can be frost tender and has been killed out by frost. Discuss hardiness with local expert. Leaves usually in threes, lanceolate, 50 to 100 mm (2 to 4 in).

Hardenbergia violacea (Native Lilac; False Sarsaparilla)

Spread-climbing: 1 to 1.5 m (3 to 5 ft).

Flowers: lilac to intense purple (but white, pink, light mauve shades have been recorded); in twos and threes in abundant clusters; winter-spring. Leaves single, smooth, undivided, toughish like eucalypt leaves. Light to heavy, clay and sandy soil. Hardier than *H. comptoniana*, but still possibly frost susceptible having been killed out by frost; discuss with local expert; also the form's suitability as a ground cover. Full sun, filtered shade tolerant.

Helichrysum bracteatum species and cultivars

Height: to 300 to 600 mm (12 to 24 in). Spread: to 1 m (3 ft).

Flowers: variable; large, 60 to 70 mm (2½ to 2¾ in), daisy flowers; varying colours and forms according to variety or cultivar but yellow best known. Some *H. bracteatum* forms considered as perennial; some as annual. Some forms or cultivars are considered possibly frost resistant, others frost tender. Good drainage and full sun needed.

Hemiandra pungens (Snake Bush)

Height: prostrate to 100 mm (4 in). Spread: 1 to 2 m (3-6 ft).

Flowers: lilac-mauve-pink; also white prostrate

form; summer; spring-autumn reported. Leaves prickly-narrow. Full sun. Well-drained clay-sand. Most milder, temperate areas with reasonable moisture.

Hibbertia pendunculata

Height: prostrate to 200 mm (8 in). Spread: 300 mm to 1 m (12 to 36 in); even wider reported.

Flowers: yellow, open; spring; possibly other times of year. Reasonably protected site. Well-drained light to medium soils. Reasonably frost resistant. Not for hot full sun or hot tropical areas.

Hibbertia scandens (Snake Vine)

Height-climbing: prostrate. Spread: up to 2 to 3 m (6 to 10 ft).

Flowers: bright yellow stars; 50 mm (2 in), and wider; mostly summer, also spring. Red berries produced in suitable climates. Quick growing. Full sun. Well-drained soil. Sand, coastal, also clay but only warm and very well drained. Can be frost tender.

Isotoma fluviatilis

Height: prostrate-creeping. Spread: up to 1 m (3 ft); possibly wider.

Flowers: numerous small stars; fragile blue, sometimes white; spring-summer. Full sun only in cool areas. Light, damp to moist soils. Possibly frost resistant.

Kennedia species

There are many Kennedia species used as ground covers, but bear in mind that certain species, e.g. K. beckxiana, K. coccinea, K. macrophylla, K. nigricans, and K. rubicunda, are very vigorous, even invasive, and could soon outstay their welcome.

Kennedia prostrata (Running Postman)

Height: prostrate to 100 mm (4 in), trailer. Spread: variable, up to 1 to 2 m (3 to 6 ft), possibly more.

Flowers (pea): brilliant red-scarlet; winter-spring-summer; abundant over plant. Clover-like leaves. Most well-drained soils. Check frost resistance with local experts.

Kunzea pomifera (Muntries)

Height: prostrate to 200 to 500 mm (8 to 20 in).

Spread: to 2 m (6 ft); possibly wider.

Flowers: cream-whitish; spring; possibly winter and summer. Open, very well-drained sandy soil; second-line coastal; dry soils.

Lechenaultia biloba

Lechenaultia biloba (Blue Lechenaultia)

Height: 300 mm to 1 m (12 to 36 in). Spread: 300 mm to 1 m (12 to 36 in).

Flowers: usually pure blue, but other shades have been recorded; winter-spring; some forms may sucker. Well-drained sandy soils preferred; plus irrigation during dry spells. Possibly frost resistant.

Lechenaultia formosa (Scarlet/Red Lechenaultia)

Height: 100 to 600 mm (4 to 24 in). Spread: 300 to 600 mm (12 to 24 in); possibly wider.

Flowers: red/yellow/orange, indeed variable colour-forms; winter-spring; possibly on. Short-lived; easily propagated. Reasonably protected light-sandy soils. Check with local expert concerning frost susceptibility.

Leptospermum rupestre (low forms only)

Height: prostrate. Spread: 1 to 2 m (3 to 6 ft).

Flowers: white to cream; summer. Reasonably hardy. Needs adequate moisture, but also good drainage.

Mazus pumilio

Height: prostrate. Spread: up to 500 mm to 1 m (20 in to 3 ft).

Flowers: on leafless stalks; small; usually purplish; tubular; late spring, also summer if soil moist. Leaves oblongish, wavy and when crushed emit an odour. Rhizome-suckering roots. Damp soil. Full or filtered sun. Possibly frost resistant. Second-line coastal; cool to cooler temperate conditions; found in certain parts of South Australia. Sufficient rain required.

Melaleuca violacea (prostrate form only)

Height: prostrate to 500 mm (20 in). Spread: 1 to 1.5 m (3 to 5 ft).

Flowers: violet; spring. Clay, sandy, damp soil. Frost tender in certain areas. Moist temperate conditions, including second-line coastal.

Myoporum debile (Amulla; Sprawling Boobialla)

Height: prostrate to 200 mm (8 in). Spread: 600 mm to 1.5 m (2 to 5 ft).

Flowers: star-like; white/blue, also pinkish recorded; spring-summer. Colourful egg-shaped fruits. Well-drained clay, medium, sandy soils; sunny, dry situation. Frost tender.

Myoporum parvifolium (Creeping Boobialla)

Possibly frost resistant. There are many forms of *M. parvifolium*, e.g. fine-leaved form, broad-leaved form, and maroon-leaved form. Use only those forms suitable as ground covers.

M. parvifolium 'Fine-leaved Form'

Height: prostrate to 300 mm (12 in). Spread: to 2 m (6 ft).

Flowers: white; spring-summer. Possibly frost resistant. Sunny, well-drained, limestone, clay, sandy and coastal soil.

M. parvifolium 'Maroon-leaved Form'

Height: 300 mm (12 in). Spread: to 2 m (6 ft).
As above.

M. parvifolium 'Broad-leaved Form'

Height: 200 mm (8 in). Spread: to 2 m (6 ft).

Rest as above except that it also tolerates swampy, saline and dry sites.

Pandorea jasminoides

Pandorea jasminoides (Bower of Beauty)

(Various cultivars are available.)
Height-spread: vigorous climber, even rampant in the right soil and climatic conditions.

Flowers: pink trumpets, deep pink-red centre; 40 mm (1½ in) wide at trumpet mouth; mid-spring-summer-autumn. Leaves glossy, lance-like to oval. Full sun, plus shelter, produces flower masses; also some partial-filtered shade. Well-drained medium, heavy soils. Can be susceptible to frost damage.

Pelargonium australe

(Select form, colour etc. before purchasing.)
Height: 200 to 600 mm (8 to 24 in). Spread: 300 mm to 1 m (12 to 36 in).

Flowers: variable; pink-streaked dark purple veins, or whitish or mauve; spring-summer. Velvety, hairy leaves, egg or heart shaped or kidney shaped. Well-drained, full sun, light to medium soil. Coastal-protected. Reasonably hardy.

Pratia pedunculata

Height-spread: creeping, mat plant 1 to 2 m (3 to 6 ft); possibly more.

Flowers: light blue, almost white; summer; also spring. Leaves almost circular to egg shaped. Suckering. Moist soil. Full sun in cool areas; lightly filtered shade. Usually frost resistant.

P. puberula is also used, as are *P. pendiculata* × *P. puberula* hybrids.

Pultenaea pedunculata (Matted Bush-Pea)

Height: prostrate-trailing—often rooting. Spread: 1 to 2 or possibly 3 m (3 to 6 or 10 ft).

Flowers (pea): usually solitary; up to 20 mm (¾ in); yellow, yellow with crimson keel, yellow-orange; spring-summer. Leaves small, mid-dark green, lance-like. Well-drained light to medium soils. Full sun in cool areas; filtered shade. Usually frost resistant.

Rhagodia spinescens (Creeping Saltbush)

Synonym *R. spinescens deltophylla*.
Height: variable; 300 to 500 mm (12 to 20 in); even taller, rampant forms are found, but are not suitable as ground cover for home gardens. Spread: 600 mm to 2 m (2 to 6 ft).

Flowers insignificant. Leaves 12 mm (½ in), mealy-white, felted, oblong to egg-shaped to almost circular, even arrow-head-like. Full sun; also filtered sun. Limestone, sandy, coastal; most soils. Usually frost resistant.

Rulingia hermanniifolia

Height: 200 to 300 mm (8 to 12 in). Spread: 1 to 1.5 m (3 to 5 ft).

Flowers: small; white (possibly some pink) stars; spring. Attractive stiff-hairy fruits. Leaves dark green, shiny, crinkled. Well-drained, acid to neutral clay or sandy soil. Full sun. Usually frost tolerant; also found by some to be frost tender.

Scaevola aemula (Fairy Fan Flower)

Height: prostrate to 150 to 500 mm (6 to 20 in). Spread: very variable according to form; 500 mm (20 in) to 1 m (3 ft) to 2 m (6 ft). (Possibly plant being subjected to species evaluation.) Check height, spread and flowering time before purchase.

Flowers: fan-shaped, variable; up to 12 to 30 mm (½ to 1¼ in) long; mauve-blue, purple, bright blue or lilac; spring-summer. Leaves small, hairy, occasionally smooth, egg to wedge-shaped to lance-like, usually toothed. Well-drained light to medium soils. Full sun in cool areas. Partial sun. Frost tender.

Scaevola crassifolia (Coastal Fan Flower)

Height: 500 mm to 1 m (20 to 36 in). Spread: 1 to 2 m (3 to 6 ft).

Flowers: fan-shaped; blue-violet; spring-summer. Leaves rounded to spoon shaped, saw-notched, to 50 mm (2 in). Well-drained limestone, sandy, coastal soils; reasonably salt spray tolerant. Usually frost resistant to frost tender.

Scaevola 'Mauve Clusters'

A popular cultivar, which flowers frequently and is frost tender.

Scleranthus biflorus (Knawel; Twin-flower Knawel)

Two forms, alpine and coastal, are known.
Height: prostrate to 150 to 300 mm (6 to 12 in).
Spread: hummocky, like a moss rock—500 mm to 1 m (20 to 36 in).

Flowers: greenish; tiny; in pairs; summer and also spring. Leaves small, bright-green, narrow, pointed. Possibly-moderately frost resistant. Well-drained clay, medium, sandy soil. Full sun in cool areas; moist, protected site.

Themeda australis (Kangaroo Grass)

Synonym Themeda triandra.
Height: 300 mm to 1.5 m (1 to 5 ft). Spread: Bunch grass to 1 m (3 ft).

Possibly Australia's most famous grass, it is now being considered as a ground cover feature; attractive rough foliage, young foliage is pale to mid greenish blue, but on maturity takes on a distinctive golden-brownish to purple-red. The seed heads are clustered in oat-like groups, bearing silky brown awns. Grows almost everywhere (protection needed in coastal areas) if it is allowed to succeed without commercial grazing. Possibly-moderately frost resistant.

Themeda australis (T. triandra) (Kangaroo Grass)

5. Exotic Plant Ground Covers

Acanthus mollis; A. mollis latifolius **(Bear's Breeches)**

Height: 600 mm to 1.8 m (2 to 6 ft).

Flowers: whitish pink possible flush of purple; hooded; mid-late spring-summer. An invasive, erect, perennial border plant having dark, glossy architecturally bold, deciduous foliage (i.e. deeply cut and divided leaves) up to 750 mm or even 1 m (30 to 36 in) long, 250 to 300 mm (10 to 12 in) wide. Well-drained, but moisture holding, fertile soil. Moderately sunny position in cool climate areas, partially shaded in others. Foliage can be damaged below −3°C. Not for dry inland area extremes.

Arctotis **hybrids**

Height: 250 to 600 mm (10 to 24 in); possibly higher. Spreading.

Flowers: white-yellow, orange, carmine tints and shades; can be large, to 75 to 100 mm (3 to 4 in) across; spring-summer-autumn depending on climate. Leaves evergreen, green or grey-green, notched-lobed. Susceptible to frost. Not for dry inland area extremes or too cold areas.

Arctotis stoechadifolia is white flowered.

Aubrieta deltoidea

Height: prostrate-mat 75 to 100 mm (3 to 4 in).

Herbaceous perennial, popular in cool-climate areas. Flowers a carpeting mass of various cultivar colours—pink, reddish, carmine, lilac, purple and white. Grey-green evergreen foliage looks straggly after flowering. Well-drained alkaline soil, sunny aspect in cool-not too warm temperate climates. Not for tropics or dry inland.

Aurinia saxatilis (Alyssum saxatile)

Aurinia saxatilis

Synonym *Alyssum saxatile*.
Height: 225 mm (9 in). Spreading.

Flowers: dense; flat-topped; deep yellow or sulphur yellow, flowers depending on cultivar; mid-late spring and possibly summer. Foliage evergreen, hummocky, grey, narrow leaved. Well-drained, moderately fertile soil; sunny aspect in cool, temperate areas; will take partial shade.

Bergenia cordifolia

Height: 450 to 600 mm (18 to 24 in). Spreading-clumping.

Flowers: dense, pink clusters, almost primrose-looking; up to 36 mm (1½ in) long; winter-spring depending on climate. Leaves evergreen, bold, green; some pink-red, glossy rounded to heart-shaped. Used as a ground cover in temperate-cool areas. Reasonably hardy, but susceptible to, and damaged by, heavy frost. Not for dry inland or hot tropics. *B. crassifolia* and *B. × schmidtii* are also grown.

Bougainvillea

(B. glabra cvs*; B. glabra × B. peruviana* cvs*)*

Rampant, scrambling-climbing (although certain other forms are available). Massed 'three-petalled' flower bracts, wrongly assumed by some to be the flowers; various colours according to cultivar—

pinkish-rose, purple, yellowish, and more; late spring-summer, autumn—also intermittently; *B. peruviana* mostly winter-dry areas. A visit to the nursery when flower-bracts are showing could prove rewarding.

Foliage egg-shaped, variable. Spiteful to vicious thorns.

Good drainage is essential. Site open, sunny. Susceptible to frost. Young plants are liable to be easily killed by frost. Root balls are easily damaged.

Usually sub-tropics to tropical but, for example, certain species-varieties-cultivars are known to grow in sheltered microclimate areas such as in Adelaide. Check hardiness and suitability of species or cultivars in your area with a local expert.

Calluna vulgaris (Ling/Scotch Heather) suitable cultivars

Height: 150 to 600 mm (6 to 24 in). Spreading.

Flowers: bell-like; 4 to 6 mm (¼ in); reddish-purplish-pink, mauve, white; massed; usually summer-autumn, depending on climate and cultivar. Many cultivars have been produced. Evergreen foliage small, fine, opposite; various coloured. Cool, moist, acidic, well-drained soils. Reasonably hardy.

Campanula portenschlagiana

Height: 100 to 300 mm (4 to 12 in); clump-forming to spreading.

Flowers: 20 possibly 25 mm (¾ to 1 in); bright-blue; bell-flowered; star-shaped; spring-summer-autumn, depending on climate. Leaves usually deciduous, small, rounded-heart to kidney-shaped, coarsely toothed. Reasonably hardy; partial shade; also open sun in cool areas. Not for hot inland or tropics.

C. poscharskyana, evergreen and more vigorous, flowers lavender-blue, is also used.

Campanula portenschlagiana

Cerastium tomentosum (Snow-in-Summer)

Height: prostrate to 150 mm (6 in); even taller, creeping plant.

Flowers: white; numerous; 13 to 18 mm (½ to ¾ in); star-like; spring-summer. Leaves evergreen, ornamental, 31 mm (1¼ in) long, lance-like, silver-grey. Plant can be rampant and invasive. Hardy. Well-drained soil. Most cool, temperate areas.

Convolvulus cneorum

Height: 300 to 900 mm (12 to 36 in).

Flowers: delicate-looking; mostly white; funnel-shaped; up to 50 mm (2 in) long; late winter-spring, depending on climate. Leaves lance-like, greyish-silverish. Half hardy. Full sun. Good drainage. Warm, temperate, suitable frost free areas.

Convolvulus mauritanicus

Synonym *C. sabatius*.
Height: trailing, spreading perennial plant.

Flowers: 13 to 25 mm (½ to 1 in) wide; funnel shaped; lavender blue; some in mid-spring—profuse late-spring, summer, possibly autumn. Leaves evergreen; green-silvery green; ovalish to almost circular. Most warm temperate sites, but only moderately to slightly hardy (half hardy), i.e. can be killed by frost.

Coprosma × *kirkii* cultivars

Height: prostratish to reasonably tall.

Flowers white, somewhat insignificant. Leaves evergreen, small—approximately 25 mm (1 in), or smaller shiny green leaves depending on cultivar. Also variegated form. Used extensively in warm, temperate areas as a reasonably fast growing plant.

Cotoneaster dammeri

Height: prostrate to 100 to 300 mm (4 to 12 in); branches can be self-rooting. Leaves evergreen, small, glossy. Flowers white. Red berries.

Cotoneaster microphyllus

Height: 300 mm to 1 m (12 to 36 in); spreading. Flowers white. Red berries. Leaves evergreen, bold-narrow-oval, ornamental; glossy above. Cotoneasters are found in many situations, except hot tropical or hot, dry inland.

Duchesnea indica (Fragaria indica)

Duchesnea indica

Height: prostrate-creeping-invasive.

Flowers: small; yellow; spring. Leaves evergreen, crinkly like small strawberry leaves. Red berries. Sunny or partial shade. Temperate to cool areas.

Erigeron karvinskianus

Height: 250 to 450 mm (10 to 18 in). Spread: reasonably rampant; rhizome roots. Evergreen usually.

Flowers: small daisies, numerous; white-pink red under; late winter onward, depending on climate. Popular in gardens where invasiveness can be tolerated. Sunny sites; partial shade; vulnerable to frost.

Eriocephalus africanus (Woolly-head)

Height: 300 to 900 mm (12 to 36 in); possibly taller.

Flowers: small, white-daisyish, followed by blobs of cotton wool seedheads; winter-spring. Leaves evergreen, savoury-fragrance, narrow, bright sheenish. Temperate areas; also coastal.

Felicia amelloides (Blue Daisy; Blue Marguerite)

Height: 300 to 450 mm (12 to 18 in), possibly taller. Erect-spreading.

Flowers: approximately 25 to 31 mm (1 to 1¼ in); mauve-blue daisies; spring-summer, depending on climate, but possibly at other times in accommodating climates. Leaves evergreen; mid-green, ovalish-oblongish. Well-drained soil. Open site. Temperate-cool moist. Not in hot tropical or too cold.

Gazania hybrids

Height: 150 to 300 mm (6 to 12 in). Clumping/spreading, depending on cultivar.

Flowers: daisy-like; 50 to 100 mm (2 to 4 in) wide; white, yellow, pink, also tints and shades; occasionally winter, depending on climate; mostly spring-summer, and then occasionally mid-summer to autumn. Leaves evergreen; ornamental; leathery, lobed or non-lobed, dark green-greyish whitish-variable. *G. linearis* also used. Well-drained sandy loam, hot sun; not hot tropics or dry inland.

Hedera canariensis (Algerian Ivy) plus cultivars

Height: creeping-clambering-climbing.

Flowers insignificant. Evergreen, bold, ornamental leaves; large kidney-shaped to heart-shaped, bright-green, lightish green; also variegated, depending on cultivar. Partial shade plant. Not as hardy as English Ivy. Rampant in fertile, moist soil but can be invasive.

Hedera helix (English/Common Ivy cultivars)

Height: creeping-clambering-climbing.

Flowers insignificant; small black fruits. Leaves bold, ornamental, evergreen, usually flat-green, but various other shades-tints, colours including variegated; egg-shaped to almost diamond-shaped; also various shapes and forms according to cultivar. Partial shade-reasonable sun. Invasive. Can destroy trees by climbing. Has aerial rootlets and can climb certain walls. Hardy.

Helleborus (various species and cultivars)

Height: 150 to 400 mm (6 to 16 in); spreading-clumping depending on species. Mostly warm-cool, temperate areas.

Helleborus niger

Flowers: 50 to 100 mm (2 to 4 in) wide; white, perhaps some greenish; sometimes touched with pink; bowl-shaped; winter or late winter to early spring. Leaves ovalish, toothed to 300 mm (12 in) wide. Shady border; cool moist soil.

Helleborus lividus corsicus and hybrids/cultivars (greenish white; winter) are also grown, as is *H. argutifolius* and *H. segitera*.

Helleborus orientalis

Flowers: white-cream, sometimes traces of pinkish; certain hybrids-cultivars can be much pinker; bowl-shaped, up to 75 mm (3 in) wide; winter-early spring. Erect. Leaves evergreen, approximately 350 mm (14 in) wide, can be palm-shaped, or with primary lobes again divided. Shady border. Reasonably hardy.

Hypericum calycinum (Rose of Sharon)

Hypericum calycinum (Rose of Sharon)

Synonyms St John's Wort, Aaron's Beard.
Height: 300 to 600 mm (12 to 24 in). Creeping plant capable of spreading over large areas, used for banks under trees and more.

Rhizomes can be very aggressively invasive.

Flowers: large, up to approximately 75 mm (3 in) across; usually borne singly; bright-yellow; star-like, centre massed with yellow stamens. Leaves evergreen, oblong to egg-shaped to ellipsoid; late-spring-summer. Reasonably frost tolerant, and all but the hottest driest-tropical climates.

Iberis sempervirens

Height: semi-flat trailing to 200 to 300 mm (8 to 12 in). Spread reasonably wide, depending on form or hybrid and soil, to 1 m (3 ft).

Flowers: small; white; massed-clustered on the stem; winter-spring-summer depending on climate. Not for dry inland. Does not tolerate harsh winters. Needs well-drained soil.

Juniperus horizontalis

Height: prostrate to 600 mm (24 in). Evergreen, creeping coniferous shrub. Ornamental, prickly, grey green-bluish leaves. Popular as a ground cover plant and rock garden feature. Many hybrids-cultivars; some spreading wider than others. Reasonably hardy. Well-drained soils. All but the hottest, driest and tropical climates.

Also check out other suitable conifer species or their cultivars used for ground cover work.

Lantana camara hybrida

Only suitable hybrids or cultivars.
Height: 0.5 to 2 m (18 to 72 in)—possibly higher. (Certain lantanas are pest plants in some states.) Cultivars used in warmer, southern temperate areas.

Flowers: clustered verbena-like at top of stems; white, yellow, pinkish, orange-red, depending on cultivar; summer-autumn; for much of the year in suitable warm conditions. Leaves evergreen, rounded-saw toothed; rough-surfaced. Hot, sunny temperate areas. Warm, moist conditions. Frost tender. Reasonably rapid growing; some cultivars can cover large areas.

L. montevidensis

Prostrate; can spread to 1 to 2 m (3 to 6 ft).

Flowers lavender purple to rose lilac; for much of the year in suitable warm conditions. Rough foliage; semi-trailing habit; aggressive. Reasonably drought resistant. Warm moist conditions. Frost tender.

Liriope muscari and cultivars

Height: 225 to 600 mm (9 to 24 in). Spreads by clumps.

Flowers: small; blue-mauve-violet; borne on leafless flower stalks like grape hyacinths; mid-late summer-autumn. Evergreen perennial; grass strap-like leaves. Variegated form. Most warm-cool temperate areas. Not tropical. Partial shade in hotter climates; sunny site or light shade in cool areas.

Mahonia aquifolium (Oregon Grape)

Height: 600 mm to 1 m (2 to 3 ft), sometimes taller, depending on species/cultivar.

Flowers: rich-yellow; in long racemes-sprays; late winter-spring; glaucous-black berries. Evergreen, bold leaves; glossy; ornamental holly-like; arranged in opposite pairs up the stalk. Suckering plant. Can take partial shade in warm temperate areas. Very adaptable in cool to reasonably cold climates. Not for tropical or hot, dry inland. Has parented varieties.

Osteospermum fruticosum

Height: prostrate to 300 mm (12 in); trailing. Spreads wide.

Flowers: 'sunshine lovers'; approximately 50 mm (2 in) daisy flowers; white-flowered form with purple-blue centre popular; winter-spring and on—depending on climate. Evergreen perennial leaves ovalish. Widespread in warm temperate areas. Frost tender.

Pachysandra terminalis

Height: 75 possibly to 450 mm (3 to 18 in). Spreading, vigorous, dense.

Flowers: white fluffs-spikes; winter-spring. Leaves 50 to 100 mm (2 to 4 in) long, evergreen, ornamental, reverse egg-shaped, coarsely toothed. Underground shoots. Shaded-under trees. *P. terminalis* 'Variegata' has white leaf margins. Moderately frost resistant; not for hot moist tropics, or hot, dry inland areas.

Pelargonium peltatum (Ivy-leaf Geranium cultivars)

Height: trailing-spreading; can be trained to climb. Flowers: 30 to 40 mm (1¼ to 1½ in) wide; white, pink, also tints and shades according to cultivar; late winter-spring-summer-autumn—depending on climate. Leaves evergreen, ornamental, glossy, ivy-like. Fast growing. Frost tender. Slightly acid to neutral, sunny, warm, well-drained soil.

Pelargonium peltatum (Ivy-leaved Geranium) cvs

Phlomis fruticosa (Jerusalem Sage)

Height: 600 mm to 1.3 m (24 to 51 in). Spreading.

Flowers: 25 to 35 mm (1 to 1½ in) long; yellow-hooded; massed in whorls around upper stem; late spring-summer.

Evergreen ornamental leaves, bold, grey, woolly and wrinkled; elliptical-lancelike-narrow egg-shaped. Full sun. Reasonably hardy except coldest areas.

Polygonum capitatum

Height: prostrate to 150 mm (6 in); spreading.

Flowers: small, clustered into attractive, small pink balls; late winter-spring-on, depending on climate. Foliage evergreen, ornamental, green changing to pinkish; 'V''shaped band. Foliage frost tender to half hardy.

Rosmarinus lavandulaceus (prostrate dwarf rosemary)

Also *R. officinalis prostratus*
Height: prostrate-mat to 600 mm (24 in). Spreading.

Flowers: small, 25 to 31 mm (1 to 1¼ in) long; blue and variations; salvia-mint like; in clusters; late winter-spring-summer depending on climate. Leaves evergreen, ornamental, herbish-scented, short—approximately 12 mm (½ in); small, blunt-sacking-needle-like. Possibly other cultivars suitable as ground covers. Moderately frost tolerant. Not for hot tropical or hot dry inland areas.

Verbena × hybrida

Often treated as an annual.
Height: 150 to 450 mm (6 to 18 in); or 300 to 750 mm (12 to 30 in); depending on form. Spreading-trailing.

Flowers: small; star-like; flat-topped clustered into impressive heads; colours various—white, pink, mauve, purple, and combinations, often with contrasting eye; late spring-summer-autumn. Leaves evergreen, narrow-toothed; leathery. Well-drained, rich organic soil. Sunny situation. Vulnerable to frost.

Verbena peruviana and hybrids

Prostrate growth; also frost vulnerable. Flowers scarlet; also mauve, pink, combinations may be available; mid-late spring to autumn, depending on climate. Sunny situation.

Vinca major (Periwinkle)

Height: 150 to 300 mm (6 to 12 in); or more. Spread: trailing-rooting to rampant; to pest plant status.

Flowers: to 40 mm (1½ in) wide; bright-blue, but white-flowered cultivars have been produced; late winter-spring-summer depending on climate. Leaves 25-50-75 mm (1-2-3 in) long; usually pointed, egg-shaped; some heart-shaped; evergreen; usually silky dark-green, but can be variegated. Temperate-cool areas. Moderately frost tolerant.

Viola odorata (Sweet Violet)

Height: prostrate. Spread: rampant.

Flowers: small, approximately 13 to 19 mm (½ to ¾ in); semi pansy-shaped, violet blue-purple; variations produced by specialist growers; any season depending on climate; fragrant. Leaves evergreen, perennial. Grows in shady, temperate sites.

Phyla nodiflora (Lippia) in flower

Plectranthus argentatus

Pratia puberula (pendunculata)

Rulingia hermanniifolia

Bougainvillea glabra cv.

Cerastium tomentosum

Convolvulus mauritanicus

Coprosma × *kirkii* variegated cv.

Erigeron karvinskianus

Eriocephalus africanus

Felicia amelloides

Festuca ovina glauca (F. glauca), Blue Fescue

Gazania hybrid ground cover

Hedera helix (English ivy)

Juniperus horizontalis cv.

Lamiastrum galeobdolon 'Variegatum'

Lantana camara hybrida cv.

Lotus berthelotii (L. bertholetii)

Osteospermum fruticosum

Polygonum capitatum

Thymus serpyllum (of gardens) cv.

Vinca major variegated leaf—white cv.

Lawn four months after laying turf

6. Supplementary Plant Lists

Lack of space means that the information on ground covers is inevitably brief, therefore a supplementary list is offered here of mat plants, small dot plants, clumps, ground covers and small shrubs; some can be one metre tall and taller.

However, it is imperative that you check suitable books, catalogues, etc., for various factors such as: form; height; spread; flower colour; flowering time(s); evergreen or deciduous; root and shoot invasiveness; frost tolerance; heat tolerance; humidity tolerance; hot inland suitability; coastal conditions suitability; drought tolerance; salt soil tolerance; damp soil tolerance; occasional flood tolerance; hot tropical-subtropical suitability; allergy causing; poisonous and/or irritating properties; pest plant status, and so on. Remember, only choose suitable prostrate/low-growing forms of species given as some 'accepted' species can be too tall for ground covers. Where garden space is limited seek information on height and spread as some mentioned below could be too vigorous or even too tall for small gardens.

Australian Native Plants

There are many more species, varieties or cultivars suitable as mat plants/ground covers etc. than given below.

Acacia acelerata; A. alpina; A. ambylgona 'Austraflora Winter Gold'; *A. bidentata; A. bivenosa; A. brownei* syn. *A. ulicifolia* var. *brownei; A. colletioides; A. cultriformis* 'Austraflora Cascade'; *A. drummondii* ssp. *affinis; A. dura; A. ericifolia; A. erinacea* low form; *A. farinosa* low form; *A. glandulicarpa; A. leptospermoides; A. luteola; A. pilosa; A. pulchella; A. shuttleworthii; A. triptera; A. venulosa.* (I repeat, choose only low-growing forms suitable as ground covers for your garden.)

Acalypha nemorum
Adenanthos cuneatus low forms
Asperula gunii; A. scoparia
Astartea fascicularis
Asterolasia trymalioides
Astroloma pinifolium
Austromyrtus dulcis
Baeckea camphorosmae prostrate-low form; *B. gunniana; B. ramosissima* prostrate form; *B. virgata* prostrate-low form
Balaustion pulcherrimum
Banksia blechnifolia; B. candolleana; B. gardneri; B. goodii; B. integrifolia prostrate-low form; *B. petiolaris; B. serrata* 'Austraflora Pygmy Possum'
Bauera rubioides low form;
Beaufortia heterophylla
Billardiera cymosa; B. scandens
Boronia pinnata
Bossiaea buxifolia; B. cordigera; B. prostrata
Brachycome angustifolia; B. iberidifolia; B. formosa; B. graminea
Brachysema aphyllum; B. celsianum; B. latifolium; B. praemorsum var. *angustifolium*
Callistemon citrinus 'Austraflora Firebrand'; *C. comboynensis; C. phoeniceus* form
Calocephalus brownii; C. citreus
Carpobrotus glaucescens
Cassia aciphylla
Celmesia asteliifolia
Chorizema dicksonii; C. diversifolium
Clematis aristata
Clianthus formosus
Commelina cyanea
Commersonia pulchella
Conospermum tenuifolium
Conostylis seorsiflora; C. setigera; C. stylioides
Correa alba low form; *C. reflexa* prostrate form
Cotula filicula

Crassula helmsii

Crowea exalata 'Austraflora Green Cape'

Cryptandra amara

Dampiera cuneata; D. linearis; D. purpurea; D. sericantha; D. tenuicaulis; D. trigona

Darwinia citriodora (prostrate form); *D. diosmoides; D. glaucophylla; D. grandiflora*

Dianella caerula; D. longifolia; D. revoluta; D. tasmanica

Dodonaea humifusa; D. procumbens

Dryandra bipinnatifida; D. calophylla; D. drummondii; D. nana; D. nivea

Drymophila cyanocarpa

Einadia hastata

Enchylaena tomentosa

Eremophila maculata (prostrate form)

Erodiophyllum elderi

Eutaxia microphylla (prostrate form); *E. obovata* (low form)

Frankenia angustipetala

Goodenia heteromera; G. hederacea

Geranium neglectum

Grevilleas (many suitable species, varieties and cultivars are used as ground covers)

Hakea myrtoides

Helichrysum apiculatum (Many other *Helichrysum* species, varieties and cultivars used.)

Helipterum albicans (Many other *Helipterum* species used.)

Hibbertia aspera (low form); *H. diffusa; H. fasciculata; H. sericea; H. serpyllifolia; H. vestita* (Other *Hibbertia* species used.)

Hypocalymma angustifolium; H. cordifolium (low form)

Hypericum japonicum

Isopogon ceratophyllus; I. petiolaris

Jacksonia sericea

Kennedia eximia; K. microphylla; K. procurrens; K. prorepens

Kunzea cambagei; K. parvifolium (low form); *K.* sp. 'Badja Carpet'

Lasiopetalum ferrugineum (prostrate form); *L. floribundum*

Leptospermum arachnoides; L. 'Clearview Fairy'; *L. juniperinum* 'Horizontalis'

Leucopogon virgatus

Lobelia alata; L. quadrangularis

Lomandra obliqua

Melaleuca calothamnoides; M. cardiophylla; M. fulgens (low form); *M. pulchella; M. scabra;*

M. violacea (prostrate form); *M. wilsonii* (low form)

Micromyrtus ciliata (prostrate form)

Oxylobium scandens; O. tricuspidatum

Pelargonium rodneyanum

Persoonia chamaepeuce; P. chamaepitys

Pimelea alpina; P. filiformis; P. linifolia

Plectranthus argentatus; P. graveolens (selected form)

Poa australis

Pratia purpurascens

Prostanthera cuneata (low form/low form cultivar)

Pultenaea capitellata; P. humilis; P. pedunculata cultivars

Ranunculus lappaceus

Scaevola hookeri; S. striata

Scholtzia involucrata; S. oligandra

Spyridium parvifolium (prostrate form/cultivar)

Stellaria pungens

Tetragonia implexicoma

Thryptomene calycina

Veronica calycina; V. gracilis

Wahlenbergia gloriosa

Xanthosia rotundifolia

Again I emphasize, check form and height as some species may be much too tall for your garden.

Exotic Plants

Achillea suitable species and cultivars

Agapanthus orientalis; A. praecox praecox cultivars

Aptenia cordifolia

Arabis albida (syn. *A. caucasica*)

Armeria maritima

Asparagus densiflorus (*A. sprengeri*)

Azalea cultivars low forms

Carpobrotus sp.

Ceanothus (only new low-growing cultivars)

Ceratostigma plumbaginoides

Chlorophytum cosmosum 'Vitattum'

Cistus species and cultivars (only prostrate-spreading forms)

Convallaria majalis and cultivars

Dabocecia cantabrica and cultivars

Dianthus species (only those suitable as ground covers)

Epimedium suitable species

Erica species including *Erica carnea; Erica* ×
    darleyensis cultivars
Frankenia laevis
Genista hispanica
Geranium suitable species
Geum × *borisii*
Hebe albicans; plus other suitable dwarf forms
    to 1 m high
Helianthemum suitable species and cultivars
Heterocentron elegans
Hosta species
Lamiastrum galeobdolon (variegated form)
Lamium maculatum

Lampranthus species and cultivars
Lotus berthelotii (L. bertholetii)
Nandina domestica (dwarf cultivars only)
Nepeta × *faassenii*
Ophiopogon jaburan
Pulmonaria suitable species/cultivars
Santolina chamaecyparissus
Sedum × *rubrotinctum*
Senecio macroglossus
Soleirolia soleirolii
Thymus serpyllum cultivars
Vinca minor
Viola species

7. Artificial (Synthetic) Lawn Surfaces

As can be seen on television, suitable artificial (synthetic grass) lawn/turf surfaces are used for certain ball-game areas. Or there may be a bowling club in your area that has an artificial (synthetic grass) green to help reduce wear and tear on the grass greens. Possibly there is also a place in your garden where a lawn will not succeed, and you want a soothing patch of green to simulate a lawn and also take a reasonable amount of wear and tear. Your local nursery may hold stocks of suitable artificial lawns, as do some carpet suppliers. Check the Yellow Pages. Discuss any problems arising from using artificial lawns with those locals qualified to answer.

Manufacturers usually issue brochures concerning their synthetic grass surface(s) explaining the type of material it is; its maintenance, its laying; the correct type of surface it is to be laid on top of. This means that some synthetic grass can be laid on a level, non-hard, porous, e.g. sand sub-surface, and top dressed with sand, whereas others have to be laid on a level solid sub-surface, e.g. concrete, using a suitable adhesive; and so on. Read the manufacturer's brochure/instructions.

Further Reading

Books

Australian Plant Study Group: *Grow What Where* Melbourne: Viking O'Neil/Penguin Books, 1990.

Australian Plant Study Group: *Grow What Small Plant,* Melbourne: Nelson Publishers, 1987.

Beard, J.B.: *Turfgrass: Science and Culture,* New Jersey: Prentice Hall, 1973.

Beckett, K.A.: *The Concise Encyclopedia of Garden Plants,* London: Orbis Publishing Ltd., 1983.

Brunning, L.H.: *Australian Home Gardener.* Ideal Home Library.

Burke, D.: *Growing Grevilleas in Australia and New Zealand.* Kenthurst NSW: Kangaroo Press, 1983.

Colls, K., Whitaker, R.: *The Australian Weather Book.* Sydney: Childs and Associates, 1990.

Crawley, M.C.: *Motor Lawnmowers Owners Workshop Manual*; U.K: Yeovil-Somerset, Haynes Publishing Group, 1980.

CSIRO Research for Australia: *Weeds, Pests and Plant Diseases.* Canberra: CSIRO, 1986.

Dawson, R.B. and Hawthorn, R.: *Practical Lawncraft.* London-Herts: Crosby, Lockwood Staples, 1977.

Decker, H.F. and Decker, J.M.: *Lawn Care, A Handbook for Professionals.* New Jersey: Prentice Hall, 1988.

Elliot, G.: *The New Australian Plants for Small Gardens and Containers.* Victoria: Hyland House Publishing, 1988.

Encyclopedia of Australian Gardening. Sydney: Bay Books, 1980.

Escritt, J.R.: *ABC of Turfculture.* London: Kaye & Ward, 1978.

Garnet, J. Ross, Conabere, E.: *Wildflowers of South-Eastern Australia.* Richmond, Vic.: Greenhouse Publications, 1987.

Greenfield, I.: *Turf Culture.* London: Leonard Hill (Books), 1962.

Handreck, K.A.: *What's Wrong with My Soil?* CSIRO Division of Soils.

Handreck, K.A.: *When should I water?* CSIRO Division of Soils/Rellim Technical Publications (Adelaide), 1986.

Handreck, K.A., Black, N.: *Growing Media For Ornamental Plants and Turf.* Sydney: New South Wales University Press, 1989.

Hassan, E. (Assisted by Swarbrick, J.T.): *Control of Insect and Mite Pests of Australian Crops.* Gatton, Queensland: Ento Press, 1983.

Australian Weed Control Handbook. 8th edn. Melbourne: Inkata Press Proprietary Limited, 1987.

Jones, D., Elliot, R.: *Pests, Diseases and Ailments of Australian Plants.* Melbourne/Sydney: Lothian Publishing, 1986.

Lord, E.E., Willis, J.H.: *Shrubs and Trees for Australian Gardens.* Melbourne: Lothian Publishing (latest revision).

McBarron, E.J.: *Poisonous Plants.* Sydney: Department of Agriculture New South Wales, 1983.

McMaugh, J.: *What Garden Pest Or Disease Is That?* Sydney: Lansdowne Press (RPLA Pty Ltd), 1985.

Molyneux, B., Forrester, S., Gammon, W., Stone, R., Talbot, A.: *The Austraflora Handbook* (plus updates). Montrose, Vic.: Austraflora Nurseries, 1986.

Monfries, M.: *Seaside Gardening in Australia.* Sydney: Methuen Australia, 1982.

New Zealand Institute for Turfculture: *Turf Culture.* Palmerston North: The Institute, circa 1971.

NZ Agrichemical Manual Partnership: *New Zealand Agrichemical and Plant Protection Manual* 1990 (plus update files). WHAM Group Ltd, (Wellington), Novasearch (Manawatu).

Parker, J.M.F.: *Motor Lawnmowers Owners Workshop Manual.* Yeovil-Somerset, UK: Haynes Publishing Group, 1985.

Petersen, F.: *Handbook of Lawn Mower Repair.* New York: Emerson Books, 1982.

Queensland Department of Primary Industries: *Herbicide Effects in Crop Plants* (compiled by J.F. Gage and H.E. Munro), Brisbane: The Department, 1987.

Rees, J.L.: *Lawns Greens and Playing Fields.* Sydney: Angus & Robertson, 1962.

Schery, R.W.: *The Lawn Book.* New York: The Macmillan Co, 1964.

Stephens, R.J.: *Theory and Practice of Weed Control.* London and Basingstoke: The Macmillan Press, 1982.

Turgeon, A.J.: *Turfgrass Management.* Virginia: Reston Publishing Co, 1985.

Voykin, P.N.: *Ask The Lawn Expert.* New York: Macmillan Publishing Co, 1976.

Wrigley, J.W. and Fagg, M.: *Ground Covers.* Sydney: Collins/Angus & Robertson, 1990.

Journals and Occasional Papers

Chandler, B. and Harris, T.Y. (compilers): *Your Australian Garden, No. 3, Mat and Ground Cover Plants.* David G. Stead Memorial Wildlife Research Foundation of Australia.

Institute of Groundsmanship (UK): various journals.

Institute of Parks and Recreation (UK): various journals.

Institute of Leisure and Amenity (UK): various journals.

New Zealand Turfculture Institute, Palmerston North, NZ: various turf management journals.

Royal Horticultural Society (UK): various journals.

Royal Australian Institute of Parks and Recreation: various journals.

Turf Research Institutes (Australian): various data.

Woods and Forests Department, SA: Nursery Catalogue Edition (latest update) plus Woods and Forests Fact Sheets.

Gardening Australia magazine.

Your Garden magazine.

Various State and Territory Departments of Agriculture, Primary Production or Primary Industries issue *Fact Sheets* or *Agnotes* on various subjects.

Choice Magazine carries articles relevant to gardeners periodically, e.g. lawn trimmers, mowers, sprinklers.

Fertilizer, seed, pesticide and irrigation firms may issue brochures.

Your local television or radio talk-back gardening programme provides useful information.

Index